**THIRD EDITION**

# Social Dance

## STEPS TO SUCCESS

### Judy Patterson Wright, PhD

**HUMAN KINETICS**

**Library of Congress Cataloging-in-Publication Data**

Wright, Judy Patterson, 1946-
  Social dance : steps to success / Judy Patterson Wright, PhD. -- Third edition.
      pages cm
1.  Ballroom dancing--Study and teaching.  I. Title.
  GV1753.5.W75 2013
  793.3'3071--dc23

                                    2012030711

ISBN-10: 0-7360-9507-1 (print)
ISBN-13: 978-0-7360-9507-5 (print)

Copyright © 2013, 2003 by Human Kinetics, Inc.
Copyright © 1992 by Leisure Press

**Acquisitions Editors:** Laurel Plotzke Garcia and Gayle Kassing; **Developmental Editor:** Laura Floch; **Assistant Editor:** Elizabeth Evans; **Copyeditor:** Joanna Hatzopoulos; **Permissions Manager:** Martha Gullo; **Graphic Designer:** Keri Evans; **Graphic Artist:** Julie L. Denzer; **Cover Designer:** Keith Blomberg; **Photograph (cover):** Alysta/Fotolia.com; **Photographs (interior):** © Human Kinetics; **Visual Production Assistant:** Joyce Brumfield; **Photo Production Manager:** Jason Allen; **Art Manager:** Kelly Hendren; **Associate Art Manager:** Alan L. Wilborn; **Illustrations:** © Human Kinetics, unless otherwise noted; **Printer:** United Graphics

We thank Stone Creek Golf Club in Urbana, Illinois, for assistance in providing the location for the photo shoot for this book.

Human Kinetics books are available at special discounts for bulk purchase. Special editions or book excerpts can also be created to specification. For details, contact the Special Sales Manager at Human Kinetics.

The contents of this DVD are licensed for private home use and traditional, face-to-face classroom instruction only. For public performance licensing, please contact a sales representative at www.HumanKinetics.com/SalesRepresentatives.

Printed in the United States of America      10  9  8  7  6  5  4  3  2  1

The paper in this book is certified under a sustainable forestry program.

**Human Kinetics**
Website: www.HumanKinetics.com

*United States:* Human Kinetics
P.O. Box 5076
Champaign, IL 61825-5076
800-747-4457
e-mail: humank@hkusa.com

*Canada:* Human Kinetics
475 Devonshire Road Unit 100
Windsor, ON N8Y 2L5
800-465-7301 (in Canada only)
e-mail: info@hkcanada.com

*Europe:* Human Kinetics
107 Bradford Road
Stanningley
Leeds LS28 6AT, United Kingdom
+44 (0) 113 255 5665
e-mail: hk@hkeurope.com

*Australia:* Human Kinetics
57A Price Avenue
Lower Mitcham, South Australia 5062
08 8372 0999
e-mail: info@hkaustralia.com

*New Zealand:* Human Kinetics
P.O. Box 80
Torrens Park, South Australia 5062
0800 222 062
e-mail: info@hknewzealand.com

E5170

To my husband, Sam Wright,
to honor all the years we've been together
and especially for sharing your zest for life
both on and off the dance floor.
With love.

# Contents

# DVD Contents (Side A)

# Waltz

Introduction

Waltz Balances

Box Step

Slow Underarm Turn

Combination A

Left Box Turn

Right Box Turn

Half-Box Progressions

Combination B

Cross Step

Weave

Rollovers

Scissors

Combination C:
On Your Own

# Six-Count Swing

Introduction

Swing Rhythmic
Step Patterns

Arch-Out/Arch-In
Transtions

Roll-Out/Roll-In
Transitions

Couple's Rotational Turns

Change of Position

Combination A

Single Under

Double Under

Brush

Combination B

Belt Loop

Shoulder Touches

Tuck and Spin

Combination C

Wrap and Unwrap

Row Step

Double Cross

Combination D:
On Your Own

# Foxtrot

Introduction

Box Step

Half-Box Progressions

Cross Step

Combination A

Box Step With Left
Box Turn

Foxtrot Basic Rhythm

Combination B

Rock Step

Left Rock Turn

Right Rock Turn

Promenade

## Foxtrot *(continued)*

## Polka

# Cha-Cha

Introduction

Cha-Cha Rhythmic
Step Pattern

Basic Cha-Cha Forward
and Backward

Transitions From Two-
Hands-Joined to Shine
Position and Shine
to Two-Hands-Joined

Combination A

Chase and Half Chase
in Shine Position

Full Chase

Cross and Hop

Combination B

Transition From Closed
Position to Two-Hands-
Joined to Closed

First Position Breaks
(Two-Hands-Joined
Position)

Parallel Breaks Forward
and Backward

Combination C

Fifth Position Breaks

Crossover Breaks

Walkaround Turns

Combination D

Butterfly

Freeze

Figure-Eight Turns

Combination E:
On Your Own

# Rumba

Introduction

Rumba Side Basic

Rumba Box Step

Half-Box Progressions

Combination A

Slow Underarm Turn

Left Box Turn

Combination B

Fifth Position Breaks

Forward Parallel Breaks

Combination C

Crossover Breaks

One-Hand
Around-the-World

Combination D

Cross-Body Lead

Open Rumba Walks

Combination E:
On Your Own

# Tango

- Introduction
- Tango Rhythmic Step Pattern
- Left Quarter Turn: Closed Position
- Combination A
- Corte and Recover
- Basic With Rock Steps
- Combination B
- Closed Figure-Eight Fans
- Basic With Open Fans
- Combination C: On Your Own

# Salsa/Mambo

- Introduction
- Salsa Rhythmic Step Pattern
- Closed Position With Cross-Body Leads
- Right Underarm Turn for Follower
- Head Loops
- Right Turn for Leader (Behind-the-Back Pass)
- Combination A
- Fifth Position Breaks
- Crossover Breaks (With Walkaround Turn Option)
- Combination B
- Side Cross Basic
- Open Break and Inside (Left) Turn (on Four Walls)
- Shoulder Checks
- Double Left Turn for Follower
- Combination C: On Your Own

# Dance Floor Etiquette

# Running Time.....................................93 minutes

# Music Tracks (Side B)

| Track | Description | Beats per min. (BPM) |
|:-----:|:-----------:|:--------------------:|
| 01 | Counting Beats in 4/4 time | 120 |
| 02 | Counting Beats in 3/4 time | 102 |
| 03 | Counting Measures in 4/4 time | 120 |
| 04 | Counting Measures in 3/4 time | 102 |
| 05 | Counting Downbeats in 4/4 time | 120 |
| 06 | Counting Downbeats in 3/4 time | 102 |
| 07 | Merengue Music | 122 |
| 08 | Four-Count Swing/Hustle Music | 120 |
| 09 | Waltz Music | 102 |
| 10 | Swing Music: Slow | 120 |
| 11 | Swing Music: Moderate | 150 |
| 12 | Swing Music: Fast | 165 |
| 13 | Foxtrot Music | 120 |
| 14 | Polka Music: Slow | 110 |
| 15 | Polka Music: Moderate/Fast | 120 |
| 16 | Cha-Cha Music | 120 |
| 17 | Rumba Music | 120 |
| 18 | Tango Music | 120 |
| 19 | Salsa/Mambo Music | 150 |

# Preface

Whether your motivation to learn to dance comes from watching dancers on popular television shows such as *Dancing With the Stars* and *So You Think You Can Dance,* or it's just something you've always wanted to do, this book and DVD package is designed just for you. Dancing is a blend of rhythm, timing, and motion. This book will help you to move efficiently to the music with a partner in social settings.

The dances in this book represent the 10 most popular smooth style and rhythm style dances used on the social dance floor in the United States today. The smooth dances follow a counterclockwise direction around the perimeter of the floor, also called the *line of dance (LOD)*. The rhythm dances are more limited within a small area, sometimes referred to as a *spot*. Both types of dances offer many rewards and challenges for a lifetime of dancing.

## STEP-BY-STEP LEARNING APPROACH

My experience with traditional methods of teaching social and ballroom dance and my research on the process of acquiring sequential skills motivated me to produce a course with a different approach. The uniqueness of this approach to learning social dance is its complete learning progression, which places skills and concepts along a continuum with uniquely designed practice drills for each learning step. So, you will find learning steps instead of chapters in this book. Each learning step gradually builds in the necessary experiences to prepare you for the final outcome—to be able to dance with a partner to music on a crowded social dance floor. The 16 learning steps are organized into three parts that outline your journey to dancing success. Part I (steps 1 to 4) introduces you to the prerequisite concepts and skills that are applied throughout the rest of the book. These early learning steps are especially helpful if you've never had any rhythmic experiences. Part II (steps 5 to 14) describes the 10 social dances covered in this book. You will learn the unique basic step for each dance, how to transition between partner positions, and how to put variations together to form combinations. Part III (steps 15 to 16) helps you bridge the gap between a practice setting and the social dance floor. These latter learning steps also help you improve your turn technique and better understand how you can add styling.

Two new dances have been added to this third edition of *Social Dance: Steps to Success*: the merengue and the four-count swing/hustle. Both of these dances are easy, beginner-level dances that provide quick success and lots of fun. All learning steps have been updated and revised as necessary to include current terminology, key concepts, more history, and a variety of footwork and timing cues for each basic step.

In each learning step, the easy-to-difficult drills are streamlined to support the concepts covered and situational drills have been added to prepare you to make spontaneous decisions on the dance floor. All of the drills provide options for increasing or decreasing the difficulty level of each drill so that you can practice at your preferred learning pace. As you meet the success goal for each drill, you are ready to move to the next drill.

Also new to this third edition are updated illustrations showing proper footwork, technique, and positioning with a partner. Lastly, a major addition is the enclosed DVD, which includes both video and music selections for practicing the 10 dance styles covered in this third edition. Use it as often as needed.

Start your journey by reading Steps to Success: How to Use This Book and DVD Package. As you proceed through this book, you'll soon find yourself pleasantly surrounded by others, enjoying their company, being challenged, and improving your fitness.

## NEW SKILL EXPECTATIONS

Sometimes it can be frustrating to learn new skills. Even if you are highly skilled at one dance, with each new dance or move you begin the learning process over again. The first stage of learning is more cognitive about what to do and how to do it. You are entering the second stage of learning when you can repeat the basic rhythmic step pattern to music and you are expanding your skills with success most of the time. As you add more moves, the challenge is how to remember them all! You'll need to choose a strategy not only to help you combine moves in a meaningful way but also to recall them on the dance floor when under pressure. The third stage of learning is when your moves are automatic and you can focus on objects around you, such as other couples on the floor. Everyone goes through these three general learning stages when learning something new. Don't expect to do things perfectly the first time you are introduced to a new skill. It takes practice to make your dancing look easy, which is the ultimate goal.

There are two general approaches to learning new skills. How do you approach learning a new skill? When someone demonstrates a new skill, do you prefer to focus on one thing at a time, add on the next part, and so forth, until the entire skill is learned? Or do you prefer to see what the entire skill involves, including the timing, rhythm, and position relative to your partner? If you prefer to focus on each part, then your attention would be only on what your feet do, then only on what your arms do, and so forth, until the entire skill is learned. This is an example of the part–whole method of approaching new skills. If you prefer to focus on the entire skill first, then you would focus on how the parts merge together, including timing, rhythm, and coordination with your partner. This is an example of the whole–part method of approaching new skills. Both methods work equally well. Neither method is better than the other. It is a matter of what you prefer and what helps facilitate your learning. Try out both methods to find your preference when viewing the enclosed DVD demonstrations. Once you know your preferred method of approaching new skills, you can be more tolerant of others who may use a different method. Again, remember that each method gets you to the same end. Be patient with your partner; it's simply a matter of using different ways of getting to the same destination.

# Acknowledgments

I wish to acknowledge the contributions of my many hundreds of students, who taught me as much as I taught them. My constant joy is to see students enjoying and expressing themselves on the floor. I am grateful for the opportunity to update my teaching methods in this third edition and thank Dr. Rainer Martens for encouraging me to write the first edition. Kudos go to Doug Fink for directing the video new to this third edition and to Roger Francisco who helped compile the music used on the enclosed DVD. This book and DVD package now presents multiple ways to learn as you can read about it, see specifics in the photos, and see things in action on the video, including how to put them into short practice combinations. My heartfelt appreciation goes to each of the accomplished dancers who modeled for both the photographs and the video segments: Allen Gehret, Charles Gibbs, Gregory Hohensee, Julie Hodson, Cassie Palmer-Landry, and Nanyan Zhou.

I especially want to thank my husband, Sam, for being my partner in life as well as on the dance floor—he is definitely my Mr. Right. I am grateful for his constant support. Finally, I give loving tribute to my late mother and father, who always encouraged me to be the best I can be.

# Steps to Success: How to Use This Book and DVD Package

Get ready to climb the staircase that will lead you to become an accomplished social dancer. You cannot leap to the top; you simply proceed one step at a time. Each of the steps is an easy transition from the one before. A total of 16 steps are grouped into three parts.

Part I, What Every Dancer Needs to Know, presents four learning steps that are prerequisites for your dancing success, each with specific concepts highlighted as follows:

- Step 1 helps you understand how to stand like a dancer, including the importance of postural alignment, centering your body's weight over your base of support for balance, and positioning your arms to create a frame. It is also helpful to know the common foot positions that are used each time you take a step (i.e., make a weight change from one foot to the other). You can enhance your balance and execution by being aware of these different foot positions.

- Step 2 helps you understand the hierarchical arrangement of beats, measures, and phrases. It also helps you identify the most reliable (as well as recognize the least reliable) cues in the music. Once you can hear and count the number of beats per measure, you will know the external speed (or tempo) and get an insight into what type of dance music is being played. The tempo of the music drives the footwork to be used.

- Step 3 helps you to connect your footwork to the tempo of the music. All dancers make a perceptual-motor match by recognizing the beats in the music and coinciding steps (or weight changes) with certain beats or counts. Your task is easier once you know and can execute the basic dance rhythm strategies used by social dancers. These dance rhythm strategies, whether used separately or combined, comprise the specific rhythmic step pattern, or basic step, unique to each dance style (to be presented in part II).

- Step 4 introduces you to the general partner dynamics that occur in social dancing, both verbal and nonverbal communication, including general tips on leading and following, proper etiquette, and partner respect. You also need to understand your role in the partnership, especially when demonstrating common partner positions, and knowing how to use your individual frame (i.e., arms and upper torso) effectively with a partner.

Part II presents the 10 social dances covered in this third edition. For each dance presented in steps 5 through 14, the following sections guide your journey:

- A brief history.

- A description of the rhythmic step pattern.

- Keys to Success illustrations with cues for both footwork and timing.

- Easy-to-difficult practice drills for executing the rhythmic step patterns, adding transitions, variations, and combinations (linking any three or more variations). In each drill, use the success goal, the success checks, and suggestions for either decreasing or increasing the difficulty level of the drill to self-pace your progress. The drills offer you successful experiences that prepare you for the next challenge.

- A summary

In part III, as you near the top of the staircase, you are ready to move from practice situations to dancing on the social dance floor. The last two learning steps help you adapt as follows:

- Step 15 introduces the floor etiquette, or the rules of the road that help you to avoid collisions with others. Unique situational drills prepare you for the spontaneous decisions needed on the social dance floor when the movement of other couples is unpredictable.

- Step 16 challenges you to improve your turn technique, demonstrate the characteristic styling associated with each dance, and be aware of timing options when dancing to unfamiliar music. The drills help you prepare for selected situations that you might encounter on the social dance floor, and they help you expand your opportunities to do more social dancing.

Before you begin your journey, read the next section, Reasons to Social Dance, to get an overview of why people dance, the benefits of dancing, and additional resources for social dancing.

At the end of this book, you may rate yourself according to the directions in the Rating Your Progress section and ask a trained observer, such as your teacher, coach, or trained partner, to evaluate all of your skills. Finally, the glossary is available for your reference.

Good luck on your step-by-step journey to developing your social dancing skills, building confidence, experiencing success, and having fun. See you on the dance floor!

# Reasons to Social Dance

**A**re you looking for a way to meet new people and expand your social skills? Are you looking for an alternative way to work out and have fun at the same time? Try social dancing! You can learn new dance skills, have an evening out, hear great music, and share common interests while you benefit from a mind, body, and spirit boost.

## SOCIAL NEEDS

Throughout history, dance forms have reflected our social needs. These social needs were first displayed in primitive courtship and tribal dances. Although primitive dances were often performed by members of the same sex with no bodily contact, social dance is essentially touch dancing and includes all forms of partner dancing done to a variety of musical styles primarily for recreation or pleasure.

The term *ballroom dance* refers to partner dances done in a ballroom to traditional ballroom music. The earliest 18th- and 19th-century forms of ballroom dance were the minuet in France, the quadrille (a dance with two, four, or more couples) in France and England, the waltz in Austria, and the polka in France. During the Renaissance it became fashionable for ladies and gentlemen of the court to dress well and have polished manners. Soon, competition to outdo others led to elaborate balls and the hiring of dance masters to teach peasant dances to the aristocracy.

The early 20th century saw the introduction of additional partner dances for pleasure, including the foxtrot, swing, tango, samba, rumba, and cha-cha. After World War II, traditional ballroom dancing and Big Band music went into a decline, but partner dancing continued in popularity throughout the rock 'n' roll era and was perpetuated by the romantic disco era. Various movies featured couples dancing, which helped to reenergize interest in even more dance styles, including the four-count swing/hustle, country two-step (a variation of foxtrot), salsa/mambo, and tango. Couples dancing continues to be popular, mainly because of the attractive benefits of social dancing.

# BENEFITS OF SOCIAL DANCE

The foremost reason for participating in partner or touch dancing is the sheer joy of moving rhythmically in unison with a partner to music, regardless of your age. Being with a partner both enhances the pleasure and highlights the social benefits of meeting others, sometimes with romance in mind. Many married couples—including my husband and me—first met on the dance floor. Through dancing, partners can get to know each other, share common interests, learn to respect each other's rights, show appreciation for each other's efforts, and get a good workout, too.

Scientific evidence supports the physical benefits of social dance for increasing muscle tone, flexibility, and cardiovascular endurance and reducing stress on the joints. The low-impact aerobic workout of dancing continuously is a major benefit of social dancing. It is a great way to blend exercise and recreation because you can raise your heart rate to 70 percent of its maximum, which boosts stamina safely. To achieve the aerobic benefit, all you have to do is gradually increase the amount of time you dance continuously. Start by dancing the length of one song, and gradually add more time until you are dancing 15 to 60 minutes nonstop, three times per week. Social dancing can add elegance to exercise. For many dancers, social dancing is becoming the preferred way to be more active and improve fitness while having fun.

Growing research also supports the mental benefits of social dancing. It helps keep the mind active, especially for older adults. A 2003 study published in the *New England Journal of Medicine* found that ballroom dancing at least twice a week makes people less likely to develop dementia.* Social dance requires that you focus, so your mind tends to wander less. For example, to keep time, you mentally count the beats of the music as you move your feet in rhythmic ways. You focus on memorizing the basic steps, learning variations, and repeating combinations or longer sequences using both short-term and long-term memory. Leading requires thinking ahead to plan what to do next. Following requires being ready to respond appropriately, so you need to know the names of the movements and be able to execute them. In a practice setting, all couples are doing the same thing. However, once you are on the dance floor, many couples are doing their own thing at the same time. This means that the leader has to be alert and constantly surveying where other couples are located and anticipate (by spontaneously adjusting the choice of variations) to avoid potential collisions on the dance floor. Potential decision-making situations are built into the drills in this book.

The spiritual benefits of social dancing come from the opportunities for social interaction, artistic expression, improved execution, and dancing in unison with a partner to music. Listening to the music requires focusing your attention on recognizing the external tempo so that you can move in time with the music, which helps you to enjoy the present moment instead of think about the past or the future. When proper etiquette is followed, it is a more pleasant experience for you, your partner, and other dancers.

You can experience great personal satisfaction from your accomplishments in dancing, including improved posture, coordination, balance, precision, timing, and concentration. Additional satisfaction comes from knowing how to ask a partner to dance (or how to accept a dance), how to lead (or follow), and how to adapt your variations to fit the traffic flow of other couples.

*Quote from Dr. Steven Karageanes, sports medicine physician, director of the Performing Arts Medicine at the Detroit Medical Center, and president-elect of the American Osteopathic Academy of Sports Medicine (reported in the *Detroit Free Press* and printed in the *News-Gazette,* Champaign, IL, June 14, 2011).

# SOCIAL DANCE TODAY

Numerous opportunities exist for social dancing, including proms, cotillions, military balls, wedding receptions, and open dances sponsored by schools, universities, colleges, parks, clubs, communities, and dance studios. Watch for flyers and other announcements in your community. During an evening of ballroom dance, an orchestra or DJ typically plays a majority of foxtrot and swing songs, a few waltz songs, and one or two songs each for rumba, cha-cha, polka, tango, and mambo or salsa. However, the selected dances vary across the country according to the theme of the social event, such as disco, Latin, swing, ballroom, or country-western, as well as with your dance style preferences.

If you would like more information on social and ballroom dancing opportunities, check out USA Dance, formerly called the United States Amateur Ballroom Dancers Association (USABDA). USA Dance is a nonprofit organization promoting the physical, mental, and social benefits of ballroom dancing as a lifetime activity. You may check out their per state listings of dance chapters for a nearby chapter and current update of events, which is helpful if you want to go dancing when traveling to other areas of the country. For information on USA Dance membership, go to www.usadance.org and locate a chapter in your area. There, you can also find more information about DanceSport, the competitive form of ballroom dancing expected soon to become an Olympic event. Try to watch the annual ballroom championships aired on PBS. After you finish this book, you will certainly be more appreciative of these dancers' stamina and expertise. Soon social dancing can bring excitement, challenge, romance, social interaction, and health benefits into your life, too!

# Key to Diagrams

CPB = Center point of balance

Center of room = Left

CW = Clockwise

CCW = Counterclockwise

FDW = Forward diagonal wall

FDC = Forward diagonal center

I = Instructor

LOD = Line-of-dance

RLOD = Rear line-of-dance

L = Left

R = Right

O = Follower

O.F. = Original front

RDW = Rear diagonal wall

RDC = Rear diagonal center

SQQ = Slow, quick, quick

SSQQ = Slow, slow, quick, quick

Wall = Right

X = Leader

⟶ = Direction of movement

= Follower's footwork (right foot shaded)

= Leader's footwork (right foot shaded)

= Foot prepares to move

= Weight on ball of foot

= No weight on ball of foot

# PART I

## What Every Dancer Needs to Know: Building a Solid Foundation

Learning to dance is like building a house; you need to start with a solid foundation. The four learning steps in part I introduce foundational concepts in social dance. These steps are essential to your success on the social dance floor, so you should read and review part I as many times as necessary to be comfortable with your body, understand music structure, recognize dance rhythms, and know how to work with different partners. The steps are as follows:

- *Step 1:* Use good posture, frame, and centering to look like a dancer. You may have recognized dancers just by their posture alone. Step 1 helps you to start with good posture and understand how the concepts of centering and frame affect your balance and appearance when stationary or in motion.

- *Step 2:* Understand music structure. Music sets the stage for how fast to move (through tempo) and provides other cues to help you recognize different styles of music. Understanding how music is structured is essential to your success on the social dance floor.

- *Step 3:* Understanding basic dance rhythm strategies gives you predictable opportunities to connect with the music and enjoy dancing. Connect your footwork to the beats of the music.

- *Step 4:* Understand partner dynamics and etiquette for effective communication. You can enhance your enjoyment on the social dance floor when you demonstrate good partner etiquette and avoid criticizing your partner. It is helpful to know the nine basic partner positions that you may use later as well.

# Posture, Frame, and Centering

## *Looking Like a Dancer*

When you watch couples on a crowded dance floor, which ones get your attention first? Most of us are drawn to dancers who move with confidence and stand tall. Whether you're on or off the dance floor, your posture speaks volumes about you to others. Check yourself now: Are you sitting or standing? Are you slumped forward or leaning back? Are your feet flat on the floor? Is your lower back straight or excessively arched? Are you standing with all your weight on one leg? Are you looking at the floor? Are your arms hanging by your sides? In other words, are you demonstrating a balanced posture?

Step 1 increases your awareness of correct body posture, which is called *alignment* when you are standing stationary or *carriage* when you are moving. Step 1 also teaches you the concepts of centering—how to place your body's center of gravity, or center point of balance (CPB), over your base of support—and individual frame—understanding where to place your arms in relation to your torso.

## IMPORTANCE OF POSTURE, FRAME, AND CENTERING

Your body is your instrument of expression. Maintaining proper body alignment is a way to express confidence. Proper body alignment also allows you to use your muscles with the least amount of effort or extra muscular tension. Your standing posture is the standard to which you add the various dance stylings, or characteristics that identify particular dances. It is critical that you correct any deviations in standing posture because they will be magnified tenfold when you move. Good dancers move with purpose and confidence, which are reflected in their posture.

The term *frame* refers to the shape or positioning of your upper body, including your arms. You have better balance when your body weight is above your base (in vertical alignment) and you curve your arms in front of you with your elbows slightly away from the sides of your body. Positioning your arms is important for balance and appearance when you dance alone and for defining your half of the space when you dance with a partner.

The concept of centering helps you to be aware of where your center of gravity is located so that you can lift it (to capture the illusion of ease that is characteristic of good dancers) and transfer your weight efficiently from one foot to the other. It is also important to align your body over your base of support, which alters with changing foot positions. Centering is important in maintaining balance when you are stationary and also when you travel on the dance floor in 10 possible directions. Good dancers make it look easy.

# MOVING LIKE A DANCER

Simply being aware of your posture while standing is only part of the image that you present to others. Dancers are movers. Thus, how you carry yourself while moving, which you do when you are walking or taking a series of dance steps, also says volumes about your self-confidence. The topics in the following sections are discussed separately, but you need to put all of them in action when you do the drills at the end of this learning step and later when you step on the dance floor.

## Posture

People often think of correct posture as they think of the weather: Everyone talks about it, but what can they do about it? If you aren't aware of your posture, then now is the time to check it and correct it. Visualization techniques are particularly effective ways to learn how to align your body. Try both of the following images. Which one helps you visualize proper vertical alignment? Perhaps other images come to mind.

1. Stand with your hands at your sides, your feet no more than shoulder-width apart, and your knees slightly flexed. As if you are balancing large blocks on top of one another, position your hips, shoulders, and head directly above your feet. Look forward with your head erect. It is helpful to look at an object that is at eye level. Think of expanding your shoulder blades, contracting your abdominals, and lengthening (rather than arching) your lower back. You are now in proper standing alignment.

2. Imagine a plumb line (a string suspended from the ceiling with a weight on it to keep it vertical) hanging along one side of your body. Adjust your posture so that the outside of your ear, shoulder, hip, knee, and ankle aligns parallel to the string. Check that your weight is evenly placed over both feet, your eyes are level, your spine is straight (especially your neck vertebrae), your shoulders are relaxed and down (not raised or lifted), your abdominals are firmly engaged, your hips are level, and your lower back is slightly and naturally curved (not hyperextended).

Figure 1.1 shows proper standing alignment with the hips and eyes level.

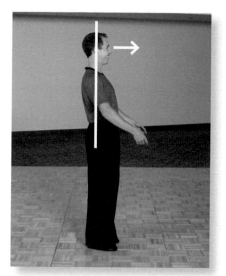

**Figure 1.1**   Proper standing alignment with hips and eyes level.

## Frame

Standing in good alignment is your first step toward understanding the concept of frame. The term *frame* refers to the placement of your arms in relationship to your torso, shoulders, and head. Often dancers don't know what to do with their arms. The narrower your base of support, the more important it is to lift your arms and to look at a point in space that is at eye level—like a tightrope walker! However, it is not necessary to extend your arms out horizontally to mimic the tightrope walker. Rather, you can improve both your balance and your appearance if you flex your elbows, lift them slightly away from the sides of your body with palms facing down, and keep them in front of your body rather than let them move behind your body. This arm positioning is an example of individual frame (see figure 1.2). Keeping your

**Figure 1.2**   Individual frame improves both balance and appearance.

individual frame helps to eliminate wasted effort (rather than lowering and extending your arms then bringing them back into position again). Keeping your frame with a partner helps to define and maintain the space between you and your partner. Ideally, each partner is responsible for half of the shared space (see figure 1.3).

A typical frame error occurs whenever you move your arms independently of your shoulder girdle. For example, a common frame error, called *spaghetti arms*, occurs when the elbows extend behind the body. Leading and following are enhanced when your arms, shoulders, and sternum (your frame) work together as a unit, but leading and following are ineffective if either partner's frame is not established and firm. You'll soon find out that leading and following are more than a matter of pushing and pulling with one's arms and hands. Rather, you need to use your whole body (and frame) to non-verbally communicate with your partner.

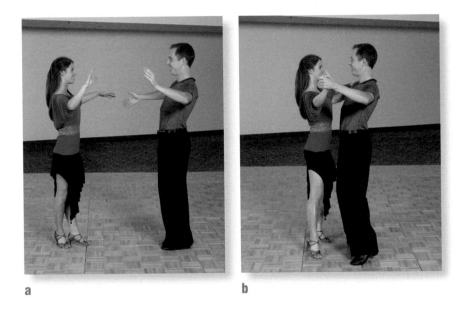

a                                      b

**Figure 1.3**    Frame with a partner helps to define your half of the shared space (*a*) when apart and facing and (*b*) when in a closed position.

## Centering and Center Point of Balance (CPB)

Once you can align your hips, shoulders, and head over your base of support (your feet), you need to become aware of where your center of gravity (COG) is located. Your COG is a point near the center of your body where your body's weight is equally divided (i.e., half of your weight is above and half is below this point). Typically, the equal division of body mass is located a bit higher in males (at or slightly above the waist) than in females (at or slightly below the waist). In dance, the more universal term *center point of balance (CPB)* refers to a point just below the diaphragm. You can feel this point by making a fist and placing it at the base of your breastbone where your ribs start to separate. Imagine a three-dimensional point behind your sternum, above your solar plexus, and aligned above your base of support. This is your CPB. If you are asked to move your *center*, then it is really your CPB that is to be moved. The advantage of the CPB is that it is slightly higher than your COG and, thus, not affected by body mass. In addition, the CPB is in the same location for each dancer and ties together the upper and the lower body to give dancers more power and control with their movements. When you move from your center, you move your entire body as a unit.

When you dance, your weight is rarely equally divided over both feet. It is more common to align or center your body's weight alternately over one foot, then the other. When your weight is on one foot, your image of vertical shifts slightly to that side of your body (see figure 1.4) and your CPB shifts toward the direction of your weight shift. Whenever your center moves too far beyond your base of support, you lose your balance. You can easily shift your center approximately 5 inches (12.7 cm) in any direction before you have to move a foot. Experiment with this shift and see how it affects your balance. To regain balance, you can take a step in the direction you shifted your center. Notice that where your CPB goes, your feet will follow.

**Figure 1.4**   When shifting weight from two feet to one foot, your image of vertical and CPB shifts slightly toward that side of your body.

## Foot Positions and Balance

How you position your feet greatly affects your balance because your feet are your base of support. You can create a stable base of support by widening your stance to approximately shoulder width apart on a side step, or in a forward–backward stride position. Also, a wider base encourages slight knee flexion, which helps to lower your CPB. Be aware that your CPB should always be above your base of support. For dancers, the relationship between foot positions and CPB is critical. The five basic foot positions are illustrated in figure 1.5. You use first position when you start with your feet together and your CPB over both feet. When you are ready to take a step, slightly shift your CPB to be above your supporting foot by lifting the heel of your starting foot (i.e., leaders lift the left heel, followers lift the right heel). You use second position when you take a step to the side and have your feet approximately shoulder width apart. This also means that you need to shift your CPB slightly forward more over the balls of the feet (to be in a ready position) and avoid leaning back on your heels. To move from first position to third position, position the instep of one foot behind the heel of your other foot, making a T. Notice that the toes of the front foot are pointing in the direction of travel. The back foot is angled slightly, approximately 45 degrees. The fourth position occurs naturally whenever you take either a forward or a backward step and your CPB shifts from one foot to the other (i.e., feet are in a forward-backward stride position). To avoid what is called *wide tracking*, keep your feet close together, no more than 2 inches (5 cm) apart, as you take each forward walking step (and alternately place each foot in fourth position). Notice also that as you step, the inside edge of each foot slightly touches each side of an imaginary line extended on the floor, somewhat like walking a tightrope. You achieve fifth position by positioning the big toe of one foot behind the heel of the other foot, again with the front foot's toes pointing in the direction of travel and the back foot angled approximately 45 degrees.

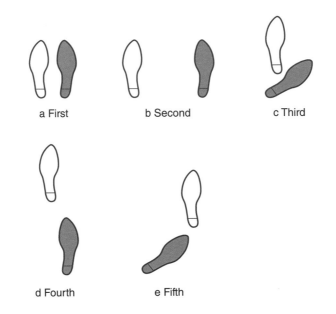

a First      b Second      c Third

d Fourth      e Fifth

**Figure 1.5** Five foot positions: *(a)* first, *(b)* second, *(c)* third, *(d)* fourth, and *(e)* fifth.

In each foot position, a slight angling-out of the toes, called turnout, is useful for improving balance and facilitating turns because it widens your base of support. When your toes are angled in preparation for turns, it is called *prepping the turn*, because the toes angle in the direction of the turn; the right toes angle out to the right when turning to the right, and the left toes angle out to the left when turning to the left. Social dancers typically angle their toes no more than 45 degrees and keep the knees aligned over the big toe of each foot.

### *Movement Directions and Balance*

If you are asked to move from a stationary location to a new location, how do you do it and where would you go? What happens to your CPB? What choices of direction do you have? The options may seem to be endless, but only 10 possible options for direction exist. The following list groups the directions according to their natural opposites:

- Forward and backward
- Right side and left side
- Diagonal left front and diagonal right back
- Diagonal left back and diagonal right front
- Counterclockwise and clockwise

Each direction is defined from where your sternum is facing before you start moving. All options for direction are interpreted either from where the front of your body is facing (see figure 1.6*a*) or from where the front of your body is facing according to the line of dance (LOD) and the walls in the room (see figure 1.6*b*). If you do dances that are more stationary (i.e., executed in a limited space on the floor such as the merengue, swing, cha-cha, rumba, or salsa/mambo), then your direction options

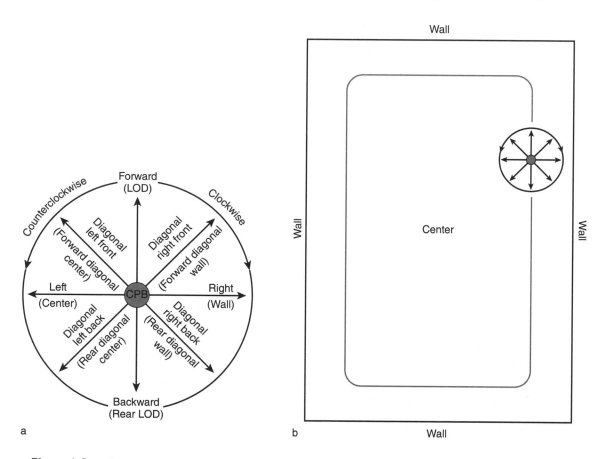

a                                        b

**Figure 1.6**     Ten movement directions defined *(a)* from where the front of the body is facing and *(b)* from the dancer's location when traveling in the LOD.

are as previously listed. However, if you do dances that progress in a counterclockwise direction around the perimeter of the room (i.e., traveling dances such as the waltz, foxtrot, tango, or polka), then your options for direction are defined according to not only where your sternum is facing, but also where you are in relationship to the LOD and the walls of the room. Whenever you execute dances according to the LOD, eight movement options exist as follows. The equivalent body directions are in brackets.

- Line of dance (LOD) [Forward]
- Rear line of dance (RLOD) [Backward]
- Wall [Right]
- Center [Left]
- Forward diagonal wall (FDW) [Diagonal right front]
- Forward diagonal center (FDC) [Diagonal left front]
- Rear diagonal wall (RDW) [Diagonal right back]
- Rear diagonal center (RDC) [Diagonal left back]

To maintain your balance when moving in different directions, it is important to slightly flex your knees to lower your CPB and/or rotate your frame toward the intended direction of movement before you take a step in that direction. Dancers move with intention. Whether you are dancing alone or with a partner, you need to plan ahead which direction you will travel, then move with confidence. When you work with a partner, the leader is responsible for indicating the LOD and body direction while the follower is responsible for holding or maintaining and continuing in the indicated LOD and body direction.

# DRILLS FOR POSTURE, FRAME, AND CENTERING

The following drills are designed to help you become more aware of how your posture, your foot placement, and your CPB can affect both your balance and movement efficiency. Try these drills by yourself, then ask a partner to observe and give you feedback. Can you demonstrate the Success Check items for each drill? If so, then you are ready to continue your journey in the next learning step.

# Drill 1
# Moving From Your Center

What part of your body moves first when you take a step forward? Most people guess that it is their foot or their knee. This drill will help you discover the answer.

Stand with your back to a wall and demonstrate good posture. Make sure that your heels, hips, shoulder blades, and the back of your head all touch the wall. Let your back curve naturally such that you can put your hand between the wall and the small of your back. Now try to take a step forward with either foot to move away from the wall. Notice what part of your body moves away from the wall first. Now, repeat and continue walking at least 4 steps forward and notice what happens to your posture. As necessary, review figure 1.1. Ask a partner to observe your actions and give you feedback.

## TO DECREASE DIFFICULTY

- Stand with your feet together away from the wall or any other objects. Gently shift your CPB in each of four directions (forward, backward, left, and right) and notice how far you can move before you have to take a step to catch your balance.
- Stand facing a partner and hold a large beach ball between you. One person shifts forward, then the other person shifts forward. Notice how your CPB initiates the momentum that gets transferred to your partner.

## TO INCREASE DIFFICULTY

- Stand facing a partner with fingertips touching. One person shifts forward to take eight walking steps, then the other person shifts forward to take eight walking steps. Notice how your CPB initiates the momentum that gets transferred to your partner.
- Stand with your feet together and slowly shift your CPB in different directions, then take a step or two in that direction.

## Success Goal

Perform 10 repetitions of maintaining vertical alignment while taking a step forward starting with your back to a wall and then on each walking step forward thereafter.___

## Success Check

- Keep your eyes focused on a point that is at eye level.___
- Imagine your body parts (hips, shoulders, and head) in proper alignment over your feet.___
- Only your CPB moves forward away from the wall before you bend a knee or lift a foot or take a step.___

# Drill 2
# Recognizing Positions of the Feet

Review the five positions of the feet shown in figure 1.5, then practice positioning your feet in each of them. After you are comfortable defining these positions, ask a partner to help you test your application of them. Take turns with your partner; one person demonstrates a particular foot position, then the other person states the name of that foot position.

**TO DECREASE DIFFICULTY**
- Start with first position and continue in numerical order.
- Use only first, second, and fourth positions of the feet.

**TO INCREASE DIFFICULTY**
- Use a random order to demonstrate the foot positions, then name that position.
- State the name the foot position, then demonstrate that position.

## Success Goal

Correctly name and demonstrate each of the five positions of the feet.___

## Success Check

- Compare your answers with the illustrations shown in figure 1.5.___
- Say and move directly in order from the first to the fifth position of the feet.___

# Drill 3
# Balance Test

Stand in proper alignment with your feet in first position and your weight balanced over both feet. Slightly bend your elbows until your forearms and hands are parallel to the floor and slightly away from the sides of your body. Use this arm position to maintain your balance. It may be helpful to stand next to a chair in case you need to support yourself. Keep your eyes focused on a spot at approximately eye level. Shift your weight onto one foot. Notice how the imaginary vertical line that divides your body along the midline when your weight is centered over both feet now shifts slightly toward and over your supporting foot (review figure 1.2). Take a deep breath from your diaphragm and feel the air under your arms.

Imagine the air enveloping your rib cage and gently supporting you (with your CPB lifted). If you are truly in balance, then you can lift the nonsupporting foot and knee even a few inches off the floor.

Challenge yourself further by gradually lifting the heel of your supporting foot off the floor. The higher you lift your heel, the more your CPB is shifted forward over the ball of your supporting foot. Hold this position as long as you can. If you lift your heel too far off the floor, your CPB will go onto the toe and beyond your base of support. If so, just catch yourself by taking a step. Repeat this one-leg, standing balance test with your weight on the other foot.

## TO DECREASE DIFFICULTY
- Hold your balance for 3 seconds per leg.
- Keep one hand on the back of a chair as you balance on one foot.

## TO INCREASE DIFFICULTY
- Hold your balance for 60 seconds per leg.
- Focus your eyes on a point at eye level and inhale to lift your CPB as you balance on one leg.

## Success Goal

Balance for 5 to 30 seconds on one foot, then repeat on the other foot.___

## Success Check

- Improving your balance takes mental concentration and practice; your CPB is a three-dimensional place.___
- Use a vertical image to help align body parts over your base of support.___

# Drill 4
# Moving Within Your Frame

You can get the feel of how your arms and shoulder girdle function as a frame in two fun ways. Both require isolating either the upper or lower part of your body. These isolations will become useful when you start leading and following.

## *Lower-Body Isolation*

Stand in front of a wall. Position both hands in front of your shoulders, palms forward, then place them against the wall for support. Move closer to the wall until you can press your weight into your palms to keep your upper torso stationary. Stand with your feet together (in first position). With your CPB lifted, twist your lower body by lifting both heels off the floor, keeping your weight on the balls of both feet and rotate the toes of both feet to one side and then to the other.

## *Upper-Body Isolation*

Move away from the wall. Stand with your feet in second position, approximately shoulder width apart. Lift your arms in front of your chest and make a circle with your middle fingers touching. Lower your hands slightly so that they are in front of your CPB. Imagine that a string connects your CPB with your fingertips. Twist your upper torso from your waist such that the string remains taut as you rotate your entire upper body as far as you can to one side, then the other side.

## TO DECREASE DIFFICULTY

- Try each isolation holding on to the back of a chair.
- Imagine reaching across your midline until your sternum is facing approximately 45 degrees by rotating towards 10 o'clock and 2 o'clock on the upper-torso twists.

## TO INCREASE DIFFICULTY

- Try each isolation facing a partner and grasping both hands firmly.
- Compare twisting your lower body with your CPB over the balls of your feet versus more flatfooted.

## *Success Goal*

Perform the drill for 60 seconds alternately twisting only the lower half of your body, then only the upper half of your body.___

## *Success Check*

- Twist from waist, keeping arms, shoulders, and sternum moving as one unit while the lower half of the body remains stationary.___
- Keep the upper torso stationary during your lower-body twists.___

# Drill 5
# Center Leads, Feet Follow

Start in a balanced stance in good posture with your feet in first position. Deliberately shift your CPB slightly beyond your base of support (your feet), and catch yourself before you actually fall (by stepping in the direction that you shifted your CPB). For example, shift your CPB to one side and take a step to that side (moving from first to second position). Come back to first position and repeat to take a step on the other side.

Experiment with shifting your CPB in eight different directions (review figure 1.6, with the exception of the two rotational directions at this point). In each case, notice how your CPB initiates the action in the intended direction. Each time, continue to walk at least 4 steps in the intended direction. As a further challenge, what happens to your CPB when you need to reverse directions? For example, experiment with four walks forward, then four walks backward. Then, combine any two opposite directions.

## TO DECREASE DIFFICULTY

- Walk 16 steps forward, then 16 steps backward.
- Walk 8 steps forward, then 8 steps backward.

## TO INCREASE DIFFICULTY

- Keep a constant pace as you walk in each direction.
- Use a decreasing number of repetitions while walking forward, then backward, such as 16/16, 8/8, 4/4, 2/2, 1/1/1/1. Repeat starting with the opposite foot.

## Success Goal

Take 4 walking steps in each of eight possible directions, then combine any two opposite directions using smooth transitions during the direction changes.___

## Success Check

- Notice that your CPB moves first regardless of which direction you move in.___
- To reverse your direction smoothly, slightly flex your knees just before taking the last step in the intended direction, keeping your CPB over both feet.___
- When reversing directions (e.g., from forward to backward, or vice versa), notice that your feet are in a forward–backward stride (fourth position).___

# SUCCESS SUMMARY FOR POSTURE, FRAME, AND CENTERING

Demonstrating good posture is your first step in looking good on the dance floor. Proper body alignment and carriage create an impression—literally an image for others that can either enhance or detract from your performance as a dancer. It is important to have your posture evaluated by your teacher or another trained observer, both when you are standing and when you are walking (as necessary, revisit the drill, Moving From Your Center).

Do you have any postural deviations? If so, begin a daily self-check of your postural alignment—which may need to be repeated up to 30 times a day—until you have a strong mental image of vertical alignment and where your CPB is located. Your CPB should move first, then your feet can follow in the intended direction. Being in balance means keeping your CPB over your base of support (either one or both of your feet). Understanding the concept of frame can help not only for balance but also for appearance (and later for leading and following). With practice, your posture, frame, and centering of your weight over your base will become automatic.

# Music Structure

## *Hearing Reliable Cues in the Music*

How do you know when to start moving with the music? The answer to this question may seem obvious to people with a musical background, who have played an instrument, or who have participated in other rhythmic activities. However, for people who have no such background or experience, the question is critical and difficult to answer. When you listen to the music, any of several aspects could grab your attention. For example, you could focus your attention on the melody or words of the song, particular instruments, the tempo, and various accents in the music. The more aspects that you can recognize, the more difficult it is to know where to focus your attention.

From a dancer's viewpoint, the beat is the most reliable cue because it has a high probability of recurring in a predictable manner. Thus, your first challenge is to separate the rhythm in the music (often called the melody) from the beat (often called the underlying beat). Once you've identified the beat, you'll know the tempo, or how much time elapses between the beats. With very few exceptions, once a tempo is established, it repeats at that same speed throughout a particular musical selection. Sometimes musicians may slow down the tempo either at the beginning or at the end of a song. However, any easy-to-dance-to song maintains a consistent tempo throughout. Additional cues that have a high probability of consistent recurrence include the number of beats per measure, the duration of each beat (the time signature), and how songs are put together (in beats, then measures, and phrases). For your convenience, practice drills at the end of this step will help you enhance your auditory discrimination skills. Finding the beat is easier than you might think.

## IMPORTANCE OF UNDERSTANDING MUSIC STRUCTURE

Social dance music is structured based on the smallest unit of time, the beat. Once you find the beat, you will know a lot more. It is advantageous to know that for all practical purposes, social dance music can be categorized into three basic time signatures: 2/4, 3/4, and 4/4. The numerator (top number) tells you the number of beats that are grouped into a measure (two, three, or four beats). The denominator (bottom number) tells you that each beat is equivalent to a quarter note that gets one count. You don't need to know about quarter notes, only that each beat in social dance music is given one count. If two beats are grouped, it is likely that either polka or merengue music is being played. Due to the fast tempos for both of these dances, it is easier to use the option of counting in multiples of four to make it equivalent to 4/4 time. It also takes two measures or four beats before your starting foot is free again in the polka. If three beats are grouped, you know that waltz music is being played. If four beats are grouped, the music being played could be appropriate for any one of a variety of other social dance styles. Most social dance music is in 4/4 time. Can you count to four? It's that easy!

If you are mathematically inclined, you will appreciate the hierarchical relationships among musical notes. But even if you are not mathematically inclined, music has an order and consistency; it is not random. You need only be able to recognize and identify which cues in the music provide order and consistency and thus provide dancers with the most reliable information. The most reliable cue in the music is the underlying beat, which is most often referred to as the *beat*. As mentioned, once you can distinguish the underlying beat, you'll be able to notice that the beats are clustered into groups of either three or four beats, which are called *measures*. Grouping two or more measures together creates a phrase, which can be grouped to create longer phrases. The following sections describe five reliable cues that illustrate the order and consistency that you can perceive and identify after listening to any one song.

# MUSIC CUE 1: UNDERLYING BEATS PROVIDE A CONSISTENT TEMPO

How can you locate the underlying beat? One way is to listen for the heavier sounds in the music, such as the bass player's or the drummer's sounds, rather than the lighter sounds. Typically, the lighter sounds reflect the melody within a song. The melody is superimposed over the underlying beats and is variable; that is, it changes the duration of certain notes. The melody is typically played by wind instruments. Because the duration of the notes within the melody may vary, the melody becomes an unreliable cue for dancers. Typically, the bass drum keeps all the musicians together at a certain consistent tempo, which is called the *underlying beat*. You may have heard band leaders say "and a 1, 2, 3, 4" to give the tempo of the underlying beat. Likewise, dancers and dance teachers often count each beat in the measure and say "5, 6, 7, 8" after mentally counting 1, 2, 3, 4 to establish the tempo.

# MUSIC CUE 2: BEATS ARE CLUSTERED INTO MEASURES

Why are beats grouped into measures? Measures provide structure and consistency. A good contrast is that of listening to a series of clicks or finger taps at a constant speed. Take a look at figure 2.1. Here, you can start and stop counting the vertical lines representing clicks, taps, or beats whenever you want. For example, you could also count by grouping these clicks in multiples of two, three, four, or any number you choose because there are no obvious starting or stopping places. This means that you might count the beats one way and your friend might count them another way, which is neither reliable nor consistent. As a result, musicians and dancers rely on grouping the underlying beats of the music into measures in order to provide a definite starting and a definite stopping point for counting the beats within a particular song.

**Figure 2.1**  Continuous beats without identifying measures.

You know why beats are grouped into measures, but do you know when to start and when to stop counting the beats that group together to form a measure? If you look at sheet music, vertical bars separate the beats into measures. Also, the specific time signature is shown at the left of the first measure. The time signature is advantageous to know because it indicates not only how many beats are in a measure, but also how much time duration to give each beat.

As mentioned earlier, common time signatures in social dance music include the fractional signs 2/4, 3/4, and 4/4. The numerator (top number) indicates the number of beats per measure, whereas the denominator (bottom number) indicates the duration of a particular beat. The numerator values in figure 2.2 signify that these examples have two, three, and four beats per measure, respectively. The denominator value, 4, signifies that each quarter-note beat in each example gets one count. In

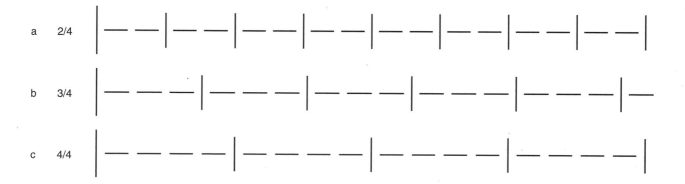

**Figure 2.2**  Underlying beats per measure for *(a)* 2/4, *(b)* 3/4, and *(c)* 4/4 time signatures.

social dance music, it is safe to assume that the denominator will be 4, which means that each beat (each quarter note) always gets one count. You might hear dancers using a shorthand version of the term, *4/4 time music*, instead of *music with a 4/4 time signature.*

# MUSIC CUE 3: TIME SIGNATURES ARE CONSISTENT WITHIN A SONG

Typically, dancers do not have access to sheet music to help them identify the time signature. Thus, you must be able to identify the time signature after hearing a portion of the music. Start by focusing your attention on the underlying beat, then identify the number of beats in each measure. Remember, in social dance music, each beat gets one count.

The easiest way to identify the number of beats grouped per measure is to count in multiples of either three or four (the most common numerators). First, try counting with the music in sets of four (1, 2, 3, 4; 1, 2, 3, 4; etc.). If counting in sets of four beats does not match the beats of the music, then switch to counting in sets of three beats. If counting in sets of three (1, 2, 3; 1, 2, 3; etc.) matches the beats of the music, then you'll know that waltz music is being played. One of these methods will work better than the other. There is a higher probability that the music is 4/4 time because only three dances, the waltz, the merengue, and the polka, have fewer beats per measure. When listening to the music for the first time, you may need to close your eyes to reduce outside distractions and focus all your attention on the music.

From a musician's viewpoint, both merengue and polka music has a 2/4 time signature; that is, two beats per measure with each beat getting one count. Yet from a dancer's viewpoint, due to the speed of merengue and polka music and the difficulty of repeatedly counting 1, 2; 1, 2; 1, 2; and so on, it is often easier to count in sets of four counts, which groups two measures of music. In addition, the footwork for the polka takes four counts before your starting foot is free again because it repeats on both sides of the body. You may memorize the fact that music with a 2/4 time signature indicates either merengue or polka music. It is your option whether to count it in sets of two or in sets of four.

The time signature gives you two important pieces of information: the number of beats per measure and the duration of each beat. Since social dance music gives each beat one count, it is a matter of knowing how many beats are grouped per measure. Once you know if the underlying beats are grouped into two, three, or four beats, there is a high probability (and reliability) that the time signature will remain constant for the length of a particular song. Thus, many dancers mentally count the beats per measure for the length of each song. Once you can identify the first beat of the measure, you will also know when to start moving—on count 1.

# MUSIC CUE 4: MEASURES ARE CLUSTERED INTO PHRASES

How might you count the measures within a song? The measures within a particular social dance song are organized in an exponential fashion that applies to both 4/4 time and 3/4 time music. For example, in 4/4 time music, one measure equals four counts. These four counts may be grouped into multiple measures as follows:

- 2 measures, or 8 counts (2 measures × 4 counts = 8 counts),

- 4 measures, or 16 counts (4 measures × 4 counts = 16 counts),

- 8 measures, or 32 counts (8 measures × 4 counts = 32 counts), or

- 16 measures, or 64 counts (16 measures × 4 counts = 64 counts),

- and so on.

Within 3/4 time music, each measure is equal to three counts. Thus, waltz measures may be grouped into multiple measures as follows:

- 2 measures, or 6 counts (2 measures × 3 counts = 6 counts),

- 4 measures, or 12 counts (4 measures × 3 counts = 12 counts),

- 8 measures, or 24 counts (8 measures × 3 counts = 24 counts), or

- 16 measures, or 48 counts (16 measures × 3 counts = 48 counts),

- and so on.

When the measures are grouped this way, they are called *phrases*. There are many ways of defining a phrase. Some might call the examples given a mini-, a minor, and a major phrase for the 2-, 4-, and 8-measure groupings, respectively. A 16-measure grouping typically, but not always, reflects a chorus or verse within a song.

Dancers and teachers tend to use mini- and minor phrases more often and to use one of the following two methods of counting the phrases: grouping either one measure or two measures. It is a matter of preference. For example, one way of phrasing 4/4 time music is to mentally count in eight sets of 4 counts (for a total of 32 counts) as follows:

**1**, 2, 3, 4
**2**, 2, 3, 4
**3**, 2, 3, 4
**4**, 2, 3, 4
**5**, 2, 3, 4
**6**, 2, 3, 4
**7**, 2, 3, 4
**8**, 2, 3, 4

Another way of phrasing 4/4 time music is to mentally count in four sets of eight counts as follows:

**1**, 2, 3, 4, 5, 6, 7, 8
**2**, 2, 3, 4, 5, 6, 7, 8
**3**, 2, 3, 4, 5, 6, 7, 8
**4**, 2, 3, 4, 5, 6, 7, 8

The two methods of counting, or phrasing, may also be used with 3/4 time music. Thus, one example for phrasing waltz music is to group eight measures as follows:

**1**, 2, 3
**2**, 2, 3
**3**, 2, 3
**4**, 2, 3
**5**, 2, 3
**6**, 2, 3
**7**, 2, 3
**8**, 2, 3

Another way to phrase waltz music is to group four sets of six counts (two measures) as follows:

**1**, 2, 3, 4, 5, 6
**2**, 2, 3, 4, 5, 6
**3**, 2, 3, 4, 5, 6
**4**, 2, 3, 4, 5, 6

The previous examples show how social dance music has structure. Dancers have less to remember when they phrase counts rather than isolate counts. It is easier to remember sets of four or eight measures than to remember individual counts of 32 or 24.

The arrows in figures 2.3 and 2.4 indicate the first count (also called the *downbeat*) within each phrase grouping for both 4/4 and 3/4 time signatures. In 4/4 time music, it may be more difficult to hear the downbeat because the even counts represent upbeats; that is, counts 1 and 3 are downbeats while counts 2 and 4 are upbeats. It is not as hard to find the downbeat in 3/4 time music because the first count typically has a stronger emphasis; it sounds heavier than counts 2 and 3. If you can also identify the beginning or end of a phrase grouping, you'll get an additional cue as to when the next measure will occur.

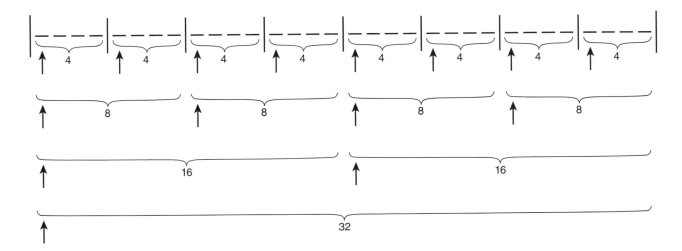

**Figure 2.3** Phrase hierarchy for 4/4 time music; arrows indicate the first beat (downbeat) either of the measure or within the selected phrases.

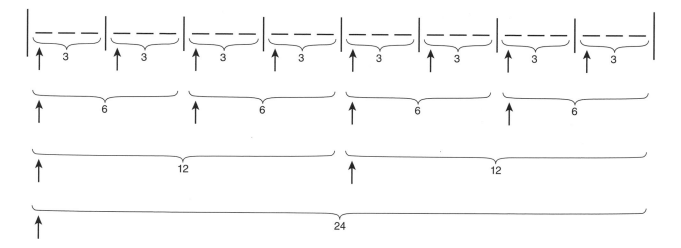

**Figure 2.4**  Phrase hierarchy for 3/4 time music; arrows indicate the first beat (downbeat) either of the measure or within the selected phrases.

# MUSIC CUE 5: TEMPO REMAINS CONSTANT DURING A SONG

How fast should you move? As discussed earlier, because each beat gets one count in social dance music, you only need to know how much time occurs between the underlying beats. Basically, social dance music uses three different speeds, called *tempos:* slow, moderate, and fast. Tempo may vary between songs, but it is highly likely to be constant within a particular song. Thus, once you have identified the tempo, you need only repeat that particular tempo consistently for the length of that song. Exceptions may occur at the end of a song when the tempo may slow down or even fade out.

Also, the tempo may be expressed as *beats per minute,* or *bpm*—literally, the number of beats counted for 1 minute. Or, you may use a shorthand method to calculate it. For example, count the number of beats for 6 seconds and multiply by 10 to get the number of beats per minute. If you counted 12, you would multiply by 10 to get 120 beats per minute. Many album labels provide the beats per minute for your convenience. Table 2.1 shows typical song tempos listed in order from slower to faster for different types of social dance music. Sometimes the tempo gives you an idea of the type of music being played.

In addition to the five reliable cues just discussed, a couple of unreliable music cues exist, too: the melody and random accents. The melody, reflected in the lyrics of a song, provides an overlying rhythm superimposed on top of the underlying beats. The melody does not provide reliable music cues because it does not have to correspond exactly to the number of beats per measure, nor does it necessarily need to fit one or more measures in a consistent manner. However, particular styling cues that are characteristic of certain types of music are introduced through the melody and its overlying rhythms. For example, a Latin flavor may be added with certain instruments, such as maracas or bongos, which often subdivide selected beats within a song that are characteristic of cha-cha, rumba, merengue, and salsa/mambo.

**Table 2.1** Typical Song Tempos for Selected Social Dances

| Social dance | Tempo (bpm) |
|---|---|
| Waltz | 90-105 |
| Foxtrot | 120 |
| Swing | 120-170 |
| Polka | 96-130 |
| Cha-cha | 120 |
| Merengue | 125-140 |
| Rumba | 120 |
| Tango | 130 |
| Salsa | 150 |

An accent occurs whenever a particular beat within a measure is made stronger, louder, or heavier or otherwise stands out differently from the underlying beats. Also, dancers may choose to accent their movements on selected beats, which can be subjective and reflective of personal styling and thus not reliable music cues. Accents are superimposed on the underlying beats whether by a dancer's styling or characteristics of selected genres of music. Thus, accents are more subjective (when compared with the underlying beats) and may be altered by different musicians' interpretations of a particular song, making this information less reliable for dancers.

However, certain accents that are consistently used within a measure can alert you to what type of dance music is being played. For example, in waltz music, count 1 is slightly different from counts 2 and 3 within a measure. In both swing and foxtrot music, both counts 2 and 4 are stronger because the upbeats are accented in each measure. In these examples, the accents are connected to the underlying beats in a consistent, recurring manner and, thus, are reliable for helping you to identify the style or type of music being played.

# WHEN TO BEGIN MOVING WITH THE MUSIC

How do you know when to begin moving with the music? Now that you can identify the underlying beat and the tempo, your next task is to identify the first beat in a measure, called the *downbeat*, so that you can eventually coordinate your footwork to start on that beat. Identifying the downbeat can be a challenge when you first learn to dance. Following are three strategies that dancers often use to find the downbeat. You can use any one, or some combination of these strategies—whichever way works best for you.

One logical strategy is to wait until after the introduction of a song is over and be ready to move on the first beat you hear. However, this may be difficult for beginners who are unfamiliar with a particular song and may not be sure when the introduction is over. Typically, an introduction lasts four to eight measures. However, song introductions have a lot of variety, so their length is an unreliable factor. As mentioned earlier, the most reliable information is the number of beats per measure.

After the introduction is over, the next strategy is to mentally start counting in multiples of three or four to see which best fits to identify the number of beats per measure. In social dance settings, the measures are typically groupings of either four beats or three beats. Once you know the number of beats per measure, then it is a matter of repeating that grouping of beats for the length of the song. For example, if you can count to four with a particular song, then it is an example of 4/4 time music with four beats per measure and each beat getting one count (or it could be 2/4 time music with two measures counted together to total four counts). Or, if you can count to three with a particular song, then it is an example of 3/4 time music with three beats per measure and each beat getting one count. In social dancing, three beats per measure is, by definition, a waltz. The majority of the music selections played during an evening of social dancing is 4/4 time music. In this case, you only need to count one measure and prepare to move on the first beat of the next measure.

A third strategy is to give yourself advance notice so that you can be prepared to move on the downbeat of any measure. Dancers can use anticipatory cues similar to the warning signals preceding the start of a race, such as *On your mark, Get set, Go.* In addition to counting the single beats within a measure, you have two more ways of giving yourself more time to locate the downbeat: using duple division or triple division of each beat. If you chose to use duple division of the beat in 4/4 time, you would mentally add an *and (&)* preceding each beat. The & divides the beat into two parts and gives you more reaction time to prepare to move. For example, &-1, &-2, &-3, &-4. If you needed even more reaction time, you could choose to use a triple division of the beat within the four-beat measure. A triple division of the beat divides the beat into three sub-parts. For example, &-a-1, &-a-2, &-a-3, &-a-4. The *&-a* can be equated to a *Ready, set* signal. The triple division of the beat is also called using a *rolling count.* Dancers often use a rolling count as a way to create flair moves by modifying the timing between the beats. Either method of dividing the beat provides a consistent structure that dancers can use to give themselves more time to shift their CPB and initiate motion—to get ready and to move with the music.

Musicians may subdivide the beat even more, but social dancers do not find further subdivisions of the beat very useful. Figure 2.5 shows an example of one measure of 4/4 time music and how dancers might subdivide it. Figure 2.6 shows an

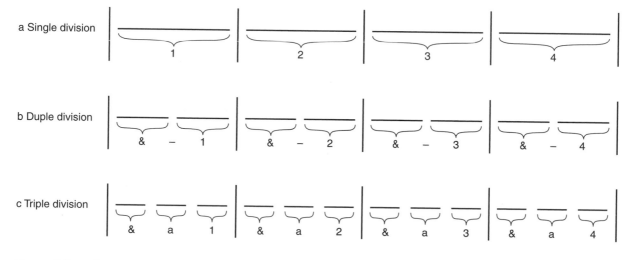

**Figure 2.5**   One measure of 4/4 time music showing (a) single, (b) duple, and (c) triple division of each beat.

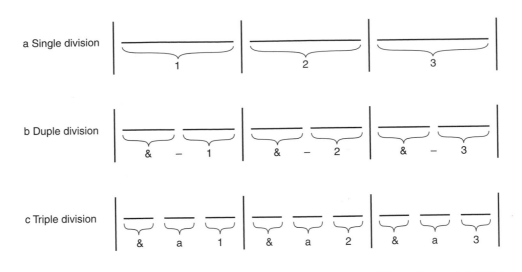

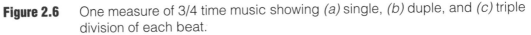

**Figure 2.6**   One measure of 3/4 time music showing (a) single, (b) duple, and (c) triple division of each beat.

example of one measure of 3/4 time music and how dancers might subdivide it. Again, sometimes a combination of these strategies is useful.

A fourth strategy is to start after hearing two measures of music, especially with waltz and polka music. Grouping two measures together corresponds to the time it takes to complete the rhythmic step pattern on both sides of the body before your starting foot is free again. It also means that you are moving *in phrase* with the music. Remember that grouping two measures equals a miniphrase of either eight counts (with 4/4 time music) or six counts (with 3/4 time music). This point will become clearer after you learn the rhythmic step patterns for the following dances: waltz, foxtrot (four-count box rhythm), polka, cha-cha, rumba, tango, and salsa/mambo (see steps 7, 9, 10, 11, 12, 13, and 14, respectively).

# DRILLS FOR MUSIC STRUCTURE

Locate the DVD bound in this book, gently remove it from the sleeve, and use it to answer the following drills. Feel free to listen as many times as necessary. You may refer to the correct answers at the end of each drill (see the Success Check). Once you get the main idea, listen to a variety of other music sources as a self-test to find out if you can transfer your auditory perception skills to different musical selections, even popular music that you hear on the radio.

# Drill 1
# Count the Beats per Measure

Listen and compare the counting examples on tracks 1 and 2. Mentally follow along as the underlying beats in each measure are vocally counted. Most social dance music is in 4/4 time with the exception of waltz music, which is in 3/4 time. The denominator of this equation tells you that each beat gets a quarter note, or one count in social dance music. Once you know the number of beats per measure, then you also know the time signature. If you can count in multiples of four, then the time signature is 4/4 time. If you can count in multiples of three, then the time signature is 3/4 time.

## TO DECREASE DIFFICULTY

- Review figure 2.2 for a visual image for grouping the beats into measures.
- Tap out each beat using your fingers, foot, or a pen.

## TO INCREASE DIFFICULTY

- Count eight measures at a time (review Music Cue 4).
- Listen to any of the tracks on the enclosed DVD, or select other songs, and repeat this drill.

## Success Goal

Be able to count using multiples of three or four to identify the number of underlying beats per measure on tracks 1 and 2.___

## Success Check

- Track 1 has four beats per measure counted as **1**, 2, 3, 4 (4/4 time signature). ___
- Track 2 has three beats per measure counted as **1**, 2, 3 (3/4 time signature). ___

# Drill 2
# Link Two Measures

Music is structured using beats, measures, and phrases. Once you can identify the number of beats per measure, the next challenge is to group two measures together, which creates a miniphrase. Listen at least twice as you mentally follow along with the vocal counts on tracks 3 and 4. On your first pass, notice that the first measure of the miniphrase is also termed a *heavy* measure because it is stronger than the second measure, which is called a *light* measure. The second time you listen to these tracks, use one hand to tap or mark the beats in one measure, then use your other hand to tap or mark the beats in the second measure.

As needed, listen for a third time and identify both the time signature and the number of beats within two measures (for the miniphrase) as used on each track. You may remember hearing instructors vocalize "5, 6, 7, 8" (the second measure) after mentally counting 1, 2, 3, 4 (the first measure) for 4/4 time signatures, or vocalize the second measure "4-5-6" after mentally counting the first measure of 3/4 time music. They were linking two measures together to create a miniphrase.

## TO DECREASE DIFFICULTY

- Review figures 2.3 and 2.4 to visualize how measures are grouped into phrases.
- Nod your head slightly to pulse on each beat you hear.

## TO INCREASE DIFFICULTY

- Listen to any of the tracks on the enclosed DVD or select other songs, and repeat this drill.
- Count the beats in sets of eight measures to identify a larger phrase. Choreographers typically use this method.

## *Success Goal*

Tap out the first measure with one hand, then tap out the second measure with your other hand and identify both the number of beats used in the miniphrase and the time signature used for tracks 3 and 4.___

## *Success Check*

- Track 3 has 4 beats per measure; eight beats of music are in each miniphrase and two measures are counted together as **1**, 2, 3, 4; **5**, 6, 7, 8 (4/4 time signature). ___
- Track 4 has three beats per measure; six beats of music are in each miniphrase and two measures are counted together as **1**, 2, 3; **4**, 5, 6 (3/4 time signature). ___

## Drill 3
# Find the Downbeat of Each Measure

When you start moving to music, you need to start on the downbeat. You can give yourself more time to react with a preparatory cue. Review figures 2.5 and 2.6, which show how to subdivide each beat of a measure. This drill demonstrates different ways of counting to locate the downbeat. Do the following to determine which way of counting works best for you:

Listen to tracks 5 and 6 for two different cuing methods. First, you will hear an & preceding the first beat of the measure or miniphrase. Next, you will hear an example using the rolling count; that is, an & a will be cued preceding the first beat of each measure or miniphrase.

As you follow along, use one hand to tap more strongly on the first beat in the measure and use your other hand to tap more softly on the other beats in the measure. You can use either method for any music.

### TO DECREASE DIFFICULTY

- Listen again to tracks 1 through 4 to hear the separate measures counted.

- Repeat this drill and verbally add a preparatory & at the beginning of each measure. For example, repeat "&-1, 2, 3, 4" with tracks 1 and 3.

- Repeat this drill and verbally add a preparatory &-a at the beginning of each measure. For example, repeat "&-a-1, 2, 3" with tracks 2 and 4.

### TO INCREASE DIFFICULTY

- Use both of the previous counting methods with tracks 1 through 4.

- Listen to any other track on the enclosed DVD and repeat this drill.

## *Success Goal*

Tap more strongly to indicate the first beat of each measure, then more softly on the other beats within each measure on tracks 5 and 6. ___

## *Success Check*

- On track 5, the downbeats occur on counts 1 and 5; four beats per measure (4/4 time signature) are counted either as **&-1**, 2, 3, 4; **&-5**, 6, 7, 8 or as **&-a-1**, 2, 3, 4; **&-a-5**, 6, 7, 8. ___

- On track 6, the downbeats occur on counts 1 and 4 with three beats per measure (3/4 time signature) and measures counted either as **&-1**, 2, 3; **&-4**, 5, 6 or as **&-a-1**, 2, 3; **&-a-4**, 5, 6. ___

- An & cue is equal to a half a count. ___

- An &-a cue is equal to two thirds of a count. ___

# SUCCESS SUMMARY
# FOR MUSIC STRUCTURE

For every song selection you hear, you need to use your auditory skills to identify the most reliable, consistent cues in the music—the beats, the duration of each beat (or tempo), the number of beats per measure, and how the measures are grouped into phrases. Basically, all social dance music can be categorized into measures of either three or four beats. If three beats are grouped, you know for sure that waltz music is being played. If four beats are grouped, the music being played could be any one of a variety of other dance styles such as foxtrot, swing, cha-cha, rumba, salsa/mambo, or tango. An exception occurs with merengue and polka music, which is in 2/4 time. Even though musicians play both the merengue and the polka in 2/4 time, giving them two beats per measure, it is often easier for social dancers to group two measures together and count these dances as if they had four beats in a measure. Moving to the music starts with finding the beat. Enjoy the process!

# Dance Rhythm Strategies

## *Connecting With the Music*

Have you ever been part of a marching band or been in the military? If so, you know the importance of recognizing an external cadence and marching to it—or how to keep the beat. These same skills are essential in social dance. The music provides the cadence, or tempo, through the underlying beats. In everyday walking, you can move at your own pace. However, with an external cadence that is provided through either a vocal count or the beats of music, you need to adjust your steps according to the tempo. As you know from step 2, once a tempo is established, it tends to remain the same throughout a particular song.

Whenever you connect your footwork to be in time with the music, three actions are integrated. First, you need to take a walking step by pushing off from one foot to the other. Each time you take a step, you make a weight change from one foot to the other. Second, you need to fully shift your CPB to be over the ball of your receiving foot. Third, you need to time your weight shift to be over the ball of your receiving foot to coincide precisely with each beat according to the tempo of the music. Walking or stepping on each beat is an example of an even rhythm that can be repeated for the length of a particular song. Other basic dance rhythms result from how your steps correspond to the beats of the music. Once you can recognize selected rhythm strategies, you'll have a head start for knowing how to execute the common rhythms that are used in all social dances.

# IMPORTANCE OF DANCE RHYTHMS

Dancing requires you to make a perceptual-motor match. That is, dancers first need to hone their auditory skills to both hear and recognize the tempo of the underlying beats of the music. Once the beat and tempo are perceived, then dancers can choose to step on each beat or to otherwise connect their footwork with the music in a rhythmic manner. Your walking steps become meaningful by how and when they rhythmically coincide with the underlying beats. When a recurring rhythm is established, you are dancing!

Your dancing is greatly enhanced when it is connected rhythmically with the music. When you ignore or don't precisely match your footwork in a meaningful way with the tempo provided by the music, it is called being *off time* with the music. When you can adjust your steps to the actual beats of the music, it becomes both intrinsically satisfying and extrinsically pleasing for others to watch. Your ability to recognize and execute the most common strategies for connecting your feet with the beats to create a rhythm will simplify your ability to learn any social dance. Don't ignore the music and your footwork; merge them in a meaningful way to create a rhythm and help you to get some positive feedback.

# RHYTHM STRATEGIES

Whether used singularly or in combination, the rhythm strategies described next provide a foundation for helping you to quickly identify how your footwork connects with the beats of the music. Each social dance has a unique basic step, or rhythmic step pattern. Once identified, the rhythmic step pattern is a consistent and recurring grouping of weight changes (or sometimes nonweight changes, such as when you tap, kick, or point a foot without shifting weight onto that foot) that is rhythmic and repeated for the length of a particular song. It can also be fun to create your own rhythmic step pattern, or you can use your analytic skills to break down the subparts of a specific rhythmic step pattern. You just need to identify the strategy used to form the rhythmic step pattern and the order if more than one rhythm is used. When someone demonstrates a specific dance's rhythmic step pattern, watch that person's foot contact with the floor and how the steps relate to the underlying beats of the music. If you can count four beats in a measure, the music is in 4/4 time. If you can count three beats in a measure, the music is in 3/4 time and a waltz.

The following strategies will give you a solid foundation for knowing how to connect your footwork rhythmically with the music. You need to become familiar with each of these rhythms; you'll meet them again when you learn the basic step, or what dancers call the *rhythmic step pattern,* for each of the social dances covered in this book. Since the majority of social dance music is in 4/4 time, those rhythm strategies are presented first, then the waltz rhythm strategy, which is commonly used with 3/4 time music, is presented.

## Step on Each Beat of 4/4 Time Music

The easiest dance rhythm to execute and to identify is the strategy of taking a step on each beat of the four-beat measure. This even-rhythm strategy alternates a weight change on each beat such that you start and end with the same foot free again. For example, if you step onto your left foot on count 1, then you would step onto your right foot on count 2, and repeat your left-right steps for counts 3 and 4, respectively. An even rhythm reflects repetitive actions that have a steady, soothing quality, such as when you walk or march at a consistent tempo. When a step is taken on each beat of the measure, you may sometimes hear these steps referred to as *quick* steps because each step takes one beat of music. Note that the use of *quick* as a cue is appropriate with only 4/4 time music; *quick* equates one count to one beat.

Walking to a steady beat sounds simple. However, your foot contact with the floor varies not only with the tempo provided, but also with the direction of travel. When walking forward, your sending foot (the foot supporting your weight) pushes back to propel your body forward and initiate a heel–ball–toe contact with the floor before stepping onto your receiving foot. It is important to keep your CPB moving forward (in the direction of travel) in order for your body's weight to be over the ball of each receiving foot on each count. Remember that your CPB leads and your feet follow, giving purpose to your walking steps.

When walking backward, the reverse happens; you create a toe–ball–heel contact with the floor as your CPB initiates the direction preceding a weight transfer from one foot to the other. Again, when asked to walk or step backward on each beat, the goal is to push forward with your sending foot in order to move backward and shift your CPB to be over the ball of your receiving foot on each beat.

## Step on the Odd-Numbered Beats of 4/4 Time Music

In this rhythm, only a single step is taken within each two beats of 4/4 time music. Thus, within a four-beat measure, you would take only two steps. Within two measures, you would take a step only on the downbeats (the odd counts 1, 3, 5, and 7). On the upbeats (the even counts 2, 4, 6, and 8), you may use a variety of nonweight options, such as a hold, a toe point, a brush, a tap, or a kick. When you take a single step on only the downbeats of a measure, the step is sometimes referred to as a *slow* step. Within 4/4 time music, a slow step typically takes two counts or beats (and is twice as long relative to a quick step).

## Step on the Even-Numbered Beats of 4/4 Time Music

You actually have two options as to when to take a single step within each two-beat grouping: either on the first count (downbeat) as in the previous example, or on the second count (upbeat). When you take only one step on the second count within two beats of 4/4 time music, your actual weight change is delayed until the upbeat. For example, you could choose from a variety of nonweight options on count 1, then step on count 2. When grouping two measures together, your delayed weight changes would occur on counts 2, 4, 6, and 8. Your footwork is more accurate when you are aware of which count your actual step should be taken on to create the desired dance rhythm. That is true whether your weight change is to be taken on count 1 with a hold on count 2, or to hold on count 1 and take a weight change on count 2 of the 4/4 time music. Within each two-beat grouping, your choices are to either take a single step on the downbeat (and hold on the upbeat) or take a delayed single step on the upbeat (and hold on the downbeat).

## Three Steps in Two Beats of 4/4 Time Music

Combining three steps together within two beats of 4/4 time music creates a triple step. A triple step in dance terminology may also be called a *chassé* (i.e., one foot follows, or *chases*, the other), or sometimes it is called a *shuffle* (again, one foot remains in the lead). The timing execution of a triple step involves three weight changes within two beats of music; one foot is in the lead on each whole count. It would be misleading to count the three weight changes as *1, 2, 3* for a triple step because you would be counting the weight changes independent of the beats within the music, implying that each weight change gets the same amount of time, which occurs only in waltz rhythm. Instead, it is more accurate to cue a triple step in terms of the timing of the weight changes in each two-beat grouping; in other words, *1, &-2*, where each cue gets a weight change in order to get the proper timing. When a triple step is counted properly, there is one weight change on count 1, while the second and third weight changes are faster and each step gets a half count on cue *&-2*. Alternatively, you might hear the cues *left, right-left* for a left-side triple step and *right, left-right* for a right-side triple step. Remember that it takes two counts on each side of your body or one measure before your starting foot is free again.

To execute a triple step within two beats of music, use a pushing action with the ball of your sending foot and step onto your receiving foot on count 1. On the *&* cue, place only the ball of your sending foot either just beside or slightly behind the heel of your receiving foot and push off; you do not have enough time to put your whole foot down. Then, take another forward step onto your receiving foot on count 2. Whether you travel to the side, forward, or backward, it helps to keep one foot in the lead and your CPB over the weighted, unit foot; that is, your left foot when executing the triple rhythm on the left side and your right foot when on the right side. Keep your knees slightly bent for more control during the push.

## Steps on Each Beat of 3/4 Time Music

The waltz rhythm strategy uses three weight changes. Although you execute three weight changes similar to a triple step, the timing is very different with 3/4 time music. In the basic waltz rhythm, each step gets one count; one weight change occurs on each beat of the measure. Because three steps correspond to the three beats in a measure, it takes two measures of waltz music before your starting foot is free again. The three steps in the waltz are repeated on both sides of the body. For example, stepping on your left, right, left; and right, left, right takes six beats of music.

# DRILLS FOR DANCE RHYTHM

The following drills help you experience the basic rhythms typically used in social dancing. Stand tall with good posture. Make sure that your head, shoulders, and hips are aligned over your feet like building blocks, one above the other. Look straight ahead with your chin level for better balance. You may refer to the suggested music tracks on the enclosed DVD or select your own music to complete the drills. Either way, listen closely to the music before moving.

# Drill 1
# Executing Three Rhythm Strategies

Listen to the 4/4 time music example on track 1. Mentally or verbally count *1, 2, 3, 4* to correspond to each beat within one measure. Imagine you are marching in place (although you don't need to lift your feet very high off the floor) and practice each of the following rhythm strategies:

a. Step on each beat as you change your weight completely from one foot to the other on each whole count. Use track 8 and sets of four beats as follows: start in place, walk forward, backward, and sideward.

b. Step on only the odd-numbered beats (the downbeats on counts 1, 3) as you change your weight from one foot to the other. Use track 8 and sets of eight beats as follows: start in place, walk forward, backward, and sideward.

c. Step on only the even-numbered beats (the upbeats on counts 2, 4) as you change your weight from one foot to the other. Use track 8 and sets of eight beats as follows: start in place, walk forward, backward, and sideward.

d. Use track 13 to group two measures together and alternately repeat sequence *a* for eight beats and sequence *b* for eight beats. Thus, for sequence *a*, make eight weight changes in place (stepping on each beat 1-8). For sequence *b*, make four weight changes (stepping in place on only the odd-numbered beats, 1, 3, 5, 7, and holding on beats 2, 4, 6, 8).

e. Use track 13 to group two measures together and alternately repeat sequence *a* for eight beats and sequence *c* for eight beats. Thus, for sequence *a*, make eight weight changes (stepping on each beat 1-8) in place. For sequence *c*, make four weight changes (stepping in place on only the even-numbered beats, 2, 4, 6, 8, and holding on beats 1, 3, 5, 7).

 **TO DECREASE DIFFICULTY**

- Execute each part separately until you become comfortable shifting your weight correctly.
- Use verbal counts (try track 3), then slowly increase the tempo.

**TO INCREASE DIFFICULTY**

- Repeat the movement sequences using a faster tempo. For example, use track 7 or 12.
- Step in place to make one long sequence using eight beats for each sequence part: *a, b, a, c*.
- Face a partner without touching and repeat sequences *a-c*. Leaders start with the left foot, and followers start with the right foot. Directions are from the leader's point of view.
- Use fingertip pressure while facing a partner and repeat sequences *a-c*.

*(continued)*

Drill 1 *(continued)*

## *Success Goal*

Perform 2 minutes of stationary stepping (a) on each beat, (b) only on the down-beats, (c) only on the upbeats, (d) alternate eight beats each of sequences *a* and *b,* and (e) alternate eight beats each of sequences *a* and *c.* ___

## *Success Check*

- Your CPB should be over the receiving foot on each weight change. ___
- Completely shift your weight from one foot to the other on the appropriate rhythm's count. ___

# Drill 2
# Walking Mixer

A mixer is an easy way to get everyone up and dancing quickly. This easy-to-follow walking mixer is a perfect choice because it uses regular walking steps, uses a set sequence, and requires no leading or following and no previous dance experience. In addition, it doesn't matter which foot you start with. A mixer calls for switching partners at some point, which facilitates social interaction. It can be used to introduce dancers during an evening of dance and to encourage dancers to be more comfortable exchanging partners. In a social setting, this mixer can be an ice breaker, a review, or a fun, culminating activity. Choose music with a strong beat such as "Good Times" by Chic, "Celebration" by Kool & the Gang, "Ring My Bell" by Anita Ward, or track 8 on the DVD.

Pair up with a partner. Stand side by side with your left shoulders toward center to form a large double circle facing counterclockwise (see figure 3.1). Walk through each part of the following sequence, gradually adding another part, until you can do the entire sequence in four sets of four beats, or 16 total counts, then to slow 4/4 time music.

This mixer uses walking steps and four directions: forward, backward, left diagonal, and a clockwise rotation. A further challenge is to accent the new direction change within each measure in order to relate to each new partner. The secret to this refinement is to group three walking steps together in any one direction, then make the second direction change on the fourth count of each measure. In total, this mixer uses four measures, or 16 counts, and the rhythm strategy of stepping on each beat of the 4/4 time music. You may start with either foot; just maintain the tempo with each weight change as you step on each underlying beat of the measure. Verbal cues for the direction changes follow:

a. *Forward and face:* Walk forward three steps, face your partner (inside circle makes a quarter turn clockwise and outside circle makes a quarter turn counterclockwise).

b. *Backward and diagonal:* Walk backward three steps and face your left front diagonal. You will be facing a new partner.

c. *Forward and hook:* Walk forward three steps in your left front diagonal direction and hook elbows with a new partner.

d. *Rotate and release:* Walk clockwise with this new partner for three steps, then release elbows and face the counterclockwise direction to start over again. (The partner in the outside circle has the greater distance to turn to be in position to start the sequence again.)

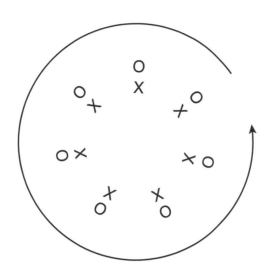

**Figure 3.1**    Double-circle formation; X = leaders or inside-circle dancers; O = followers or outside-circle dancers.

 **TO DECREASE DIFFICULTY**

- Substitute a do-si-do (pass right shoulders, move back-to-back) around your partner (in place of the elbow hooks).
- Use a verbal count and no music until you can match the tempo of the desired music.
- Without a partner, assume you are on the outside or the inside of the double circle, and walk to a verbal count as you repeat the set sequence. This becomes a great low-impact aerobics routine.

**TO INCREASE DIFFICULTY**

- Introduce yourself during the mixer and thank each partner before switching to the new partner.
- Add an accent as you move backward, such as a clap on count 4.
- Experiment with substituting a three-step turn to your left as you move diagonally left to a new partner.

*(continued)*

Drill 2  *(continued)*

## *Success Goal*

Keep your feet moving to step on each beat during the walking mixer first to slow 4/4 time music, then to faster 4/4 time music. ___

- Keep your feet moving, as if you are marching, in order to take a step on each verbal count or beat of the music. ___
- Change to a new direction on count 4 of each measure. ___
- Take small backward steps to avoid bumping into others (if on the inside of the circle) or getting too far apart (if on the outside). ___

# Drill 3
# Triple Rhythm

The triple rhythm is sometimes referred to as a *triple step,* and sometimes shortened to a *triple.* Notice that the phrase *tri-ple step* can be broken into three syllables, which is an easy way to remember the number of weight changes in a triple step—three. However, within 4/4 time music, these three steps are executed within only two beats of music. The second and third steps are executed with only a half beat per weight change. When doing continuous triple rhythm steps, any one measure (four beats within 4/4 time music) is cued 1, &-2, 3, &-4. Each cue represents a weight change, which means that you are making six weight changes in four beats.

When you start with your left foot (for leaders), keep your CPB over that foot as you group three weight changes within two beats (stepping left, right-left). When you start with your right foot (for followers), also keep your CPB over that foot as you group three weight changes within two beats (stepping right, left-right). Advanced dancers add a bit more rhythm to the triple step especially with swing music by using the rolling count (&-a). Their strategy is to keep the & cue silent and delay taking the second weight change until they hear the *a* (e.g., 1, a-2).

Try your triple rhythm steps while stationary until you are comfortable with executing three weight changes within two beats. Then, use track 10 and sets of eight beats to execute four triples in the following sequence: to each side, to move forward, and to move backward.

### TO DECREASE DIFFICULTY

- Repeat each subpart to slow counts, keeping one side in the lead for two counts, then the other side in the lead for two counts.
- Gradually increase the tempo until you can move to slow music.

## TO INCREASE DIFFICULTY

- Increase the tempo of the 4/4 time music. For example, try tracks 11, 14, and 15.
- Repeat the drill starting with your right foot.
- Repeat the sequence two ways: first facing a partner without touching, then with fingertip pressure. Leaders start with left foot and followers start with the right foot. Directions are from the leader's point of view.

## Success Goal

Perform 2 minutes of continuous triple rhythm steps (a) while stationary, and (b) while sequencing the following: four triple steps in place and alternating sides, four forward triples, and four backward triples; in other words, move eight counts in each direction. ___

## Success Check

- Execute three weight changes within two beats. ___
- Execute six weight changes within four beats. ___
- Keep your CPB over your left foot on a left-side triple step, then over your right foot on a right-side triple step. ___

# Drill 4
# Waltz Rhythm

First, you need to identify the number of beats per measure within a particular song. If the song's measures are grouped in three beats, then it is waltz music (listen to tracks 2, 4, and 6). The waltz is the only social dance that uses 3/4 time music with three beats per measure. In the basic waltz rhythm, each beat gets one count and one weight change. You might think that because there are three weight changes that the waltz rhythm uses a triple rhythm; however, it does not. A true, basic triple rhythm occurs only within 4/4 time music (see the previous drill).

Using the waltz rhythm, it takes two measures, or six beats (and six weight changes), before your starting foot is free again. For practice, start with your left foot and step in place corresponding to each beat of the measure (left, right, left). For the second measure, continue stepping on each beat (right, left, right). After two measures, you will end up with the left foot free.

It is actually more difficult to execute this drill when you are stationary. So, starting with your left foot, add a forward direction (stepping forward, together, in place), then a backward direction for three steps starting with your right foot (stepping back, together, in place). Both partners do the same footwork, but when facing a partner, the follower starts with the right foot and reverses the directions to execute the backward waltz rhythm, then the forward waltz rhythm. These steps are called *balance steps;* the feet are together in first position on counts 2 and 3.

*(continued)*

**Drill 4** *(continued)*

The waltz rhythm may be executed to each side as well. Leaders start with the left foot to step to the left side, bring the feet together, and step in place. When moving to the right side, step with the right foot to the right side, bring the feet together, and step in place. Again the feet alternate, left-right-left and right-left-right to maintain the tempo and a weight change on each count of the three-beat measures. Use track 9 to practice the waltz rhythm.

## TO DECREASE DIFFICULTY

- Use a slow verbal count.
- Transfer your weight over the ball of each foot on each whole count.
- Face a partner without touching and mirror the waltz rhythm steps forward-backward and sideward. Leaders start with the left foot and followers start with the right foot.

## TO INCREASE DIFFICULTY

- Use fewer repetitions before changing directions, such as one forward–backward, then one side left and one side right waltz basic.
- Repeat the sequence above while facing a partner and using fingertip pressure.

## Success Goal

Execute the waltz rhythm for 2 minutes (a) alternately moving forward one measure and backward one measure, (b) alternately moving to the left side on one measure and to the right side on one measure, (c) combine parts a and b with two repetitions (or four measures) each, and (d) alternate four waltz steps forward, then four waltz steps backward. ___

## Success Check

- One weight change is made on each beat. ___
- The forward waltz rhythm starts with the left foot and takes three beats or one measure. ___
- The backward waltz rhythm starts with the right foot and takes three beats or one measure. ___
- Move (forward or backward or sideward) on count 1, and keep your feet together (in first foot position) on counts 2 and 3. ___
- You can rise on the balls of your feet on counts 2 and 5 to add styling. ___

# Drill 5
# Combining Rhythms Into Patterns

The previous drills have given you a chance to practice selected dance rhythms for the length of a particular song. If you mix and match these basic dance rhythm strategies, you can come up with traditional as well as some original combinations that match the music and provide a recurring pattern. Below are some choreographic ways of establishing a specific rhythmic step pattern using 4/4 time music.

One way is to put two dance rhythms together. For example, within one measure of four beats of music, you might combine the following:

- Two steps (one on each of two beats) + A single step in two beats

- Two steps (one on each of two beats) + A triple rhythm step

Another way is to reverse the order, such as in the following combinations:

- A single step in two beats + Two steps (one on each of two beats)

- A triple rhythm step + Two steps (one on each of two beats)

A third way is to put three rhythms together (again, note the order of appearance). Combining three rhythms is grouping more than one measure of 4/4 time music, such as one and a half measures, or six beats of music as follows:

- A single step in two beats + A single step in two beats + Two steps in two beats

- A triple rhythm step + A triple rhythm step + Two steps in two beats

A fourth way is to put four rhythm strategies together. Combining four rhythms is grouping two measures, or eight beats of music. Within social dance, you will rarely find a rhythmic step pattern composed of more than four dance rhythms. The tango is the best example of this choreographic strategy because it uses an eight-count rhythmic step pattern that is subdivided into four sets of two beats as follows: a step on the upbeat, a step on the upbeat, two steps, and a close or foot drag (using a nonweight-change ending).

A fifth way is to combine slow and quick cues to create a rhythm pattern. A *slow* takes two beats with only one weight change that may be taken either on the downbeat or on the upbeat. A *quick* takes one beat of music and one weight change. Mix and match the 4/4 time dance rhythm strategies to form two different six-count rhythm patterns composed of (a) *quick, quick, slow, slow*, then (b) *slow, slow, quick, quick*. Can you detect the timing differences when the slow weight change is executed on the downbeat versus the upbeat? In part II, you will learn the specific rhythmic step patterns that are traditionally associated with each dance style covered in this book. Be aware of how the dance rhythms are utilized to form these specific rhythmic step patterns.

Select any one of the preceding rhythm strategy examples and use it to establish your own rhythm pattern that can be repeated for the length of one song. Use any 4/4 time music or select from tracks 10, 11, 12, 13, 16, 17, 18, or 19.

*(continued)*

Drill 5 *(continued)*

### TO DECREASE DIFFICULTY

- Take one example at a time, using the first strategy only.
- Remain stationary to try out your selected pattern.

### TO INCREASE DIFFICULTY

- Add direction changes within your selected pattern.
- Use a variety of nonweight options where possible.
- Combine any two or more strategies to establish your own pattern.
- Explain how your solution to the problem fits the criteria (many possible solutions exist).

## *Success Goal*

Repeat your selected rhythm pattern to 4/4 time music for 2 minutes. ___

## *Success Check*

- Keep the rhythm constant. ___
- Use the appropriate weight changes to match the appropriate beats for your selected rhythm pattern. ___
- Many possible solutions to this drill exist, if you can meet the preceding criteria. ___

---

# SUCCESS SUMMARY FOR DANCE RHYTHMS

Blending your perceptual-motor skills for hearing the beat and coordinating your steps with the tempo of the music requires both timing and practice. A rhythm is a recurring pattern that is established when your footwork connects in a meaningful way with the beats of the music. With practice, you can learn to time your CPB shift onto the ball of your receiving foot to coincide precisely with a specific beat or count—once you know the recurring rhythm, or rhythm pattern. It takes concentration to be able to walk or step in a rhythmic manner according to the tempo of the music rather than to your own pace.

All social dances are composed of a few dance rhythms. You are dancing when you can repeat either a dance rhythm, or the rhythmic step pattern universally associated with a particular dance style, for the length of a song. Being able to recognize and execute the common strategies for connecting your feet with the beats to create a rhythm will simplify your ability to learn any social dance. Whether used singularly or in combination, the selected dance rhythm strategies provide a foundation for success for knowing how to connect your footwork rhythmically with the music.

# Partner Dynamics and Etiquette

## *Communicating Effectively*

Before dancing with a partner, feeling uncertain is natural. Here are common questions about partner dancing: *How should you ask a partner to dance? Who asks whom to dance? What do you do if a partner does not want to dance? Will your partner know how to give the proper leads? What do you do when your partner doesn't follow? Why does the man always get to be the leader and the woman has to follow? What do you do if your partner doesn't know the basic step? What do you do if your partner criticizes you?* You can be more in control of these uncertainties if you know your responsibilities and how to communicate effectively in a social dance setting.

You can communicate with your partner verbally and nonverbally. Both ways contribute to making the *social* in social dancing a more pleasant experience. Verbal communication includes knowing and practicing proper social dance etiquette as well as promoting and practicing a respectful attitude toward your partner and others. Nonverbal communication includes knowing and practicing how to connect with a partner, how to lead, how to follow, and how to create a three-way partnership involving you, your partner, and the music.

# IMPORTANCE OF PARTNER DYNAMICS AND ETIQUETTE

Social dancing involves traditional roles for partners as well as proper etiquette. Just as driving a car requires only one driver at the wheel, social dance requires only one leader in the partnership. The leader's primary role is to *drive;* that is, to plan and signal direction changes to a partner and to initiate choreography (put moves together) without bumping into other couples. However, neither partner is literally a car, so this analogy must be modified a bit. Thus, the interpretation of leading has evolved from thinking of it as a dictatorship situation to viewing it as a partnership. A successful partnership combines an awareness of moving not only yourself, but of moving both yourself and your partner in unison to the tempo of the music. Blending these three elements together is intrinsically satisfying.

It is said that good communication is made up of 7 percent words, 38 percent voice quality, and 55 percent body language. On the dance floor, your actions speak louder than your words! When you say something to a partner, how you say it is as important as what you say. We all like to receive positive strokes. If you are polite and respectful of both your partner's and other dancers' space, they are more likely to treat you in the same manner. A social setting presents numerous opportunities to practice social etiquette, such as introducing yourself to others, politely asking a partner to dance, graciously accepting a dance invitation, thanking your partner for the dance, and generally working well with a partner. The main advantage of demonstrating these social graces is that they encourage positive interactions and continual interchanges. A sponsored evening of social dancing is similar to a group date because the group members constantly interrelate with each other, fulfilling the role of a good host or hostess.

# GENERAL PARTNER ETIQUETTE

In a social setting, it is considered good etiquette to introduce yourself to someone new. Likewise, whenever you meet a new partner, make it a point to introduce yourself. At least three potential situations exist where you may demonstrate social dance etiquette: prior to dancing with a partner, while dancing with a partner, and after sharing a dance with a partner.

## Before Dancing With a Partner

Traditionally the male is expected to take the initiative, but either partner may ask the other to dance. It is most important that both partners be polite to each other, such as in the following examples. When asking someone to dance, use phrases such as these:

- "May I have this dance?"
- "Would you like to dance?"

Accept an invitation graciously with phrases such as these:

- "Certainly."
- "Yes, you may."

- "Yes, I would like to."
- "I would love to."

The following rules provide some examples of etiquette practices typically found in sponsored, nondate events.

- It is more polite to ask a partner to dance than to stand on the sidelines watching.
- Politely ask a partner to dance.
- The follower should accept graciously. If the follower truly does not want to dance, she can say so, but she should not dance with another partner until that particular dance is over.
- Follow the *no monopolizing* rule, meaning that the follower may excuse herself after two successive dances to provide the leader with an opportunity to ask another partner. This rule encourages mixing and more opportunities for all to dance.
- A leader should not cut in on a dancing couple without first asking any follower who is not dancing whether she would like to dance.
- Followers should not huddle in groups; it makes it harder for the leaders to ask them to dance.
- Introduce yourself, as well as other people you know who do not know each other.

## When Dancing With a Partner

Once on the dance floor, one partner needs to lead and the other needs to follow. Traditionally, the male takes the initiative to lead and invites the female to follow. In this case, tradition is practical in that one person, the leader, becomes the designated driver. Especially in waltz and foxtrot, the leader may extend his left hand to the follower who moves forward to accept the invitation by grasping his open left palm with her right hand and by moving into a closed dance position with the leader in preparation to move together with the music. Following are selected social etiquette tips to use when dancing with a partner:

- Be considerate of your partner. Avoid giving hints, criticizing, or dancing for the benefit of onlookers—showing off at the expense of your partner.
- Move in unison with your partner. Avoid leading your partner as you would an object; you are dancing with a person.
- The leader is responsible for choreography on the dance floor. Avoid elaborate and complex combinations with a new partner. Focus on the basic steps to the music, then gradually add variations.
- Be considerate of other couples. Avoid executing long routines and horizontal arm extensions, especially when the floor is crowded.
- The follower should let the leader lead; have patience that the leader is doing his best.
- Do not offer advice on the dance floor unless you are specifically asked for your opinion.

- The follower's arms should not rest heavily on the leader's arm and hand.
- The leader's right hand should not slip down below the follower's left shoulder blade.
- Avoid singing, counting out loud, or chewing gum to the music as you dance.
- If you accidentally bump someone, offer an apology.
- Inconspicuously and gently lead a partner through an unknown step, or move to the side to avoid blocking traffic.
- Do not eat, drink, or stand and talk on the dance floor when others are dancing.

## After Dancing With a Partner

Etiquette doesn't stop when the dance is over. Following are some examples of how to treat a partner after sharing a dance:

- The leaders escort their partners back to where they asked them to dance.
- Both partners thank each other for the dance.
- During an evening of dance, share the fun by dancing with many different partners.
- At the end of the evening, thank the official host or hostess.

# CONNECTING WITH A PARTNER

When you dance with a partner, you are sharing space that includes both of you. The basic partner positions used in this book are commonly used in social dancing (see figure 4.1, *a-i*). Each partner position described in the following paragraphs requires you to connect with a partner in a slightly different manner.

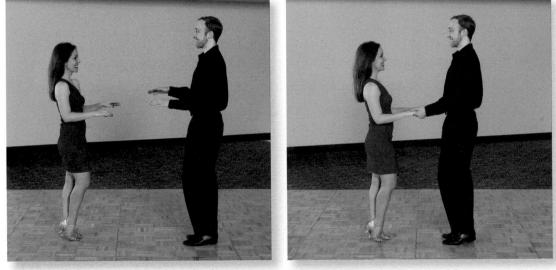

a Shine

b Two hands joined

**Figure 4.1**   Basic partner positions.

**c** One hand joined

**d** Inside hands joined

**e** Closed

**f** Promenade, or semiopen

**g** Sweetheart

**h** Right parallel

**i** Left parallel

## Shine Position

The shine position (figure 4.1*a*) is used whenever you are facing a partner but not touching hands. It is called *shine* because each partner has more freedom to express him- or herself when apart and not touching. Another interpretation of the shine position is that a spotlight is shining on your chest and you are in the spotlight to present your moves with flair. The shine position is typically used in the cha-cha and the salsa/mambo.

## Two Hands Joined

In the two-hands-joined position (figure 4.1*b*), the partners face each other at a comfortable distance apart. The leader opens his palms for the follower to put her hands into them with the palms down. The leader then gently grasps the follower's hands. Avoid gripping too tightly. A modification of this two-hands-joined position is used in the cha-cha. Specifically, the leader separates his thumb from his fingers with his palms down (as if wearing a hand puppet), extends his elbows out from his sides slightly and grasps the follower's hands on each side with his thumbs under her palms.

## One Hand Joined

Start with two hands joined, then release one hand (figure 4.1*c*). Typically, this position is used for leading either sideways or rotational moves. For example, the leader's left hand may be brought across his midline toward his right side, or conversely, the leader's right hand may be brought across his midline toward his left side.

## Inside Hands Joined

This position (figure 4.1*d*) is most often used in the polka. Stand side by side with your partner; the leader is on the left side. The leader extends his right hand, palm up, toward his partner. The follower places her left hand, palm down, in his hand. Another characteristic of the polka is for each partner to place the outside hands on the hips.

## Closed

The closed position (figure 4.1*e*) is a very regal position reflecting the origin of ballroom dancing in the royal courts of Europe when soldiers wore swords on the left hip. Thus, the follower is positioned more on the leader's right side so as to keep the sword out of the way. An offset position also keeps the leader from stepping on the follower's toes and from stepping around the follower with his feet too widely spaced. In social dancing and within the American styling, the *closed position,* or closed hold, consists of at least four points of contact between partners: The leader's right hand is placed on the follower's left shoulder blade; the follower's left arm is gently placed on top of the leader's right arm; the follower's left elbow is resting on, or slightly touching, the leader's right elbow; the leader's left hand is extended with palm up for the follower to place her right hand with palm down. The clasped hands are held approximately level with the follower's shoulders when in closed position.

In international style, an additional contact point is required; that is, the right side of each partner's diaphragm must be touching. Because the international styling requires closer contact, it is not commonly used on the social dance floor, especially when dancing with a variety of partners. In Latin dances, the closed position is modified to have the forearms almost touching. Also, the clasped hands are held higher, approximately level with the leader's left ear.

## Promenade, or Semiopen

This position (figure 4.1*f*) is a modified closed position with outside shoulders angled toward the joined hands. To get into the semiopen position, keep your frame firm as both partners rotate the lower half of their body to face their extended hands. Both partners look toward the extended hands.

In the swing, the joined-hand position changes slightly such that the hands are lower and the leader rotates the fingers of his left hand clockwise approximately 90 degrees to have his thumb on top before grasping his partner's fingers.

## Sweetheart

This position (figure 4.1*g*) is used in the polka and the cha-cha. Other names for this position include *cape* and *varsovienne*. It starts with a right-to-right hand grasp. The leader then brings his right hand to his right side to guide the follower in front and to his right side. The follower's palms are facing out and placed at approximately shoulder height. The leader's fingers gently connect with the follower's fingers. The follower stands approximately a half step in front of the leader.

## Parallel Left and Parallel Right

The two parallel positions are based on the leader's position. Start in a closed position, then modify it by bringing the follower to one side of the leader. For a right parallel position (figure 4.1*h*), bring the follower to the leader's right side. The leader's right shoulder is next to the follower's right shoulder. For a left parallel position (see figure 4.1*i*), the follower stands outside the leader's left side with left shoulders closer together and parallel.

Notice that within each position a center point exists between the partners. If either partner gets too far away from or too close to the other, it is more difficult to lead and follow. You can use your arm positions to give your partner a reference base for where you are. If you permit your arms to hang freely at your sides whenever you are in an open or apart position, it will be difficult to find your partner's hand whenever a hand grasp is needed. Or, if you bend your elbows and keep your forearms more parallel to the floor, you are splitting the distance between you and your partner such that your hands can meet in the middle, such as in a two-hands-joined position. Thus, your arm placements, or positions in space, provide a frame that defines your personal space. Following are three example situations where one's frame affects how partners connect with each other.

## Example 1

From a closed position (figure 4.2*a*), if the leader signals a forward direction move, the leader will not be effective if the follower lets her arms collapse, which permits the leader to move into her space (figure 4.2*b*). Conversely, if the leader moves in a backward direction and lets his elbows collapse, the follower moves into his space (figure 4.2*c*). Basically, each partner is responsible for maintaining his or her half of any partner position. The amount of pressure or tension to maintain is often a matter of trial and error. It is not necessary to tense your arms all the time. Rather, it is a matter of not letting your partner move into your space, and vice versa. In the example of a forward direction lead, once the leader moves forward, the follower can feel the movement initiation and can move backward with arms defining her space. She only needs to hold her arms up against the pull of gravity and avoid letting her elbow extend back behind her body. The follower needs to avoid resting the weight of her arms on her partner, and the leader needs to avoid letting his elbows droop toward his sides. For both partners, holding the arms up and not dangling them becomes an isometric exercise that will strengthen the triceps muscles (posterior upper arms). Note that these same points apply to the sweetheart position, too.

a                                    b                                    c

**Figure 4.2**  *(a)* Starting in closed position with individual frame, each partner's half of the shared space may be invaded when the leader wants to travel *(b)* forward and she doesn't hold her half or *(c)* backward when the leader doesn't hold his half of the shared space.

## Example 2

From a two-hands-joined position, avoid straightening your elbows, which increases the distance or space between partners. Figure 4.3 shows the results of this common error. Notice that straightening your elbows permits your head and upper torso to lean backward, throwing you off balance and slowing down your timing with the music. Correct this potential error by using your elbows like shock absorbers; that is, keep your elbows slightly bent with enough tension or resistance to keep them in front of your body. Be aware that this error may also occur when using a one-hand-joined position.

**Figure 4.3** Avoid straightening your elbows and letting your upper body lean back when using a two-hands-joined position.

## Example 3

On rotational moves, the distance between partners should also be split. For example, stand beside a partner and find the center point between your feet. Imagine stretching a string from this center point and drawing a small circle on the floor connecting both partners' feet to outline both an inner and an outer circle. Now both partners may take walking steps either clockwise or counterclockwise within this small circular floor path (figure 4.4). By splitting the distance that either partner has to travel, you are connecting with your partner to make the entire rotational move look effortless. On the other hand, if one partner acts like a post, the other partner must walk around this post, which is more awkward. By splitting the distance that each partner has to move, you are working together, which is an important part of social dancing.

**Figure 4.4** On rotational moves, imagine a small circular area that connects both partners' feet.

# LEADING AND FOLLOWING A PARTNER

The ultimate goal on the social dance floor is to dance with your partner in time to the music. This shared experience provides intrinsic rewards. Once you go to a dance, you may become aware of spectators watching you dance. However, you need to shift your focus away from any observers and instead focus first on the music for the tempo, then on moving with your partner to that tempo. The ideal three-way partnership consists of you, your partner, and the music. If only one or two elements come together, then you'll experience a feeling of being at odds with either your partner or the music. If all three elements mesh together, then dancing becomes a pleasure to do as well as enjoyable to watch. You can better maintain this three-way partnership once you know your role and responsibilities within the partnership. Keep the following points in mind when you begin leading and following.

## Leading a Partner

To be a good leader, you first need to be able to repeat your basic steps (or rhythmic step patterns) until you can do them almost without thinking. Once you can repeat the rhythm pattern to the music without looking at your feet, you are ready to think about other aspects of dancing with a partner such as how much force to use on leads, when to signal a lead, how to smoothly connect any two or more partner positions, and how to combine steps into short sequential combinations. As the leader has a lot to think about, it helps to focus on only one aspect at a time and to gradually add another aspect as you execute the appropriate basic steps.

How much force should you use to lead? In general, leads involve gentle pressure to indicate a direction change. They are subtle, nonverbal indicators of where you intend to move next. Typically, a lead is comprised of a combination of actions. For example, from a closed partner position, the leader may initiate a couple's turn by facing, or rotating, his frame (upper torso, including arms) in the intended direction, either clockwise or counterclockwise. This example lead involves upper-body isolation to twist the upper body in the direction of the desired turn. The leader should keep his arms curved and move his entire frame (i.e., shoulders, arms, and torso move as one unit) until his sternum is facing the intended direction. It is important to maintain a solid frame; the lead is less effective if either partner lets only his or her arms move.

When does the leader give the lead? All leads must be given immediately preceding the intended move so that the follower has enough time to respond. If you intend to stay in the direction indicated, then it is not necessary to give a new lead until you want to move in another direction. Thus, the leader is always thinking ahead to what direction to move in and signaling the lead early enough that the follower can recognize and respond to it. In general, leads occur at the end of a rhythmic step pattern. It is helpful for the leader to repeat the rhythmic step pattern at least twice—using a minimum of two measures, or typically four measures, before signaling a new lead. The advantages of this strategy are that the leader has time to think about the next move and the follower has time to react to the lead before another lead is given. Use this strategy when dancing with a new partner for the first time or in any other situation where you find it helpful.

As the leader, you are responsible for doing the following:

- Executing the rhythmic step pattern in tempo with the music

- Adjusting the length and width of your steps to match your partner's (you may need to use shorter steps if your partner is shorter than you are, or if the tempo is very fast, or if the partner is less skilled)

- Keeping your elbows positioned against gravity (slightly bent, away from the sides, and in front of your body to establish a frame)

- Signaling the lead preceding the next rhythmic step pattern (i.e., indicating the direction)

- Signaling a turn by lifting your hand above your partner's shoulders and head

- Ending a turn by lowering your hand below your partner's shoulders and head

- Keeping your weight centered over the balls of your feet (in a ready position)

## Following a Partner

A good follower also needs to be able to repeat the basic steps (or rhythmic step patterns) without much thinking. In addition, the follower must be ready to respond to various nonverbal signals. This means that the follower must be versatile in order to reverse directions and sides of the body from that used by the leader. The follower potentially may move in the same eight directions that the leader may move in. However, whenever the follower is facing a partner, the follower's directions are the mirror opposite. For example, the follower travels backward in response to the leader's signal to move forward, or the follower moves to her right side in response to the leader's signal to move to his left side. Or, from a closed position, the leader moves forward with his left foot while the follower moves backward with her right foot.

At first, followers can be confused because instructors typically call out cues for the leaders to know when to give the lead. The order of sequence should be hearing the instructor's cue, giving the lead, then following, which means that you can expect a subtle delay after the instructor's cue and the actual lead before the follower needs to respond. Otherwise, a common error for followers is to anticipate the lead (as given by the instructor's verbal cues to the leader) and move to the vocal cues. Neither anticipating the leads nor responding early will help the leader understand how to lead a particular move when the instructor's verbal cues are not given.

How can followers pick up the leads for direction changes? One tip is to use your peripheral vision to focus on your partner's shoulders, because they indicate direction changes, especially rotations. Avoid the habit of watching your own feet, which indicates that you need more practice without a partner to become proficient in the basic dance rhythms and rhythmic step patterns. If the leader is moving forward, backward, or sideways, his shoulders will be perpendicular to the line of dance (LOD). On couple's turns, the leader's shoulders typically angle approximately 45 degrees either clockwise (to face diagonal toward the wall) or counterclockwise (to face diagonal toward the center) from the LOD.

As the follower, you are responsible for the following:

- Executing the rhythmic step pattern at a consistent tempo (set by the leader)

- Waiting for the lead (versus anticipating or trying to help the leader)

- Repeating the rhythmic step pattern until given a new lead

- Holding your own frame (arm positions) against gravity (versus resting weight on your partner's arms)

- Maintaining your frame so as to provide gentle feedback to define your space (avoid either very rigid or very limp, *spaghetti* arms)

- Keeping your weight over the balls of your feet (in a ready position)

- Executing the turn (after the leader signals when to start; the leader then stops the turn)

- When traveling in the LOD, reaching backward from the hip (versus bending your knees)

## HANDLING CRITICISM

"You're hard to lead." "Dancing with you is like moving a tank around the floor." "When are you going to add a turn?" "You didn't do that right—you need to lift your arm like this." "You're pushing too hard." "You can't lead." "You can't follow." Perhaps the worst scenario on the dance floor is hearing criticism from a partner, even if it is well intended. You've probably either heard others disagree or been involved in disagreements about the so-called "correct" order, timing, way to move, and so on. It is not a pleasant experience.

The best way to handle criticism is to make it a practice to notice what your partner is doing right and compliment him or her on it. Have patience that your partner is doing the best he or she can at any point in time. Have confidence and trust that your partner will get there eventually and at his or her own rate. It is not helpful to provide verbal reminders to your partner as to what to do or how to do it. Your role is to cooperate with your partner. You can only be responsible for your own actions. The only time advice is welcome on the floor is when a partner specifically asks for it. Otherwise, social dancing should be for meeting others, practicing and improving your own skills, accepting differences, and sharing the experience of dancing with a partner. It is a great way to have fun and get some exercise, too.

With experience, you'll soon find that couples dancing has an evolution of blame starting from directly criticizing your partner to taking responsibility for your own actions to finally acknowledging that something didn't work out as planned and laughing about it or just trying it again, as follows:

| | | |
|---|---|---|
| "You did that wrong." | *Or* "You made a mistake." | *Or* "You're off." |
| "I did that wrong." | *Or* "I made a mistake." | *Or* "I'm off." |
| "We did that wrong." | *Or* "We made a mistake." | *Or* "We're off." |
| "Let's try that again." | *Or* "That didn't work." | *Or* "That's one way." |

At both the third and fourth levels, the blame is shared, so there are often a few laughs at the same time as the couple acknowledges that things didn't go right and decides to try it again. No one person is to blame; rather, it is a consequence of a particular trial. We all learn by trial and error. Give yourself some leeway to make mistakes on the dance floor; it is how you learn and have some fun along the way. Some suggestions for handling criticism follow:

- Compliment your partner on something he or she did correctly (e.g., "I liked the way that you timed the lead for my turn. I knew just which way to turn.") or mention something about the experience that you enjoyed (e.g., "That was fun," or "I really like this song," or "Thanks so much for the dance.").

- Use a cooperative approach (e.g., "Would you try it again?" or "Let's do that again.").

- Ask an unbiased observer, ideally an instructor, to watch and provide constructive criticism (e.g., "When should I give the lead?" or "Where should I be standing in relationship to my partner?" or "What should my footwork be?").

- Take a time-out if at an impasse (e.g., "Time for a break. Let's try it again later.").

- Take responsibility for your own contribution to the partnership (e.g., "I missed that lead. Would you please try it again?" or "I was trying to lead a turn. Let me do it again.").

- State your position, then use *would* instead of *could* in your comments (e.g., "I'm a beginning dancer. Would you please go easy?" or "I don't like to go that fast. Would you please slow it down?" or "I want to make sure that I understand my part. Would you please walk through that again?"). The use of *would* is more polite and assertive. I "could do" something, but "would I do it" requires a commitment.

Notice that the previous suggestions assume that it is unacceptable to offer advice or criticism on the social dance floor. It is more important to appreciate different role responsibilities and to cooperate with your partner. It will not matter in 5 years whether one person or the other was right. On the other hand, it could matter greatly if you're establishing a new friendship or meeting a potential life partner.

# DRILLS FOR PARTNER DYNAMICS AND ETIQUETTE

Leading and following is more than pushing and pulling with your arms. Good dancers use the least amount of effort when leading and following because they understand how to maintain frame and how to use and respond to whole-body leads. Try the following drills to experience these concepts.

# Drill 1
# Whole-Body Leads

Face a partner and match both your facing palms such that your fingers are pointing toward the ceiling, like a stop sign. Adjust your facing palms so that only your fingertips are touching. The best leads are those that are subtle. One partner can be designated as the leader, who starts this drill by shifting his weight (center point of balance, or CPB) forward to signal the forward direction. For example, once the leader has shifted his weight forward over the balls of his feet, the follower can detect this subtle shift forward—even before the leader can take a step. Walk 4 to 8 steps in the leader's forward direction (which is backward for the follower).

After a few trials, alternate roles such that the follower initiates the direction forward by shifting her CPB forward over the balls of her feet. The leader should be able to detect this subtle shift forward (which is backward for the leader). Walk in the direction indicated. Notice that this drill does not work if either partner lets the elbows or arms move in isolation from the rest of the body. The term *frame* refers to the entire hand, arm, and shoulder relationship with elbows positioned in front of the body and hands in the middle to define each half of the shared space.

Next, the leader can practice subtle whole-body leads to indicate travel to either side. Remember that the CPB should shift in the direction of travel. The follower should be able to pick up the leader's weight shift from both feet to one foot before actually taking a step to that side, all without any verbal cues from the leader. Walk to the side indicated by the leader. After a few trials, reverse roles and let the follower initiate the side direction (either right or left) before you both step to that side so that the leader may feel the lead. Again, this does not work if either of you isolates and only moves your arms (versus moving from your center).

## TO DECREASE DIFFICULTY

- Start the drill with the leader standing with his back to a wall, then repeat the drill.
- Both partners place hands on a beach ball positioned between them. Feel the transfer of weight as the leader initiates walking forward 8 steps, then backward 8 steps (as the follower initiates the motion).

## TO INCREASE DIFFICULTY

- Start on the outside of the room with a partner such that the leader can travel forward in a counterclockwise direction around the perimeter of the room (which is the line of dance, or LOD). Practice walking to the beats of any 4/4 time music or at a set pace with a partner and notice how you need to incrementally angle your center (much like turning the wheel of a car) on the curves.
- When multiple couples are on the floor, the leader must be aware of other couples and safely maneuver the follower in the LOD to avoid the feeling of playing bumper cars.

## Success Goal

Perform 10 repetitions of shifting weight to indicate direction first either forward or backward, then either left or right. ___

- Shift your CPB in the intended direction before actually taking a step in that direction. ___

- When facing a partner, shift your CPB forward to indicate the follower should move backward___

- When facing a partner, shift your CPB to the left side to indicate that the follower should move to the right side, and vice versa.
___

- Maintain your half of the shared space between you and your partner instead of letting only your arms move. ___

# Drill 2
# Frame and Rotational Leads

Whether you are dancing in a shine position or with a partner, it is important to establish and maintain your frame. Stand without a partner. Notice where you have positioned your arms. If they are dangling by your sides, then you do not have frame. Make a conscious effort to bend your elbows and lift your forearms until they are parallel with the floor with your palms facing downward. This is the arm position used in the two-hands-joined position. What differs is that you need to maintain this position even when you rotate to either side. For example, rotate your upper torso 45 degrees both left and right. Notice that your entire upper torso rotates from your spine or midline. As your sternum faces either side, your arms move as well. It is not a matter of reaching your arms across your body.

Another critical position for frame is in the closed position. Stand in the closed position with a partner. Now take at least 2 steps backward and away from your partner. You may lower your arms slightly to make the position more comfortable, but keep the same semicurved shape from your fingertips through your arms and shoulders. Imagine that you are holding a large beach ball so that you become aware of the space inside the semicircle. Maintain this shape as you rotate your upper torso 45 degrees both to the left and to the right. Think of turning your sternum in the direction of the turn, and your arms will follow if you keep them moving as one unit.

*(continued)*

Drill 2 *(continued)*

### TO DECREASE DIFFICULTY

- Check yourself in a mirror to see whether you have positioned your arms correctly.
- Start in a closed position with a partner and rotate your upper torso 45 degrees to either side while keeping a circular shape with your partner; that is, each partner's arms create a semicircle that together with the partner's makes a full circle.

### TO INCREASE DIFFICULTY

- From a two-hands-joined position, alternately practice rotating your upper torso and arms to one side (e.g., to leader's left side) and release one hand (e.g., leader's left hand) to make the transition to a one-hand-joined position (leader's right hand holding follower's left hand). Face your partner to resume a two-hands-joined position, then continue rotating to face the opposite side and release one hand to make the transition to a one-hand-joined position (leader's left hand holding follower's right hand).
- In closed position, the leader can practice rotating his sternum to face 45 degrees to his left front diagonal, then toward his right front diagonal.

## Success Goal

Perform 10 repetitions of demonstrating frame while rotating your upper torso to one side, then to the other side first alone, then with a partner. ___

## Success Check

- Maintain an arm position whether dancing alone or with a partner. ___
- Keep your forearms parallel to the floor when in a two-hands-joined position. ___
- Create a semicurved shape that slopes in a descending manner from your shoulders to your elbows to your hands. ___
- Initiate a turn by rotating your upper torso and arms in the direction of the turn. ___

# Drill 3
# On Your Own: Practicing Partner Etiquette

Imagine that you are at a social dance with the goal of dancing with a variety of partners. If you are the leader, plan how you might ask a partner for a dance. If you are the follower, plan how you might accept a dance with a partner. How would you introduce yourself before the dance? What would you say if you wanted to compliment your partner and avoid any criticism? Do the following:

a. Introduce yourself to a new partner.

b. With a partner, name and demonstrate each of the nine basic partner positions shown in figure 4.1.

c. Thank each partner. If you are the leader, practice how you would escort the follower back to the location where you asked her to dance.

## TO DECREASE DIFFICULTY

- Challenge yourself to dance with at least two new partners each time you go social dancing.

- Demonstrate at least four different partner positions.

## TO INCREASE DIFFICULTY

- Dance with a variety of partners.

- From a closed position, indicate a forward direction lead in the LOD and step on each beat using a consistent tempo, then try stepping to slow 4/4 time music.

- From a two-hands-joined position, review the dance rhythm strategies on the DVD, then try at least one of the dance rhythms to music.

## Success Goal

Use appropriate dialogue for meeting at least five different partners and correctly demonstrate the nine partner positions with each partner. ___

## Success Check

- Politely ask a partner to dance.
  ___

- Graciously accept a partner's invitation to dance. ___

- Thank your partner after the dance. ___

# SUCCESS SUMMARY FOR PARTNER DYNAMICS AND ETIQUETTE

Social dancing may be both exciting and a bit unnerving if you've never done it before. You can be more in control of the uncertainties if you know your responsibilities on the dance floor and know how to communicate effectively with your partner. Verbal communication is important when asking for or accepting a dance and generally making the time shared on the dance floor enjoyable for both partners. Nonverbal communication is important for indicating direction of travel, connecting with a partner, and moving in unison with the music. What you say and how you move with a partner can show either respect or lack of it. Obviously, the goal is to work together to make dancing a more pleasant experience for everyone.

How you get from any one partner position to the next makes a big difference in your presentation of any particular dance style. Transitions function as bridges to connect any two partner positions. Many dancers either ignore or forget about transitions in their rush to learn as many *cool* moves or variations as they can. It is important to take time to understand how transitions can make your dancing look more polished and flowing. Smooth transitions also make it easier for leaders to lead and for followers to follow. Now you are ready to start applying your foundational knowledge to specific dance styles. You'll be amazed at how soon you begin dancing specific dances.

# PART II

## 10 Social Dances: Rhythmic Step Patterns, Transitions, and Variations

You've started your journey through the four foundational learning steps in part I. Now you are ready to get more specific instructions for each of the 10 social dances presented in this book. To guarantee your success, the easiest-to-learn dances are presented first. Each learning step provides step descriptions, footwork and timing cues, illustrations, and practical applications. The drills help you to practice your execution of the appropriate rhythmic step pattern, selected variations, and sample combinations for each dance style. Steps 5 through 14 outline these social dances:

- *Step 5:* Merengue—As easy as marching, the merengue will be part of your dance repertoire in no time.

- *Step 6:* Four-count swing/hustle—If you can walk and count to four, you can do this dance.

- *Step 7:* Waltz—This is the only social dance with three beats per measure.

- *Step 8:* Six-count swing—Learn three basics for three tempos of swing music.

- *Step 9:* Foxtrot—Long walking steps and two basics to select from will get you traveling in the LOD ASAP.

- *Step 10:* Polka—Lively and robust, polka music makes you want to dance.

- *Step 11:* Cha-cha—Latin styling that contrasts slow and quick actions makes the cha-cha exciting to watch and to do.

- *Step 12:* Rumba—The slow, romantic music of the rumba sets the stage for this dance of love.

- *Step 13:* Tango—If you have a flair for the dramatic, you'll love the tango.

- *Step 14*: Salsa/mambo—If you want to learn a *hot* dance, these dances are for you.

# Merengue

## *Joining the Party*

The fast, energetic Latin music appropriate for dancing the merengue brings an atmosphere of gaiety and fun to any occasion. This dance is one of the easiest and quickest to learn. It is ideal for a crowded dance floor because it doesn't take up much space. The fun in this dance is keeping your feet moving as you step on each beat of the fast music. Once you get the rhythm down, the movements include turns without letting go of hands and rotations both clockwise and counterclockwise as a couple. The music is in 2/4 time, but dancers typically count the beats in multiples of four.

Both music and dance are important within the culture of the Dominican Republic. The Dominican Republic is the second largest Caribbean nation (after Cuba) and shares the eastern two thirds of the island of Hispaniola. Haiti occupies the western third of the island. It has a blend of cultures, including Spanish (originating from colonists), African (from slaves), and Taino (natives). Spanish is the primary language taught in the schools and English is the secondary language. Merengue music was internationally promoted starting in the mid-1930s, which helped the dance to gain popularity also. Merengue music is engaging; it has a fast tempo and sometimes an even faster pace near the end of a song. The dance was introduced to the United States in the 1980s and 1990s and became especially popular in New York, New Jersey, and Florida, where many Spanish-speaking cultures gained prominence.

Considered the Dominican Republic's national dance, the merengue has controversial origins. One version is that this dance was created in the honor of a famous war hero returning home, who had injured one leg and could not bend that leg. During a victory celebration upon his return and to make him feel more comfortable, the Dominicans also moved with one stiff leg. The shifting of weight from one bent knee to a straight leg produced more hip action. Another version is that this dance originated with slaves in the sugar cane fields. Because they were chained to each other by a chain on one leg, they were forced to drag one leg in unison. It was more efficient to work to a drum beat, which created a tempo to pace their steps and coordinate their movements. A third version is that the merengue resulted from a combination of African dance and the French minuet. The slaves mimicked what they saw their masters doing, but they found these dances boring so they added a more upbeat tempo through the drums.

# RHYTHMIC STEP PATTERN FOR MERENGUE

You can learn and be dancing the merengue in just a few minutes. Start by keeping your feet flat and close to the floor, almost as if there is honey on the floor and you can barely lift your feet. Remain in one place and shift your weight from one foot to the other in a constant tempo, giving each weight change one count, or beat in the measure. On each count, press into the floor and notice that one leg is bent at the knee while the other leg is straight. The straight leg has the weight, which means that you could lift the other foot off the floor, but instead you need to keep both feet close to the floor and remain flatfooted. Avoid lifting the heel of either foot higher than the ball of that foot. It is helpful for beginners to start with eight counts, or weight changes, while remaining stationary to get connected with the tempo and a partner before moving in a new direction. Later, you can group your weight changes in any multiple of two counts before changing directions; that is, when the leader's left foot and the follower's right foot is free again.

Once you can keep the tempo while stationary, add motion; step to the side on the downbeat and bring your feet together on the upbeat. Repeat these side–together steps, changing weight on each count. The merengue is associated with celebrations, so it is common to move your body with the music and naturally rock your weight to each side, letting your upper torso lean toward the side that has the bent knee. When you first learn merengue, both the side steps and the counterclockwise rotations are the easiest directions to execute. Later, you can add other directions. Almost any turn with your partner works in the merengue. The only rule in merengue is that your feet never stop moving! Figure 5.1 shows the various ways you might organize the counts and footwork for the basic merengue side steps. Some cues may be more helpful than others. Select those cues that you find most relevant for helping you to remember and execute the basic rhythmic step pattern to the side. Then, complete the drills in the next section to see how you can transition to other directions while repeating the rhythmic step pattern.

## Figure 5.1 **MERENGUE RHYTHMIC STEP PATTERN TO THE SIDE**

### Footwork Cues

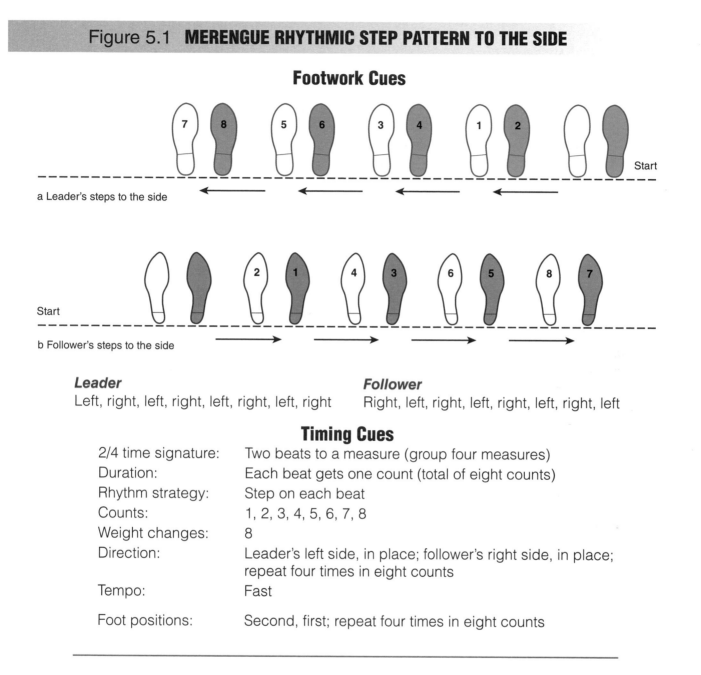

a Leader's steps to the side

Start

Start

b Follower's steps to the side

*Leader*
Left, right, left, right, left, right, left, right

*Follower*
Right, left, right, left, right, left, right, left

### Timing Cues

| | |
|---|---|
| 2/4 time signature: | Two beats to a measure (group four measures) |
| Duration: | Each beat gets one count (total of eight counts) |
| Rhythm strategy: | Step on each beat |
| Counts: | 1, 2, 3, 4, 5, 6, 7, 8 |
| Weight changes: | 8 |
| Direction: | Leader's left side, in place; follower's right side, in place; repeat four times in eight counts |
| Tempo: | Fast |
| Foot positions: | Second, first; repeat four times in eight counts |

You can choose from many partner positions when doing the merengue. Two popular positions are a two-hands-joined position and a closed position. A closed position within Latin dances brings the elbows closer together, keeping the forearms almost vertical. Figure 5.2 shows the higher grasped hands and arm adjustment for Latin dances.

**Figure 5.2** Modified closed position for Latin dances.

# DRILLS FOR MERENGUE

The merengue is similar to walking; you take a step on each beat. Once you get the rhythm going by using your flatfooted marching steps, almost any variation works. The following drills and the engaging music can help you have fun. For each drill, read the directions, and watch the video demonstrations on the enclosed DVD to see (a) how to execute the selected merengue variations, and (b) how to combine them into short practice combinations. Then, practice until you can meet the Success Goal for each drill. Listen, then use track 7 or start with a slow verbal count until you can match your footwork with the fast tempo characteristic of the merengue.

## Drill 1
## Eight in Place and Eight to the Side

Merengue music has a fast tempo of 2/4 time, so a good starting place is to group your weight changes in sets of eight counts. Once you are more comfortable with the tempo and footwork, you may choose to execute your weight changes in sets of either four counts or two counts before changing to a new direction. Obviously, the more counts, the more time to react and execute the steps in any one direction. The purpose of this drill is to help you to practice stepping (i.e., making a weight change) on each beat or count while remaining in place, then while moving to the side. Try each of the following practice segments.

a. Start by stepping in place. Without touching, stand facing a partner about an arm's length apart. The leader starts with his left foot, while the follower starts with her right foot. Set a tempo with slow counts in sets of eight, then step in place on each count.

b. Next, try moving in a sideward direction. Extend a flexed foot and knee to the side and shift your weight onto that leg on the first count. On the second count, drag your other foot and shift your weight onto it with the feet together. Repeat these two actions four times to the side for a total of eight counts. Notice that the leader is moving to his left side while the follower is moving to her right side. This sideward direction takes you both to one side of the floor, so you'll need to move back to your original starting location to repeat the drill once you run out of room to move any further to the side. Don't worry about stopping and restarting again at this point.

c. Combine a and b. Alternate eight steps in place, then eight steps to the side while facing and not touching your partner. Continue to adjust your starting location after each repetition of this combination. The next drill gives you the transition to move back to where you initially started by using another direction change option.

## TO DECREASE DIFFICULTY

- Start in a two-hands-joined position.
- Use a slow tempo.

## TO INCREASE DIFFICULTY

- Repeat the drill combination in a closed position.
- Repeat the combination using sets of four counts.

## Success Goal

Alternate eight steps in place and eight steps to the side in time with the music. ___

## Success Check

- Fully change your weight from one foot to the other on each beat. ___
- Maintain the tempo. ___
- Mirror reverse your steps while facing a partner. ___

## Drill 2
# Rotational Turn Options for Couples

This drill gives you the transition moves to rotate either clockwise or counterclockwise with your partner. Either rotation option is a good choice whenever you have no more room to move to the leader's left side or to the follower's right side. Start in a closed position with your partner, repeat the two-direction combination from the previous drill, and then alternately add on one of the following direction options.

a. *Counterclockwise couples turn.* Continue to rock your weight from one foot to the other as you take 8 steps in place, 8 steps to the side, then 8 steps to rotate 180 degrees counterclockwise with your partner. Sometimes called a couple's left turn, this rotation has your left shoulder moving backward with each left-foot weight change. The leader needs to rotate his sternum with a firm frame toward his diagonal left front to initiate the counterclockwise rotation. Take your time and don't rush the rotations.

b. *Clockwise couples turn.* Let your upper body rock from side to side on each weight change to help you get into and maintain the rhythm. Take 8 steps in place, 8 steps to the side, then take eight counts to rotate 180 degrees clockwise to complete a half turn. Notice that your right shoulder rotates back with each right foot change on a clockwise couples' turn, which is also called a couples' right turn. The leader needs to keep a firm right hand on the follower's back to reinforce the clockwise rotation direction. It helps to step in place on the first count, then slowly rotate clockwise in small increments. After eight counts, the leader can then determine whether to continue another 180 degrees in the same direction or to repeat the entire combination facing the back wall.

### TO DECREASE DIFFICULTY
- Repeat each practice combination twice before changing to a new order.
- Combine three directions using a set order such as in place, sideward, and couples' right turn or in place, sideward, and couples' left turn.

### TO INCREASE DIFFICULTY
- Vary only the rotation direction in the previous combinations. For example, one variation could be sometimes repeating the same direction.
- The leader may use any order to combine all four direction options covered so far.
- Change the direction whenever the leader's left foot is free again, such as after four counts or a minimum of two counts.

## Success Goal

Take eight steps to complete each rotational 180-degree couple's turn moving either clockwise or counterclockwise. ___

- Keep your feet moving as you step on each beat. ___
- Group your direction changes in sets of eight, four, or two counts. ___

# Drill 3
# Follower's Right Underarm Turn

Start in a closed position with a partner. After taking 8 steps in place, the leader can lift his left hand and arm to create an arch to signal the follower's right underarm turn. Both partners keep the tempo for eight more counts while the follower rotates clockwise doing small side-together steps. To avoid getting dizzy, the follower needs to take her time and use the entire eight counts as she rotates clockwise until she faces her partner again.

To facilitate the turn, the leader may gently press with the heel of his right hand on the follower's left shoulder blade to guide her under the arch and indicate the clockwise direction. As the follower does the turn, the leader releases his right hand, then he reestablishes contact on her left shoulder blade when her right shoulder is facing him. Also, the follower needs to avoid dropping her left arm as she rotates. Instead, the follower needs to keep her left arm curved when turning so that she can place it on top of the leader's right arm again to resume a closed position at the end of her turn.

During the turn, avoid holding the raised hands too tightly. It is your choice as to which of two strategies to use. Both use fingertip pressure. One way is using a flat palm-up position for the follower (similar to holding a tray in one hand over head), while the leader uses a flat palm-down position. Another way is that the follower can cup her hand while the leader holds one or two fingers downward for her to rotate around. The follower also needs to avoid straightening her right elbow as she turns; rather it needs to be slightly bent as she maintains contact with her right hand and the leader's left hand.

 **TO DECREASE DIFFICULTY**
- Keep your weight changes in sets of eight counts.
- Start in a two-hands-joined position.

**TO INCREASE DIFFICULTY**
- Vary the number of steps in place (e.g., 6, 4, or 2 steps) before leading the follower's underarm turn (i.e., use the entire eight beats of music on the turn).
- Add this variation to the combination from the previous drill.
- After the follower's turn, the leader can rotate counterclockwise under his arched arm (while it is the follower's turn to keep the rhythm in place).

*(continued)*

**Drill 3** *(continued)*

## *Success Goal*

Perform eight counts in place, then eight counts for the follower's right underarm turn. ___

## *Success Check*

- Both partners keep their feet moving at all times. ___
- Match your weight changes to the tempo of the music. ___

# Drill 4
# Head Loops

The transition to head loops requires a right-to-right handhold. So, at the end of the follower's underarm turn, the leader brings his left hand down to waist level and passes the follower's right hand into his right hand. You should be in a handshake position facing your partner. Then, grasp the left hands, keeping them below the right hands. Take eight steps while in this crossed-handshake position.

For the next set of eight counts, take four counts to gently lift the leader's right hand up and loop over the follower's head, making sure that you both release the right hands and continue the curved path in the air as if you were caressing the hair. Then, take four more counts to lift the leader's left hand up and loop over the leader's head as you both release the left hands and continue the curved motion. Resume a closed position for the next set of eight counts in place.

**TO DECREASE DIFFICULTY**
- Do each set of eight counts, gradually adding another set.
- Begin with a slow tempo and gradually increase it.

**TO INCREASE DIFFICULTY**
- The leader may choose the number of steps both before and after the follower's underarm turn (i.e., 8, 6, 4, 2).
- Eliminate the third set of eight counts in place and go directly into the head loops.

## *Success Goal*

Perform four sets of eight counts to execute (a) basic in place, (b) follower's underarm turn with hand change, (c) basic in place, and (d) head loops. ___

## *Success Check*

- Keep the feet moving to step on each count. ___
- Match your weight changes with the tempo of the music. ___
- Right hands go over the follower's head during the first half of the head loops. ___
- Left hands go over the leader's head during the second half of the head loops. ___

# Drill 5
## She–He–She Turn Combination

Start in a closed position with your partner. As in the previous drill, do eight steps in place, then eight steps for the follower's right underarm turn. The follower's right underarm turn is the *She* portion of this combination. Then, this drill substitutes a fancy way to transition into a right-to-right hand grasp—at the end of the leader's turn, or *He* portion of the sequence. Thus, on the third set of eight counts, the leader rotates clockwise as he lowers his left hand behind his back and passes the follower's hand into his right hand as he continues to rotate to face his partner. On the fourth set of eight counts, the leader uses his right hand to circle clockwise above the follower's head as *she* does another right underarm turn. On the fifth set of eight counts, face your partner with crossed-handshake grasps (right-to-right on top and left-to-left on the bottom) and step in place. On the sixth set of eight counts, finish the combination with head loops by looping right hands over the follower's head for four counts, then looping left hands over the leader's head for four counts. Resume a closed position to be ready to repeat the entire combination.

### TO DECREASE DIFFICULTY
- Slowly practice the hand positions and turn order without worrying about your feet, then add the steps.
- Use a slow tempo.

### TO INCREASE DIFFICULTY
- Eliminate the steps in place on the fifth set of eight counts and move directly into the head loops after the follower's second underarm turn.
- Use a fast tempo.

## Success Goal

Perform six sets of eight counts to execute (a) basic in place, (b) follower's right underarm turn, (c) leader's behind-the-back pass, (d) follower's right underarm turn, (e) basic in place, and (f) head loops. ___

## Success Check

- The leader needs to pass his hands low behind his back to avoid sharply bent elbows that may hit the follower. ___
- Remember to use fingertip pressure on the underarm turns. ___
- Keep a sustained flow of movement using the entire six sets of eight counts. ___

# Drill 6
# Cuddle Turn

Start in a closed position with your partner. Do eight counts in place as the leader gently extends out his arms to slide out to a two-hands-joined position facing each other. During the second set of eight counts, the leader needs to give two leads as follows: He extends his right hand low and out to his right side, then brings his left hand toward his right shoulder and counterclockwise above the follower's head. Keep holding both hands; you will be in a wrap, or cuddle position with the follower on the right side of the leader. It is helpful to keep the follower a half step in front of the leader with the front hands away from and curved in front of the bodies for balance and control. If you get too close and collapse the arms, it is difficult to move or lead properly.

During the third set of eight counts, remain in the wrap position. To initiate rotation, the leader steps forward, while the follower steps backward as you both rotate clockwise. Sometimes this rotation move is called a *wheel*. In swing dancing, it is also called a *walking wrap*. Continue holding both hands as you come out of the wrap on the fourth set of eight counts. All it takes is for the leader to lift his left hand to form an arch for the follower to turn clockwise out to face the leader.

## TO DECREASE DIFFICULTY

- Add more steps in place whenever more time is needed.
- Start in a two-hands-joined position and eliminate the first set of eight counts.

## TO INCREASE DIFFICULTY

- The leader may move forward to initiate the rotation at the same time that he leads the wrap position; in other words, merge actions *b* and *c* into one set of eight counts.
- Reverse the wrap to be on the leader's left side and both dancers move counterclockwise; the leader steps backward and the follower steps forward.

## Success Goal

Perform four sets of eight counts to (a) slide out to two hands, (b) wrap position (on leader's right side), (c) rotate clockwise, and (d) unwrap (back to two hands). ___

## Success Check

- Use fingertip pressure in the wrap position with the follower moving as far right into her left hand as possible, and her right hand (and his left hand) curved about waist level in front. ___
- Avoid rushing into a position; take the full eight counts. ___

# Drill 7
# On Your Own: Linking Three Merengue Moves

You have enough moves to start having fun on your own. It is time for the leader to put together any order and any sequence that he wishes. The catch is that he needs to let the follower know what to expect. Be aware of the transition when making a direction change. A direction change begins whenever the leader's left foot (and the follower's right foot) is free. Remember that it takes a minimum of 2 steps before the leader's left foot (and the follower's right foot) can be free again. Technically a new direction can be signaled after any two counts. However, you can give yourself more reaction time by grouping your steps in either four or eight counts before making a direction change. The fewer the number of steps before changing directions, the more quickly the leader needs to plan ahead. Grouping eight beats in each direction gives the leader and follower time to react and adjust to the tempo and rhythm.

Put together any three or more moves or direction changes to create an original sequence, or *combination.* If you are looking for ideas, try any of the combinations that you know so far (review drills 1 through 6) and experiment with different orders and different numbers of weight changes before leading a new move. When making your selections, use the following points as a reminder of the merengue variations:

- Basic (in place and to the side)
- Couples turn (clockwise and counterclockwise)
- Follower's right underarm turn
- Head loops
- She–he–she turn combination
- Cuddle turn

## TO DECREASE DIFFICULTY

- Select any one combination from the previous drills to repeat for the length of one song.
- Select any two combinations from the previous drills to repeat for the length of one song.

## TO INCREASE DIFFICULTY

- Select any three combinations from the previous drills to repeat in different orders for the length of one song.
- Select any four or more combinations from the previous drills to repeat in any order for the length of one song.
- Create your own variation within a minimum of eight counts to add to any three combinations from the previous drills to repeat for the length of one song.

*(continued)*

Drill 7 *(continued)*

### *Success Goal*

Perform 2 minutes of constant moving to the tempo of the music using at least three combinations in any order. ___

- Both partners need to keep the tempo with a weight change on each count. ___
- You must have a minimum of two weight changes before leading a new move or a new direction.
  ___

# SUCCESS SUMMARY FOR MERENGUE

The merengue is one of the easiest dances to learn and it is a lot of fun, too. As if walking, you step on each beat. For practice, begin by grouping the steps in sets of eight counts. Then, later the direction changes may be made whenever the leader's left foot is free, which occurs after grouping 2, 4, 6, or 8 steps. The merengue music is engaging with its fast tempo, which has helped this dance gain popularity. Considered the national dance of the Dominican Republic, the merengue is important in cultural celebrations. Today, the merengue dance and music are both recognized internationally. After completing the drills in this learning step, you, too are ready to join the party and enjoy the celebration!

# Four-Count Swing/Hustle

## *Keeping the Rhythm*

Sometimes called a *two-hand rhythm dance,* the four-count swing/hustle is useful at weddings and other social events because it fits many popular songs and music styles. It has other names as well, such as the *four-count hustle* (as compared to a three-count hustle), the *four-count swing,* the *two-hand salsa* (in the late 1970s), the *mélange* (the Golden State Dance Teachers Association gave it this name for their teaching syllabus in 1995), and the *cherkessia step* (from Israeli folk dancing). All have in common that they are referred to as *even-rhythm* steps because the rhythm strategy of stepping on each beat takes an even number of beats before your starting foot is free again, which is very easy to repeat.

A versatile dance, the four-count swing/hustle fits well with music that ranges from 120 to 180 beats per minute. It also fits well with most popular music today across a variety of styles of music including swing, Latin, hustle, country, and contemporary. For each style the dance easily takes on the character or style of that music. For example, in the 1970s John Travolta popularized one version of the hustle in the movie *Staying Alive.* Disco music was also popular in the 1970s. It has its roots in swing and Latin music. The four-count swing/hustle prepares you for a variety of moves that transfer to other social dances. If you can hear a strong underlying beat, then you can try the four-count swing/hustle!

# RHYTHMIC STEP PATTERN FOR FOUR-COUNT SWING/HUSTLE

An easy dance to learn and to lead for non-dancers, the four-count swing/hustle uses one measure of 4/4 time music—four counts. With a partner, start in a two-hands-joined position. The leader starts with the left foot and the follower starts with the right foot. The rhythmic step pattern is composed of four walking steps taken in a repetitive pattern using the following directions: forward, backward, backward, forward. You need to give each step one count. On count 1, both dancers step forward at the same time. On count 2, step back and in place (keeping that foot in the same location). On count 3, both step backward, keeping weight only on the ball of the foot. On count 4, step forward and in place. Another term for a step in place is a *replace*. A *replace* means to lift, then lower your foot keeping it in the same location as you shift your weight onto that foot. Thus, small steps are needed. Just like marching, the four-count swing/hustle helps you to keep the rhythm or external tempo because you make a weight change on each count of the four-beat measure.

Now check your hand and arm positions. Start facing your partner. The leader places his hands about waist level and curved as if holding two cups. The follower places her fingertips in the leader's fingertips, keeping her palms down and both elbows close to her sides. The leader's fingers should be firm like a wall that defines the center and separates and maintains both his and her space. On count 1, the follower gently presses in with the heel of her palms as the leader keeps both hands firmly in the center. Go back to a neutral, two-hands-joined position on count 2. Both partners step back onto the ball of the foot on count 3 and they keep both elbows flexed as they gently pull back with fingertips. Resume a neutral position again on count 4.

Next, check your foot positions. Start with your feet in first position. Execute the four weight changes of this rhythmic step pattern while keeping your feet in a forward–backward stride position (fourth foot position with feet parallel). Notice that the leader's right foot becomes his reference foot in that his downbeat weight changes taken with his left foot (on counts 1 and 3) are taken either forward or backward of his right foot. On counts 2 and 4, the leader steps in place with his right foot. The follower does the mirror reverse: Her left foot becomes her reference foot in that she steps on her right foot either forward or backward of her left foot on the downbeats (on counts 1 and 3). On counts 2 and 4, the follower steps in place with her left foot. Figure 6.1 shows the ways that you might organize the counts and footwork cues for the four-count swing/hustle.

## Figure 6.1  RHYTHMIC STEP PATTERN FOR FOUR-COUNT SWING/HUSTLE

### Footwork Cues

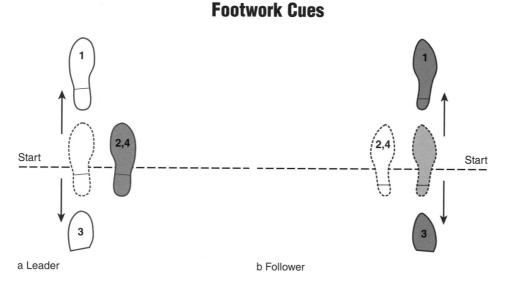

a Leader                    b Follower

***Leader***
Left, right, left, right

***Follower***
Right, left, right, left

### Timing Cues

| | |
|---|---|
| 4/4 time signature: | Four beats to a measure (one measure for basic pattern) |
| Duration: | Each beat gets one count (total of four counts) |
| Rhythm strategy: | Step on each beat |
| Counts: | 1, 2, 3, 4 |
| Weight changes: | 4 |
| Length of steps: | Small |
| Direction of steps: | Forward, backward (replace), backward, forward (replace) |
| Foot positions: | Fourth, fourth, fourth or fifth, fourth |

# DRILLS FOR FOUR-COUNT SWING/HUSTLE

The following drills will soon get you on the dance floor doing the four-count swing/hustle. For each drill, read the directions, and watch the video demonstrations on the enclosed DVD to see (a) how to execute the selected four-count swing/hustle variations, and (b) how to combine them into short practice combinations. Then, practice until you can meet the Success Goal for each drill. Try track 8 on the enclosed DVD for practice music or select any song with strong four-beat measures, which is the case with most disco music and with popular music.

## Drill 1
## Execution Challenge for the Four-Count Swing/Hustle

Review figure 6.1 and repeat the rhythmic step pattern to a slow four-count tempo. Think about the rolling count, then add an *&-a* preceding each whole count. Continue to use the rolling count to help you transfer your body weight from your sending foot to your receiving foot on each whole count. This means that you will be moving your body in each of two directions (forward/backward, then backward/forward) versus just moving your feet. Keep your CPB over your base of support, which in this case is both feet, to facilitate the transition shift to the opposite direction. After you are comfortable doing the basic step pattern without a partner, repeat the basic step pattern while facing a partner and using a two-hands-joined position. Position your hands between yourself and your partner in order to define each partner's half of the shared space. Both partners press in toward the center on count 1, step in place on count 2, gently pull back or away from your partner on count 3, and step in place on count 4.

### TO DECREASE DIFFICULTY
- Move to a slow verbal count and gradually increase the tempo.
- Remember to initiate movement from your center preceding each step.

### TO INCREASE DIFFICULTY
- Repeat the rhythmic step pattern with different partners.
- Vary the music tempo or the music type.

## Success Goal

Execute the four-count swing/hustle in place to music for 2 minutes first without a partner, then facing a partner in a two-hands-joined position. ___

- Flex your knees slightly to prepare for the direction changes. ___

- Keep weight on only the ball of your foot on count 3. ___

- Make a weight change on each count. ___

- Keep your starting foot in a forward–backward stride position on counts 1, 2. ___

- Keep your starting foot in a backward–forward stride position on counts 3, 4. ___

# Drill 2
# Change of Position

A change of position involves a 180-degree, clockwise rotation to literally change places with your partner. Start facing your partner in a two-hands-joined position. This drill combines two repetitions of the rhythmic step pattern, or eight counts. During the first repetition, the leader sets up the rotation that occurs on the second repetition of the pattern. Thus, execute one repetition of the basic rhythmic step pattern with one exception for the leader. On the fourth count, the leader needs to move his right foot slightly to his left (and still be in fourth position with his right foot forward). This puts him offset with the follower in order to give both partners room to rotate.

On the second repetition of the basic rhythmic step pattern, both partners step forward on count 1. Notice that your right hips and shoulders are closest to each other's. Keep your center over this foot and swivel clockwise to face your partner again as you step in place on the second count. Step backward onto the ball of your foot on count 3 and shift your weight forward to step in place on count 4.

In addition, the arms can facilitate the change of position by extending both arms horizontally out to the sides (approximately waist or hip level) on count 1, which automatically brings the right sides of your bodies closer together as you both step forward and swivel. The leader facilitates this rotation by pulling more strongly with his right hand as if he is turning the wheel of a car to turn to the right. Keep your feet in a forward–backward stride during the rotation so that you can face your partner on counts 2 through 4. It may seem easier for the leader to step across on count 2, but it is sharper when the leader steps behind and brings his shoulders around to be parallel with his partner's shoulders.

*(continued)*

**Drill 2** *(continued)*

### TO DECREASE DIFFICULTY

- If the floor is sticky and doesn't permit you to swivel, just angle each foot as you walk clockwise two steps (forward on count 1, then backward on count 2) to face your partner again.
- Do a slow clockwise turn by each time angling your center slightly to the right preceding count 1, then remain facing your partner as you execute the four-count rhythmic step pattern.

### TO INCREASE DIFFICULTY

- Vary the number of repetitions in place before leading the change of position.
- Try two changes of position in a row without any rhythmic step pattern in between.

## Success Goal

Perform 2 minutes of alternating the rhythmic step pattern in place with a change of position. ___

## Success Check

- Use small steps. ___
- Foot positions: fourth, fourth, fourth or fifth, fourth. ___
- Shoulders facing and parallel with partner's shoulders on counts 3, 4. ___

# Drill 3
# Inside (Left) Turn for Follower

On this turn, which is approximately 180 degrees, both partners switch sides. The leader does the same footwork as he did in the Change of Position drill. However, the lead is different on the first repetition of the basic step pattern. Start in a one-hand-joined position (his left and her right). To signal the inside turn, the leader starts bringing his left hand toward his right shoulder on count 3, then drops two fingers and lifts his left hand higher on count 4 to form an arch. On the second repetition, the follower moves under the arched hands traveling toward her left diagonal on the first step, then does a half turn to the left (counterclockwise) on the second step, and partners face each other on counts 3 and 4. Check that the hand grip is not so tight that it hinders the follower's ability to turn. Either use a palm-to-palm hand position (follower's palm up, leader's palm down) or the follower's hand cups around the leader's fingers, which are extended downward.

### TO DECREASE DIFFICULTY

- Practice alone to a slow count, checking your position on each count.
- Repeat the rhythmic step pattern at least twice in place before leading the inside left turn.

### TO INCREASE DIFFICULTY

- Alternate a change of position with an inside turn for the follower.
- Lead two inside left turns in a row without any rhythmic step patterns in place.

## Success Goal

Alternate the rhythmic step pattern in place with an inside left turn for the follower for 2 minutes. ___

## Success Check

- Switch sides with your partner during the inside turn. ___
- Face your partner on counts 3 and 4. ___

# Drill 4
# Outside (Right) Turn for Follower

From a one-hand-joined position, the goal is again to switch sides or change positions with your partner. However, this time, the leader turns in the opposite direction (than in the previous drills) and the nonverbal lead is different. During the repetition of the rhythmic step pattern in place, the leader just needs to start extending his left hand out to his left side on count 3 and lift it to make an arch by count 4. The follower moves along a diagonal right front path on count 1, rotates a half turn clockwise on count 2 (under the raised hands), and faces her partner on counts 3 and 4. The leader moves forward on count 1, rotates a half turn counterclockwise on count 2, and faces his partner on counts 3 and 4. Keep the grip loose during the turn.

Imagine a triangle on the floor with each partner on the ends. The follower moves toward the tip of the triangle as the leader moves to her vacated spot. You can both get back to your original spots (and adjust the awkward hand position at the end of the outside turn) if an inside turn is immediately led. Thus, a natural combination is to lead an outside turn immediately followed by an inside turn without a rhythmic step pattern in between. In between these turns, it is important that the leader keeps the hands held high to let the follower know that the turns are not over.

### TO DECREASE DIFFICULTY

- Slowly walk through your footwork alone, then with a partner and check your body positioning on each count.
- Followers should angle their right foot approximately 45 degrees toward the direction of the turn on count 1.

### TO INCREASE DIFFICULTY

- At the end of the turns in this drill, add an inside turn so that the follower does three consecutive turns.
- Add in a change of position to the previous combination.

*(continued)*

Drill 4   *(continued)*

## *Success Goal*

Combine an outside (right) turn for the follower, and an inside (left) turn for the follower for 2 minutes. ___

## *Success Check*

- Maintain the rhythmic step pattern with a weight change on each count. ___
- Both partners switch places (turn approximately 180 degrees) on each turn. ___
- Avoid getting too far apart. ___
- Face your partner on counts 3, 4. ___

# Drill 5
# Wrap and Unwrap

In this drill, the leader does not have to move from his original starting location. Start in a two-hands-joined position with your partner. Do one repetition of the rhythmic step pattern in place to connect with your partner. On the second repetition executed in place, the leader gives the nonverbal leads on counts 3 and 4. On count 3, he extends his right hand to his right side. This indicates to the follower that the leader wants her to move to his right side. Without this lead, there is a tendency to move directly toward (and into) the leader, which is not desired. On count 4, the leader brings his left hand toward his right shoulder, then lifts it higher to form an arch. The follower does the equivalent of an inside left turn with one difference: Partners remain holding both hands. The follower moves diagonally left front to end up in a wrap position. Once in the wrap position, the follower needs to move as far as possible to her right and into her left hand at her waist. The other hands and arms are curved in front for balance. Avoid letting the extended hands and arms collapse onto your stomachs. You'll have a better lead if the leader's left hand is extended a bit in front and at waist level.

On the third repetition, the leader lifts his left hand on count 4. On the fourth repetition, the follower moves clockwise under the arch to unwrap the arms and to resume a two-hands-joined position facing her partner.

## TO DECREASE DIFFICULTY

- Using arms only, try the wrap and unwrap slowly to get a feel for where to move in relationship to your partner.
- Repeat the rhythmic step pattern while in the wrap position (especially with a fast tempo).

**TO INCREASE DIFFICULTY**

- To get out of the wrap position, the leader may choose to release his right-hand grasp and use the inside of his right wrist to gently roll out the follower to end up in a one-hand-joined position.
- Add any of the other moves covered so far in any order.
- Experiment with a wrap to the leader's left side, then unwrap.
- Extend this variation to a walking wrap; once in the wrap position, the leader walks forward four steps as the follower walks backward four steps, then arch the arms to unwrap.

## Success Goal

Alternate the rhythmic step pattern in place with a wrap and unwrap for 2 minutes. ___

## Success Check

- Make a weight change on each count of the four-count rhythmic step pattern. ___
- Start and end in a two-hands-joined position. ___

# Drill 6
# Belt Loop (Left) Turn for Leader

Now it is time for the leader to have some fun! From a one-hand-joined position with a partner, do one rhythmic step pattern at a slow tempo to get connected with your partner. The footwork for the leader is the same preparation as for an inside turn for the follower, but the hands remain at waist level. Once the leader has moved slightly to his left on count 4 of the first measure, he also brings his free right hand and arm above his left hand (and angled diagonally left). On the second repetition of the rhythmic step pattern (and the second measure of music), the leader steps along a diagonal left front path as he places the follower's right hand near the right side of his waist or belt area, releases her hand,

and continues to make a half turn counterclockwise (turning into his own left arm). The follower rotates clockwise to face the leader as she slides her right hand around the leader's back (or just above his belt area) keeping in contact so that the leader can pick up her right hand with his left hand when he faces her at the end of his turn. Depending on the hand grip at the end of the belt loop turn for the leader, he may need to immediately lead an inside turn for the follower to naturally correct the hand positions. The addition of the inside turn helps you to avoid any fumbling and rolling hands around to resume the one-hand-joined position again.

**TO DECREASE DIFFICULTY**

- Slowly walk through the hand and body positions for the belt loop turn without doing the rhythmic step pattern.
- Do more repetitions of the rhythmic step pattern in place to prepare for the belt loop turn.

*(continued)*

**Drill 6**   *(continued)*

### TO INCREASE DIFFICULTY

- Lead a right outside turn, a left inside turn, then a belt loop turn.
- Combine any three moves covered so far in any order.

### *Success Goal*

Combine the rhythmic step pattern in place, a belt loop turn for the leader, and an inside turn for the follower for 2 minutes. ___

### *Success Check*

- The follower rotates clockwise to face leader as she keeps her right hand sliding across the leader's back. ___
- The leader rotates counterclockwise toward (and inside) his left arm, and re-grasps with his left hand to the follower's right hand on count 3. ___

# Drill 7
# Inside Turn With a Slide to Two Hands

This drill provides an easy way to either remain in or get into a two-hands-joined position. Start in a two-hands-joined position with your partner. Do one repetition of the rhythmic step pattern in place. On the second repetition of the rhythmic step pattern, the leader's left hand indicates an inside turn, while he releases his right hand and slides it across the follower's back and under her left elbow to re-grasp her left hand. During this second repetition, the leader does a clockwise half turn to switch positions with the follower. Repeat this variation starting from a one-hand-joined position.

### TO DECREASE DIFFICULTY

- Substitute an inside turn for the follower (i.e., release one hand completely) and eliminate the slide to two hands.
- Slowly walk through the positions without doing the rhythmic step pattern.

### TO INCREASE DIFFICULTY

- From a one-hand-joined position, combine an inside turn and slide to two hands with a wrap and an unwrap.
- Experiment with the leader turning left as he lifts his right hand to form an arch and as he places the follower's right hand at the right side of his waist, then continues his counterclockwise turn to face the partner as she slides across his back, both resuming a two-hands-joined position.

## Success Goal

Alternate a rhythmic step pattern in place with an inside turn and slide to two hands for 2 minutes. ___

- Maintain the tempo with a weight change on each count of the four-count rhythmic step pattern. ___

- Face your partner on counts 3, 4. ___

# Drill 8
# On Your Own: Combining Four-Count Swing/Hustle Variations

Your challenge is to put the variations you've learned into clusters of at least three moves. A cluster helps you remember the variations and gives the leader time to plan the next move or just enjoy the moment. As you've noticed, some moves naturally link together. Experiment and come up with at least three different short combinations. Use the following points as a reference when selecting your moves:

- Rhythmic step pattern executed in place
- Change of position
- Inside (left) turn for the follower
- Outside (right) turn for the follower
- Wrap and unwrap
- Belt loop (left) turn for the leader
- Inside turn with a slide to two hands

### TO DECREASE DIFFICULTY

- Start with one combination that you can repeat for the length of one song, then add another, then another, and so on.
- Review the previous drill combinations and start with your favorite one.

### TO INCREASE DIFFICULTY

- Add any moves covered so far to create a longer combination.
- Try your combinations with a variety of partners.
- Using a two-hands-joined position, experiment with an outside turn followed by an immediate inside turn; reverse it, each time keeping the joined hands high in between the two turns.

*(continued)*

Drill 8  *(continued)*

## *Success Goal*

Execute three different short combinations, each linking any three moves to music for 2 minutes. ___

## *Success Check*

- Maintain the tempo with a weight change on each count of the four-count rhythmic step pattern.

    ___

- Write out your favorite clusters.

    ___

# SUCCESS SUMMARY
# FOR FOUR-COUNT SWING/HUSTLE

The four-count swing/hustle is one of the easiest dances to learn and do. It has four weight changes—one on each count of a four-beat measure. The rhythmic step pattern is like walking or marching (without lifting your feet or knees as high as a majorette or drum major). The music gives the external tempo, or how fast you need to step. Just step on each beat of the music to keep the rhythm going and you are dancing! The four-count swing/hustle fits popular music from the 1970s to today. With its versatile music and simple rhythmic step pattern, the four-count swing/hustle will soon be your new favorite choice on the dance floor.

# Waltz

## *Moving Stately*

The waltz is a smooth, graceful dance that became popular after two Austrian composers, Franz Lanner and Johann Strauss, created beautiful waltz music in the early 1800s. With songs such as "The Blue Danube," their music set the standard for the Viennese waltz with its fast tempo that is still popular today. The Viennese waltz alternates multiple left and right turns and requires stamina to keep up with the music. Waltz music (with its unique 3/4 time signature) has three beats per measure: one downbeat and two upbeats. With the evolution of a slower version of the Viennese waltz, dancers began to take a longer step to accent the first count of the music. Two tempos of the waltz are recognized and danced today: a fast tempo and a slower tempo. In general, the waltz is characterized by its stately posture and a wavelike rise-and-fall motion. Although there are two different tempos of waltz music, only the slow-tempo American waltz will be described in this book for two reasons: It is the easiest to learn, and it is the version that you will most likely encounter on the social dance floor. The waltz has a rich and long history.

For over 300 years, a version of the waltz has been danced. Its early origins were in the 17th century (1600s) when peasants danced a *weller*, or turning dance, in Austria and Vienna. The word *waltz* comes from the old German word *walzen*, which means to turn, to glide, or to roll. In the 18th century (1700s), the upper class danced primarily open-couple dances such as the slow and stately minuet and other court dances. Napoleon's soldiers helped spread the waltz from Germany to Paris and eventually to England. After the French Revolution, the minuet gradually declined in France and even in England with the advent of the Industrial Revolution, and it was replaced by less complicated dances with more natural movements. The main reasons were that the minuet required practice, complex figures, suitable postures, and proper carriage—all things that had to be taught by a dancing master. Dancing masters were held in high esteem by the upper class for teaching dance technique and manners to adults and children. In Germany and England, the court balls protested the dance and Wilhelm II forbade the waltz until 1812.

In the mid-18th century (1750s), another early version of the waltz, the allemande, became popular in France. It began as one of the figures within the contredanse (dance done in a formation of two facing lines). The allemande was danced with arms on each other's shoulders. It soon became an independent dance with a close hold—the first time that the man placed his right hand around the woman's waist.

Women were criticized on moral grounds for dancing the waltz during this time-frame. According to religious leaders and society morals, the waltz was considered vulgar and sinful because of the closer hold and rapid turning movement. By the end of the 18th century, the scandal associated with the waltz only increased its popularity and it was accepted by high society.

In the 19th century (early 1800s), the waltz was introduced to the United State where two more modifications occurred. The first was the *Boston,* a slower waltz with long, gliding steps, fewer and slower turns, and more forward and backward movement (compared to the Viennese waltz, in which dancers constantly turned at a fast tempo). The second modification was taking one step to three beats of music, or a *hesitation.* The use of hesitation steps is popular today, especially with faster tempos.

By the 20th century (early 1900s), over three fourths of all dance programs were waltzes. All levels of society were now dancing the waltz. However, dance masters thought the slow version of the waltz was a threat to their profession because it was so easy to learn. Then, the waltz had a brief decline in popularity around World War I when a new craze from the United States, the foxtrot, spread to Europe and over-shadowed the waltz. In response in 1921, leading dance teachers and masters determined the standard technique as *walk, side, close.* This unification in teaching along with the shift toward more natural body movement resulted in an entirely new style waltz that is danced by old and young people today. In particular, the previous insistence of turnout of the feet (still useful with the faster Viennese waltz) was replaced with more comfortable foot positions as used in walking, more forward–backward movement was included, and the slower-tempo waltz became less stylized; it was friendlier for all to learn and enjoy.

# WALTZ RHYTHMIC STEP PATTERN

The waltz's 3/4 time music has three beats per measure. Each beat gets one count and one weight change. The waltz's three-count rhythmic step pattern needs to be repeated on both sides of the body before your starting foot is free again. Thus, when counting the waltz, it is helpful to group two measures, or six counts, together.

The waltz uses a half-box floor path that can be executed in different directions. The two foundational rhythmic step patterns are the box step and the half-box progression. The box step in the waltz is composed of two half boxes in two directions, either forward or backward. Initially, the leader starts with the left foot and executes one half-box forward, then one half-box backward. The follower starts with the right foot and executes one half-box backward, then one half-box forward. The half-box progression is composed of consecutive forward half boxes (for the leader) or backward half boxes (for the follower).

## Forward Half-Box Step Pattern

To execute the forward half-box step pattern, stand with your weight more on your right foot. Imagine a rectangular box on the floor. Bend your right knee, then push backward against the floor to take a long stride forward onto your left foot to the left front corner of the box. Move your right foot diagonally to the right front corner of the imaginary rectangle on the floor and step onto your right foot. Bring your left foot beside your right foot and change weight (onto your left foot) as your feet come together. These three weight changes comprise the forward half-box step pattern.

## Backward Half-Box Step Pattern

To execute the backward half-box step pattern, stand with your weight more on your left foot. Bend your left knee, then push forward against the floor to take a long stride backward onto your right foot to the right back corner of the box. Move your left foot diagonally to the left back corner of the imaginary rectangle on the floor and step onto your left foot. Bring your right foot beside your left foot and change weight (onto your right foot) as your feet come together. These three weight changes comprise the backward half-box step pattern.

Figure 7.1 shows the various ways you might organize the half-box counts that are used in two waltz rhythmic step patterns: the box step and the half-box progression step. Some cues may be more helpful than others. Select those cues that most help you retain how to execute these basic waltz step patterns.

---

## Figure 7.1 **WALTZ RHYTHMIC STEP PATTERNS**

### Footwork Cues

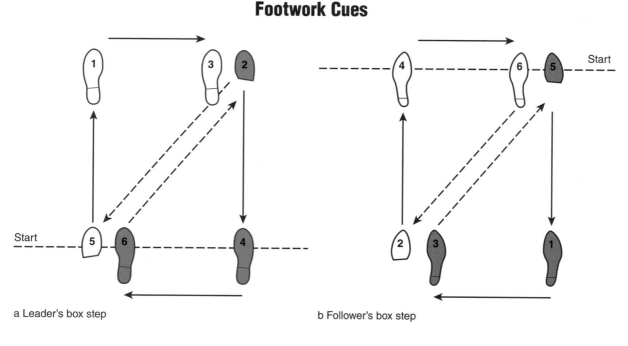

a Leader's box step

b Follower's box step

### *Box Step*

| *Leader* | *Follower* |
| --- | --- |
| Forward, side, together; backward, side, together | Backward, side, together; forward, side, together |

*(continued)*

## Figure 7.1 WALTZ RHYTHMIC STEP PATTERNS *(CONTINUED)*

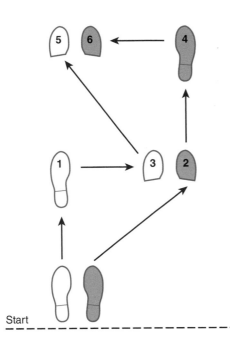

c Leader's half-box progression forward

d Follower's half-box progression backward

### *Half-Box Progression*

| Leader | Follower |
| --- | --- |
| Forward, side, together; forward, side, together | Backward, side, together; backward, side, together |

## Timing Cues

| | |
| --- | --- |
| 3/4 time signature: | Three beats to a measure (group two measures) |
| Duration: | Each beat gets one count (total of six counts) |
| Rhythm strategy: | Step on each beat |
| Counts: | 1, 2, 3; 4, 5, 6 |
| Weight changes: | 6 |
| Direction of steps: | Box step—Forward half box, then backward half box (leader); or backward half box, then forward half box (follower) |
| | Half-box progression—Forward half box, forward half box (leader); or backward half box, backward half box (follower) |
| Foot positions: | Half-box forward or backward—fourth, second, first |
| Floor contact: | Half-box forward—Heel, ball, ball flat; half-box backward—toe, ball, ball flat |
| Styling: | Rise and fall motion (subtle lowering and rising) |

# DRILLS FOR WALTZ

The appeal of the waltz has stood the test of time and is still popular today. The following drills will help you to become proficient in the waltz rhythm in 3/4 time. For each drill, read the directions, and watch the video demonstrations on the enclosed DVD to see (a) how to execute the selected waltz variations, and (b) how to combine them into short practice combinations. Then, practice until you can meet the Success Goal for each drill. Use track 9 to practice your waltz moves.

## Drill 1
## Waltz Balance Options

The waltz balance is a good review of the basic waltz rhythm because it uses three steps, one on each count of the three-beat measure. The waltz balance can be executed in four different directions, giving the leader more options. In each case, two directions are contrasted: forward and backward or left and right sides. It is also a versatile option that permits you to remain relatively in place, which is especially useful for getting started, or any time that you want to slow down a bit such as when another couple is blocking your forward movement. Starting in a closed position with your partner, the footwork is the same for both partners, only the follower does the mirror reverse. Thus, the leader starts the forward half of the waltz balance with his left foot (then right, left steps in place) and the backward half of the waltz balance begins with his right foot (then left, right steps in place). The follower starts with her right foot to do the backward half of the waltz balance, then she uses her left foot to do the forward half of the waltz balance. It takes six weight changes—three in each direction—and two measures of waltz music before your starting foot is free again. Try each of the following direction options.

a. *Forward–backward balances.* To execute a forward balance, step forward onto your left foot on count 1. Step forward onto your right foot with feet together on count 2. Step in place onto your left foot on count 3. To execute a backward balance, step backward onto your right foot on count 1. Step backward onto your left foot with feet together on count 2. Step in place onto your right foot on count 3. Notice that each direction is executed within one measure, and it takes two measures (six counts) to execute the combined forward–backward balances. For practice, repeat each direction at least twice, using four measures, before changing to another direction.

b. *Side balances.* To execute a left-side balance, step to your left side onto your left foot on count 1. Step to the left side with your right foot, bringing your feet together on count 2. Step in place onto your left foot on count 3. To execute a right-side balance, step to your right side onto your right foot on count 1. Step to your right side with your left foot, bringing your feet together on count 2. Step in place onto your right foot on count 3. Again, each direction takes two measures (six counts) before your starting foot is free again. For practice, repeat each side at least twice, using four measures, before changing to another direction.

*(continued)*

Drill 1 *(continued)*

### TO DECREASE DIFFICULTY

- Practice the footwork without a partner.
- Verbally count the beats to help maintain the rhythm as you step on each count.

### TO INCREASE DIFFICULTY

- Repeat the combination using only one measure in each direction.
- Substitute a hesitation step (step, touch, and hold) on each measure in each direction.

## Success Goal

Alternate forward–backward balances (for four measures) and side balances (for four measures) for 2 minutes. ___

## Success Check

- Step on each count. ___
- On forward–backward balance steps, use fourth, first, first positions of the feet.___
- On side balance steps, use second, first, first positions of the feet. ___

# Drill 2
# Box Step

The box step is a popular variation in the waltz that evolved from the more natural movements of *walk, side, close* that was introduced around 1921 in the United States. Review figure 7.1, *a* and *b* for the box step footwork and timing cues. Imagine a rectangular box on the floor. The width should be approximately the width of your own shoulders. You will actually step in each corner of this box shape. To outline the forward half of the rectangle, the first step is taken along the length of this rectangle with your left foot, whereas the two *side, together* steps are executed along the width of

the rectangle in the top right corner. To complete the bottom portion of the imaginary rectangle, step backward with your right foot along the length of the rectangle, then take two steps in the back left corner. Both halves form the rectangular floor shape, which is called the box step. After you can easily repeat the box step alone, try it with a partner in closed position. Leaders start with the left foot and a forward half-box, while followers start with the right foot and a backward half-box. The box step is a stationary move in that it permits you and your partner to remain in one location.

### TO DECREASE DIFFICULTY

- Prepare yourself to move by using extra cues such as *&-a-1.* The *&* alerts you to be ready, the *a* signals you to bend your supporting knee and push off to stride forward (or backward), and the *1* is the first count, or first weight change.
- Face a partner, match fingertips, repeat the box step, and feel the momentum when your center moves first and your feet follow.

### TO INCREASE DIFFICULTY

- Practice with different partners.
- Add a rise-and-fall motion (i.e., bend on count 1, rise onto the ball of your foot on count 2, and lower on count 3).
- Alternate the forward–backward balance steps with the box step.

## *Success Goal*

Execute the waltz box step for 2 minutes.

___

## *Success Check*

- Make six weight changes in two measures of music for the waltz box step. ___
- Lower your center of gravity (flex your knees) and push off with your supporting foot before taking your first step (within each measure of three counts). ___
- Take a long forward or backward step on counts 1 and 4. ___
- Take the side steps on counts 2 and 5. ___
- Blend both half-boxes into a fluid waltz box step. ___

# Drill 3
# Slow Underarm Turn

Start in a closed position with your partner. The leader's part is to execute two box steps (or four half-boxes for a total of 12 counts). It is easiest to group four half-boxes when executing the slow underarm turn for the follower. Both partners do the first half-box together and the first count of the second half-box when the leader lifts his left arm to form an arch.

On counts 2, 3 (of the second half-box), the follower moves clockwise a half turn (and under the arched hands) to be on the leader's left side. She continues to curve her forward traveling steps to face the leader on the third half-box. Both partners reconnect on the fourth half-box to be back in closed position.

### TO DECREASE DIFFICULTY

- Check your positions on each of the four half-boxes.
- Use slow counts without music, then use music with a slow tempo.

### TO INCREASE DIFFICULTY

- Alternate the balance steps with the box step and the slow underarm turn.
- The leader can rotate to face the follower on the third half-box (cutting off the follower's turn to be a quarter turn instead of a half turn).

*(continued)*

Drill 3 *(continued)*

## *Success Goal*

Alternate two waltz box steps and a slow underarm turn for 2 minutes. ___

- Maintain the tempo with a step on each count. ___
- The lead is given on the first count of the second half-box step. ___
- The follower moves under the arched hands on counts 2 and 3 of the second half-box step. ___

# Drill 4
# Left Box Turn

The left box turn is a variation of the box step. It is composed of four counterclockwise (CCW) quarter turns. A forward quarter turn is combined with a backward quarter turn, or vice versa. From a closed position, the leader initiates the left box turn by rotating his upper body 45 degrees CCW until his shoulders and sternum are facing his left front diagonal direction. The leader starts with the forward direction while the follower starts with the backward direction. Visually, a diagram of the complete left box turn gets complicated. Thus, if you think about breaking it down into a quarter turn that faces each wall of the room using alternating directions for each half-box, it is easier to conceptualize. Or, if you start facing the LOD, your quarter-turn orientation is as follows: center, reverse LOD, outside wall, and LOD. Try each of the following segments separately, then blend them together.

a. *Forward CCW quarter turn.*
From a closed position, imagine a 45-degree diagonal line on the floor extending from the leader's left foot along his left

front diagonal direction. After the leader's upper body CCW rotation toward the left front diagonal, he steps forward with his left foot along his left front diagonal on count 1. The leader can use a toes-angled-outward foot placement for better balance. Continue to rotate to face a new wall as the leader steps to the right with his right foot (feet in parallel second position) on count 2, then he brings his feet together (left foot beside right foot) and changes weight onto his left foot with feet in parallel first position on count 3. At the end of this half-box (three counts), notice that the leader has made a quarter turn and is facing a new wall.

b. *Backward CCW quarter turn.*
From a closed position, imagine a 45-degree diagonal line on the floor extending backward from your right heel. The leader's upper-body rotation lead facilitates his right foot's step backward along his right back

diagonal path on count 4. The leader continues the rotation to face a new wall as he steps to his left side with his left foot on count 5, then he brings his feet together (shifting your weight onto his right foot) on count 6.

The third and fourth half-boxes repeat the movements previously described. After the fourth quarter turn, the leader may end the turn by firmly keeping his

frame (upper torso and arms) facing the LOD. Avoid any tendencies to under- or overrotate on the first step of each measure. A diagonal direction is more efficient (see figure 7.2, *a* and *b*). When starting in a closed position with your partner, the follower starts with her right foot and does the backward half-box rotation, which is the mirror reverse of the leader's start with his left foot and a forward half-box rotation.

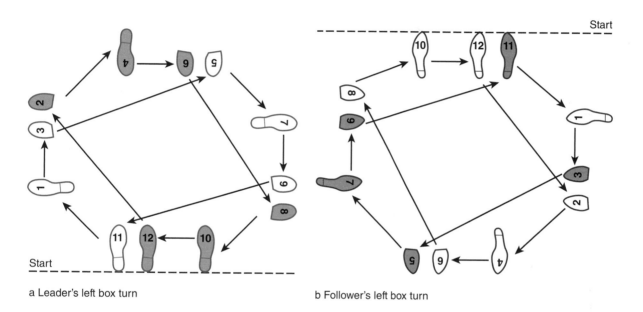

a Leader's left box turn                    b Follower's left box turn

**Figure 7.2**    Left box turn footwork for the waltz (12 total counts).

 **TO DECREASE DIFFICULTY**

- Practice the footwork and upper torso rotation without a partner.
- Do a half-box forward, then angle only on the backward half-box to make a CCW quarter turn. Repeat these two half-boxes facing each wall.

**TO INCREASE DIFFICULTY**

- Add a slow underarm turn at the end of this combination.
- Alternate forward–backward balances with a left box turn.

*(continued)*

Drill 4   *(continued)*

## Success Goal

Alternate two box steps and a left box turn for 2 minutes. ___

- Face a new wall on each quarter turn. ___
- Four CCW quarter turns (using four half-boxes) comprise a left box turn. ___
- Angle the toes of the left foot outward on forward CCW quarter turns, then angle the toes of the right foot inward on backward CCW quarter turns. ___

# Drill 5
# Right Box Turn

A right box turn is a clockwise (CW) turn from a closed position with your partner. Like the left box turn, it also takes four half-boxes to complete the turn. However, the right box turn requires two more half-boxes—one to set up the turn and one after the turn. As the leader starts with his left foot, he executes a forward half-box while facing in the LOD. With the leader's right foot now free, he can rotate his upper torso (frame) 45 degrees to his right initiating a quarter turn (to face the wall) on the second half-box. Continue rotating CW a quarter turn on the third, fourth, and fifth half-boxes. When the leader is back facing the LOD, he may execute either a forward or a backward half-box (on the sixth half-box). Thus, much like a sandwich, the right box turn is both preceded and ended with a half-box as follows: a forward half-box, four CW quarter turns, then either a backward or a forward half-box. These directions are cued for the leader. The follower does the mirror reverse.

## TO DECREASE DIFFICULTY

- Practice the footwork and upper torso rotation without a partner.
- During the turn to the right, take as many basic steps as needed to revolve 360 degrees.
- Do a half-box forward, then angle 45 degrees forward only on the second half-box to make a CW quarter turn. Repeat these two half-boxes facing each wall.

## TO INCREASE DIFFICULTY

- Add a slow underarm turn at the end of this combination.
- Combine two left quarter turns with two right quarter turns. Notice that this combination moves in the LOD.

## Success Goal

Alternate two box steps and a right box turn for 2 minutes. ___

## Success Check

- A total of six half-boxes comprise the right box turn. ___
- A forward half-box sets up the four CW quarter turns and either a forward or a backward half-box is executed after the four CW quarter turns. ___
- The toes of the right foot angle outward on forward CW quarter turns, then the toes of the left foot angle inward on backward CW quarter turns. ___

## Drill 6
# Half-Box Progression

The half-box progression is a good option when dancers have room to travel. Start in a closed position. Do one forward half-box. On the second half-box, continue traveling forward. Leaders start with the left foot and travel forward on each half-box, stepping left foot forward, side, together and right foot forward, side, together. Followers do the mirror reverse, starting with the right foot and traveling backward on each half-box progression. Review figure 7.1, c and d to identify each partner's basic footwork and timing execution. Once in motion, continue moving at the same pace, especially at the end of the first half-box progression to resist the tendency to remain stationary. If the momentum pauses or slows down in between the two measures, then the follower thinks that a box step (versus a half-box progression) is being led. Travel in a CCW direction around the perimeter of the floor, gently curving your movements at each end of the room. Or, you might experiment with half-box progressions forward along the length of the room. In the corners of the room, execute only one CCW quarter turn, then continue with half-box progressions forward again.

### TO DECREASE DIFFICULTY

- Use slow verbal counts until you can execute six weight changes in six counts (or two measures of music) without pausing in between.
- Modify the starting position to face a partner and match facing palms and fingertips in order to be more aware of the CPB shift forward (for the leader) or backward (for the follower).

### TO INCREASE DIFFICULTY

- Alternate two box steps with four half-box progression steps.
- Use a variety of slow waltz music.
- Switch partners frequently.

*(continued)*

Drill 6 *(continued)*

## Success Goal

Perform half-box progressions in the LOD for 2 minutes. ___

## Success Check

- Lower your CPB and push off with your supporting foot before taking your first step of each three-count measure. ___

- Before taking the side step on counts 2 and 5, your free foot should follow a diagonal path as you move your foot directly into a corner of the rectangular box. ___

- Maintain a constant forward motion in between each half-box progression. ___

# Drill 7
# Cross Step

In the waltz, the cross step is composed of two half-boxes using two measures of music, or six counts. The cross step starts in a closed position, transitions to a promenade, or semiopen position, and ends in a closed position (review figure 4.1, *e* and *f*). What makes this transition to the promenade position more challenging is that it requires isolation such that your hands, torso, and arms remain stationary while your lower body angles 45 degrees. To get an idea of what this rotation entails, stand facing a wall without a partner. Place your hands against the wall at about shoulder height. Position your weight over the balls of your feet and swivel such that your toes alternately face each side. You don't need to be extremely flexible because you'll only need to rotate your hips 45 degrees to either side (or 90 degrees total). The most common error is moving the arms versus keeping them firmly in frame with your partner. The second most common error is rotating too far to the side beyond

45 degrees. Practice this subtle lower-body rotation on your own, then with a partner.

The first half-box is used to move into a promenade position (also called an *open twinkle* as the follower opens to face the extended hands), then another half-box is used to move back to a closed position. Keep your frame firm as you execute the following two measures.

a. *First half-box (transition from closed to promenade).* From a closed position, start to execute a half-box. Both partners take a normal step on the first count, followed by a regular side step on count 2. At the end of the side step, the leader needs to swivel on the ball of his right foot so as to rotate his lower body CCW approximately 45 degrees and to gently press with the heel of his right hand on the follower's left shoulder blade. Thus, in the waltz, the lead occurs at the end of count 2 and preceding count 3. Both partners look toward their extended hands and bring their feet together on the third weight change to be in a promenade position.

b. *Second half-box (transition from promenade to closed)*. When in the promenade position, both partners' inside feet should be free (his right foot and her left foot) to start the second half-box. On the first weight change, the leader crosses his right foot over his left foot while the follower crosses her left foot over her right foot. At the end of this step, both partners swivel on the ball of the weighted foot in order to face each other in closed position again. Then both partners execute their *side, together* steps (their second and third weight changes) in the closed position. Both of these transitions comprise the cross step (see figure 7.3).

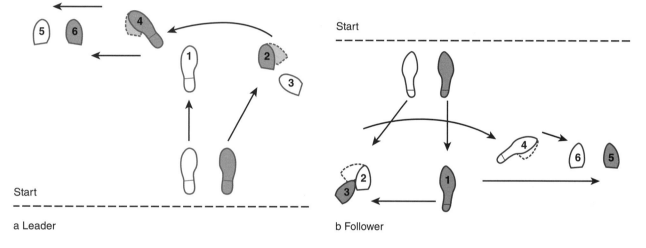

a Leader

b Follower

**Figure 7.3** Waltz cross step.

 **TO DECREASE DIFFICULTY**

- Place your hands on a wall at approximately shoulder height. Keep your weight on the balls of your feet as you practice the entire cross step in place without a partner.
- Repeat the cross step at least twice before changing to something different.

 **TO INCREASE DIFFICULTY**

- Repeat the cross step only once.
- Combine the cross step with any other variation covered so far.

*(continued)*

Drill 7  *(continued)*

## Success Goal

Alternate two box steps and two cross steps for 2 minutes. ___

*First Half-Box*

- Leader: Forward (left foot), side (right foot and CCW swivel), together (left foot). ___
- Follower: Backward (right foot), side (left foot and CW swivel), together (right foot). ___
- Angle your lower body and sternum 45 degrees toward the extended hands when in the promenade position. ___

*Second Half-Box*

- Inside feet cross on the first weight change, then swivel preceding the *side, together* steps. ___
- Square up the hips (to be parallel) with your partner on the *side, together* steps and resume the closed position. ___

# Drill 8
# Weave

The weave is an extension of the cross step. After the first half-box (open twinkle), the cross step is repeated three times, alternating from side to side in an open position. In the open (side-by-side) position, the outside hands (furthermost from your partner) are released when facing each side. Starting in a closed position, the follower does the mirror reverse. The follower needs to keep both arms lifted throughout so that the leader can find her shoulder blades. The leader alternately presses with the heel of his right, left, and right hand on the follower's shoulder blades. The weave uses four half-boxes that permit you to mark time or maintain your location instead of travel.

## Leader

- *First half-box:* Open twinkle and release your left hand (face the left side with left arm opened to the side).
- *Second half-box:* Cross your right foot, step your left foot to the left side, swivel and release your right hand (face right side with right arm opened to the side), and step onto your right foot.
- *Third half-box:* Cross your left foot, step your right foot to the right side, swivel and release your left hand (face left side with left arm opened to the side), and step onto your left foot.

- *Fourth half-box:* Cross your right foot, step your left foot to the left side, and bring your feet together as you step onto your right foot (resume a closed position).

## Follower

- *First half-box:* Open twinkle (backward half-box with a swivel) and open right arm (face right side).
- *Second half-box:* Cross your left foot, step your right foot to the right side, swivel and open your left arm (face left side), and step onto the left foot.
- *Third half-box:* Cross your right foot, step your left foot to the left side, swivel and open your right arm (face right side), and step onto the right foot.
- *Fourth half-box:* Cross your left foot, step your right foot to the right side, and bring your feet together as you step onto your left foot (resume a closed position).

 **TO DECREASE DIFFICULTY**

- Practice without a partner, then with a partner to match symmetrical arm positions when facing each side.
- Use a slow tempo.

 **TO INCREASE DIFFICULTY**

- Combine the weave with any two additional waltz variations in any order. For example, combine box step, slow underarm turn, and weave.
- Practice with a variety of partners.

## Success Goal

Alternate two box steps and the weave step to slow waltz music for 2 minutes. ___

## Success Check

- The weave is composed of four half-boxes. ___
- When facing each side, shoulders angle approximately 45 degrees. ___
- Keep your extended arm curved with the elbow and hand in front of your shoulder. ___
- Followers need to keep both elbows up and in frame throughout so that the leader can locate her shoulder blade before each of the crossing steps. ___

# Drill 9
# Rollovers

Rollovers are similar to the weave, but both partners travel in the LOD in an open position. Once in a side-by-side position, the rollover results when the partner on the inside (left side) rolls in front of (faces) and moves diagonally across to the opposite side (right side) while the other partner does the basic in place. As in the leads used with the weave step, the leader will alternately hold the follower's left shoulder blade with his right hand, then hold the follower's right shoulder blade with his left hand, keeping the opposite arm extended in a curved and open position. Arms open to face the LOD as the rollovers progress in the LOD. Start in a closed position with your partner and do at least one box step and angle to face diagonally toward the outside wall. Then, do the following.

## Leader

- *First half-box:* Open twinkle and release your left hand (face LOD).
- *Second half-box:* Step with your right foot diagonally in front of the follower (toward the front diagonal wall), step onto your left foot to the left side (face your partner), continue CW and release your right hand (leader is on the right side with his left hand on the follower's right shoulder blade) to step onto the right foot.
- *Third half-box:* Step in place (left, right, left) and release your left hand and slide down her right arm to grasp her hand

(face LOD in promenade position with your right hand on the follower's left shoulder blade as she moves to your right side).
- *Fourth half-box:* Use your right hand and frame to bring the follower back into closed position during this forward half-box.

## Follower

- *First half-box:* Open twinkle (backward half-box with a swivel at the end of count 2) and open your right arm on count 3 (face LOD and be on the leader's right side).
- *Second half-box:* Step in place (left, right, left) as the leader rolls over by moving CW across to the right side of the follower and you open your left arm on count 3 (both face LOD).
- *Third half-box:* The follower now rolls over starting with the right foot diagonally in front of the leader, step your left foot to the left side (face leader), continue CW across to the right side and into a promenade position after the leader slides under your right elbow to grasp your right hand (both face LOD) as you step the right foot in place.
- *Fourth half-box:* Step forward with your left foot and angle it to facilitate a half turn to your left to face the leader and be in a closed position.

### TO DECREASE DIFFICULTY

- Imagine a triangle with the leader on the left, the follower on the right, and the LOD at the top of the triangle. Walk through the changing side positions, alternating the leader rolling across as the follower remains stationary, then switch roles.
- When the follower is on the inside or left side of the leader, he can practice sliding his left hand down the arm and under the elbow prior to grasping hands to be in the promenade position.

### TO INCREASE DIFFICULTY

- Do any multiple of two repetitions of the rollovers.
- Alternate the rollovers and the forward half-box progressions.

## Success Goal

Alternate box steps and rollovers to slow waltz music for 2 minutes. ___

## Success Check

- Keep your extended arm in a curved shape, symmetrical with your partner's extended arm. ___
- Keep your arms lifted in frame throughout. ___
- On the rollovers, your sternum should face diagonal front, either toward the wall or toward the center. ___
- The inside person (on the left side) rolls across first. ___

# Drill 10
# Scissors

The scissors variation may also be called *spirals, serpentines,* or *zigzags* because it follows a diagonal floor path that alternates toward the center, then toward the outside wall (see figure 7.4). It takes at least four half-boxes to execute the scissors variation. Both the first and the fourth half-box basics are transitions into and out of the zigzag floor path that is characteristic of the scissors step. The scissors starts in a closed position, which gets modified by rotating 45 degrees to move into a right parallel position with the right shoulders together (to travel toward the center of the room), then by rotating 90 degrees to move to a left parallel position with the left shoulders together (to travel toward the outside wall). Once in these parallel positions (review figure 4.1, *h* and *i*), step outside your partner's feet and on the diagonal (either left front or right front for the leader). Notice that the follower remains slightly ahead or in front of the leader throughout. Using a diagonal path permits travel in the LOD, while overrotating keeps you in one location. The purpose of this variation is to travel in the LOD.

*(continued)*

Drill 10 *(continued)*

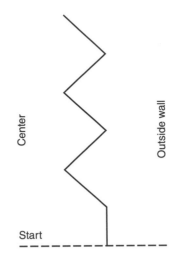

Center

Outside wall

Start

**Figure 7.4** Zigzag floor path used in the scissors variation.

## Leader

- *First half-box:* Closed twinkle (forward half-box with a CCW swivel) to right parallel position (follower on right side with right hips together).

- *Second half-box:* Step forward toward the diagonal center with your right foot, left to the side, CW swivel, and bring your feet together into a left parallel position (follower is on the left side).

- *Third half-box:* Step forward toward the diagonal wall with your left foot, right to the side, CCW swivel, and bring your feet together into a right parallel position (follower is on the right side).

- *Fourth half-box:* Step forward toward the diagonal center with your right foot, left foot to the side, feet together, and resume a closed position (facing your partner in LOD).

## Follower

- *First half-box:* Closed twinkle (i.e., backward half-box with a CCW swivel on count 2) to right parallel position (right hips closer together; follower is a half step in front of the leader).

- *Second half-box:* Step backward toward the diagonal center with your left foot, right to side, CW swivel and bring your feet together in the left parallel position (follower is on the leader's left side with left hips closer together).

- *Third half-box:* Step backward toward the diagonal wall with your right foot, left to the side, CCW swivel and bring feet together to be in the right parallel position (follower is on the leader's right side with right hips closer together).

- *Fourth half-box:* Step backward toward the diagonal center with your left foot, right to side, feet together and face your partner (closed position).

**TO DECREASE DIFFICULTY**

- Place your hands on your partner's shoulders to become aware of the diagonals and to keep the follower in front of the leader with a clear right (or left) parallel position.

- Without a partner, practice pivoting no more than 90 degrees to face each diagonal direction and to travel in the LOD.

 **TO INCREASE DIFFICULTY**

- Use any even number of repeats of the zigzag floor path, such as four, six or eight half-boxes.

- Slide apart to use an open two-hand position (extend arms to sides at shoulder level) during the scissors.

- Lead a right underarm turn on the last diagonal zigzag to come out of the scissors. The follower's turn should occur on count 5.

## *Success Goal*

Alternate box steps with the scissors to slow waltz music for 2 minutes. ___

## *Success Check*

- The scissors' long, reaching step (first beat of the second and third measures) is taken with the leg closest to the LOD, or the leg opposite the diagonal direction of travel (the leader's right foot moves toward his left front diagonal; the follower's left foot moves toward her right back diagonal). ___

- Footwork cues for the scissors: diagonal, pivot, together. ___

- Step outside your partner's feet as you alternate a right, then left parallel position (with right-to-right hips closer together, then left-to-left hips closer together). ___

# Drill 11
# On Your Own: Combining Three Waltz Variations

The purpose of this drill is to combine at least three waltz variations. The advantage of combining or clustering moves is that once you start any particular cluster, with practice the rest of the moves flow automatically without your having to think about them. Try each of the following three-variation practice combinations with a partner to waltz music:

- Two boxes, a slow underarm turn, and a left box turn
- Two boxes, a left box turn, and four half-box progressions forward
- Two boxes, six half-box progressions forward, and scissors step
- Two balance steps (forward and backward twice), a box step, and a weave step
- Two CCW quarter turns, two CW quarter turns, and a cross step

Now, select from the following points as you experiment with the order to make your own combinations of any three variations:

- Half-boxes (forward and backward)
- Half-box progressions (forward and backward)
- Balance steps (forward, backward, and sideward)
- Box step
- Slow underarm turn
- Left box turn
- Right box turn
- Cross step
- Weave
- Rollovers
- Scissors

## TO DECREASE DIFFICULTY

- Repeat each variation at least twice to give the leader more time to prepare for the next lead and to get in sync with your partner.
- Do as many repetitions of each of the variations within the combinations listed as needed.
- Practice at least two of the previous sample combinations.

## TO INCREASE DIFFICULTY

- Do four consecutive repetitions of each of the previous sample combinations.
- Create your own clusters of three variations.
- Link any four to six variations together to create a longer combination.

## Success Goal

Perform four consecutive repetitions of any three of the previous combinations as you practice proper etiquette with at least three different partners. ___

## Success Check

- Maintain the waltz rhythm. ___
- Write down at least two of your favorite combinations to trigger your memory later. ___

# SUCCESS SUMMARY FOR WALTZ

The waltz is a graceful, smooth, and stately dance. It has a three-count rhythm pattern with a weight change taken on each count. Waltz music is in 3/4 time with a down-beat and two upbeats in each three-beat measure. Because it has an odd number of counts and corresponding weight changes, you can best match your footwork to the music by grouping two measures, or six counts, together to account for both sides. For example, step left, right, left; and right, left, right. The closed position is used primarily, but it is helpful to be able to make the transition to a promenade position, then back to closed position again. Two common transition moves are the open twinkle (used in the cross step, the weave, and the rollovers) and the closed twinkle (used in the scissors step). Characteristic of the waltz is its subtle rise and fall motion created by bending your supporting knee to lower the body preceding the first step, then rising onto the ball of the foot on the second step, and gently lowering to level on the third step. After completing the drills and practicing the suggested combinations (review the enclosed DVD), it is time to take your waltz moves to the social dance floor!

# Six-Count Swing

## *Looking Jazzy*

The six-count swing's name is often shortened and referred to as simply the *swing*. It is fun to do because of its styling freedom. Erect posture is not as important in the swing. Rather, the swing is characterized by torso leans and a jazzy, syncopated style. The swing is a spot dance; each couple stakes out a small circle, or spot, on the dance floor. The many variations within the swing allow partners to rotate around each other within a circle approximately 10 feet (3 m) in diameter. The basic six-count rhythm of the swing may be cued as *slow, slow, quick, quick* in that each *slow* gets two counts and each *quick* gets one count. The swing is danced to Big Band 4/4 time music with four beats per measure and three different tempos: slow, moderate, and fast. Thus, the basic six-count swing takes one and a half measures of music and has three different rhythmic step patterns, each suited to fit the tempo of the swing music. The swing is an American dance with a rich history.

The swing evolved from the jazz era of the 1920s and was first known as the *jitterbug*. The first jitterbug step, the shag, was inspired by the boogie-woogie. The shag had a *slow, slow, quick, quick* rhythm that is still used today. Later, another American dance evolved. It was called the *lindy hop* in honor of Charles Lindbergh, who flew solo across the Atlantic Ocean in 1927. In time, the lindy hop became known simply as the *lindy*. Typically, lindy steps involve eight-count patterns executed in a circular area on the floor. However, sometimes these patterns were interchanged with the earlier shag step—according to the tempo of the music—with a single, a delayed single, or a triple step taken on each *slow* count. Because of the popularity of swing bands during the 1930s and 1940s, the lindy became known simply as the *swing*. Swing was also popular throughout the rock 'n' roll era of the 1950s and 1960s.

Then, two additional forms of swing emerged, the East Coast swing and the West Coast swing, which remain popular today. The East Coast swing is a circular dance also known as the triple swing because it uses a triple step on each *slow* count, which is very effective with slow swing music. The West Coast swing is a slot dance that uses both six- and eight-count patterns done to either medium or slow tempos. A European version of the East Coast swing is called the *jive*. Characterized by sharp kicks and flicks, the jive is typically used in competitions and is done to a fast tempo with knees lifted high. Neither of these latter dances are covered directly in this book. As you gain more experience and confidence, you may want to try the East Coast swing's triple steps to a very fast tempo, but remember that it is easier to practice with slow tempos first.

The terminology for the swing has also evolved. In the 1950s, the Arthur Murray studios denoted the three different rhythms that may be used on each of the *slow, slow* rhythm cues in swing dancing as follows:

- *single-time swing*—Step, touch; or step, hold.
- *double-time swing*—Tap, step.
- *triple-time swing*—Step three times.

Skippy Blair modified these terms for the Golden State Teachers Association in 1964 and again in 1978 when her book, *Contemporary Social Dance: Disco to Tango and Back,* introduced the following rhythm terms to be used with each *slow* cue:

- *single rhythm*—Step one time in two beats.
- *delayed single rhythm*—Step once only on the upbeat or second count in two beats.
- *triple rhythm*—Step three times in two beats.

How do you know when to use any one of these rhythmic pattern strategies? Each rhythmic step pattern is best suited for one of three tempos as follows:

- *fast*—Single swing rhythmic step pattern.
- *moderate*—Delayed single swing rhythmic step pattern.
- *slow*—Triple swing rhythmic step pattern.

For each of the three rhythmic step patterns in the swing, the same footwork actions occur on the *quick, quick* rhythm cues, or counts 5, 6. You might have heard these two weight changes called a *rock step,* but the term *ball–change* is more accurate. In particular, the term *ball–change* presents a better image for shifting your weight onto the ball of your foot (rather than the entire foot) on count 5 and for keeping your upper torso above your base of support when changing your weight on count 6. Two common errors are to let your upper torso lean backward beyond a vertical alignment or to step back onto a flat foot on the ball, change. Both of these errors greatly affect your balance and your timing with the music, causing you to be late or behind the tempo. Be aware that in some geographic locations, it is preferred to start the rhythmic step pattern with the ball–change. On the social dance floor, either way is acceptable.

You may find that you have certain tempo preferences, which is fine. Feel free to start with the tempo you prefer. Once you know all three rhythmic step patterns for the swing, you may select the one that best fits the tempo of the swing music being played. Think of it as three ways to have more fun on the dance floor. Typically, the three rhythmic step patterns for the swing are initiated either from a two-hands-joined position or in a semiopen position with a partner. Figure 8.1 shows the triangular partner orientation when in a semiopen position. The leader is on the left side, the follower on the right side, and the hands are placed in the middle toward the top of the triangle. Notice that the hand position is a bit different in the swing in that the hands are grasped at approximately waist height with the leader's thumb on top (his palm is up and fingers are pointing toward his midline).

**Figure 8.1**   Suggested hand grasp in the semiopen starting position for the swing.

# RHYTHMIC STEP PATTERNS FOR SIX-COUNT SWING

The swing has three six-count rhythmic step patterns to choose from. The rhythm for each pattern may be cued as *slow, slow, quick, quick* with different timing options during the *slow, slow* portions. Each pattern ends with a ball–change on the *quick, quick* portion. Each pattern is addressed according to its fit with the three tempos of swing music—fast, moderate, or slow. At some point, you should be able to distinguish and execute all three rhythmic step patterns, which will give you more options on the dance floor. Or, you may choose to focus on only one at a time and gradually increase your repertoire.

## Single Swing (Fast Tempo)

Listen for the tempo; it should be fast. Mentally count in sets of four counts to identify the tempo, and prepare to step on any first count with your starting foot (left foot for the leader, right foot for the follower).

### Leader

In a two-hands-joined position, stand with your feet together and shift your weight onto your right foot in order to free your left foot. Take a small side step onto your left foot on count 1 and hold on count 2, then take a small side step onto your right foot on count 3 and hold on count 4. Keep your steps no wider than shoulder-width apart. Both of these weight changes take two counts during each of the *slow* timing cues. Two more weight changes follow for a ball–change. On count 5, place the ball of your left foot about 2 or 3 inches (5-8 cm) from your right heel and change your weight. On count 6, shift your weight back onto your right foot, which remains in place (replace it to be in the same place as it started). Thus, the ball–change steps are similar to *left, right* marching steps taken in place. The ball–change steps move you away from and then toward your partner as if stretching a rubber band.

### Follower

In a two-hands-joined position, stand with your feet together and shift your weight onto your left foot in order to free your right foot. Take a small side step onto your right foot on count 1 and hold on count 2, then take a small side step onto your left foot on count 3 and hold on count 4. Keep your steps no wider than shoulder-width apart. Both of these weight changes take two counts during the *slow* timing cues. Two more weight changes follow for a ball–change. On count 5, place the ball of your right foot approximately two to three inches from your left heel and change weight. On count 6, shift your weight back onto your left foot, which remains in place. These actions are similar to a mirror reverse except during the ball–change steps, when both partners move away from and then toward each other.

For styling and to maintain the tempo, you may add a slight knee bend on counts 2 and 4 instead of pausing or holding these counts. Figure 8.2 shows the two-hands-joined position footwork and timing cues for the single swing rhythmic step pattern.

---

### Figure 8.2  RHYTHMIC STEP PATTERN FOR SINGLE SWING (FAST TEMPO)

**Footwork Cues**

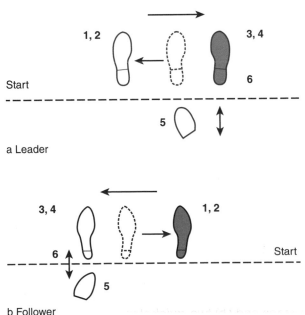

a Leader

b Follower

**Leader**
Left/hold, right/hold, ball–change
(left, right)

**Follower**
Right/hold, left/hold, ball–change
(right, left)

## Timing Cues

| | |
|---|---|
| 4/4 time signature: | Four beats to a measure (group 1 1/2 measures) |
| Duration: | Each beat gets one count (total of six counts) |
| Counts: | Six; 1, 2, 3, 4, 5, 6 |
| Rhythm: | Slow, slow, quick, quick |
| Weight changes: | Four (on counts 1, 3, 5, 6) |
| Direction of steps: | Two-hands-joined position—Side, side, backward, replace; Semiopen position—Forward, backward, backward, replace |
| Foot positions: | Two-hands-joined position—second, second, fifth; Semiopen position—fourth, fourth, fifth |

In the semiopen position (review figure 8.1), when both partners angle 45 degrees toward the middle, you use the same timing but the direction changes. Now both partners take a small step forward, then shift their weight backward and do a ball–change (step backward, then replace your weight in the same position). See figure 8.3 for foot diagrams when in the semiopen position with your partner. You may start either with your feet together (in parallel first position) or with one foot slightly ahead of the other (in third position) for better balance. The forward and backward (*slow, slow*) steps are taken in fourth position (see figure 8.3*a*), while the ball–change (*quick, quick*) steps should be in either third or fifth position (see figure 8.3*b*).

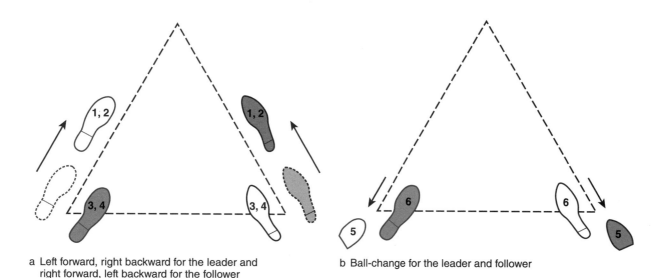

a  Left forward, right backward for the leader and right forward, left backward for the follower

b  Ball-change for the leader and follower

**Figure 8.3**    Single swing footwork from a semiopen position for the leader and the follower showing (*a*) two *slow* steps and (*b*) two *quick* steps.

For both partners and in any position, add the characteristic upper-torso leans on both *slow, slow* rhythm cues. Let one shoulder dip slightly lower in the same direction as your single weight change and knee bend (see figure 8.4, *a* and *b*). After you step onto the other foot, slightly bend that knee, which again gives you two actions to fit two counts of the music. On the *quick, quick* (counts 5, 6), keep your torso more upright so that you can execute your ball–change steps under your center of gravity (see figure 8.4c). When making these two weight changes, you might think of marching in place rather than actually rocking your weight.

**a** Forward lean on slow (counts 1, 2)

**b** Backward lean on slow (counts 3, 4)

**c** Upright posture on quick, quick (counts 5, 6)

**Figure 8.4**    Swing torso leans demonstrated from a semiopen position.

## Delayed Single Swing (Moderate Tempo)

The difference between the single swing and the delayed single swing is when you take your steps within the *slow, slow* rhythm cues. Thus, if you take one step on the first count and no step or weight change on the second count of each of the *slow* cues, you are doing the single swing rhythmic step pattern. If you delay your one step until count 2 on each of the *slow* cues, you are doing the delayed single swing rhythmic step pattern. An alternative to holding count 1 in the delayed single swing is to add a nonweight action on counts 1 and 3, then take a step (or weight change) on counts 2 and 4. This option is useful with moderate- to fast-tempo music. You may select from a variety of nonweight actions preceding the actual weight change, including a toe-heel, a touch step, a tap step, a point step, and a kick step. The selected nonweight option and a step are executed twice preceding the ball–change—for a total of six counts. The kick step option is also called the *retro swing*. From a one-hand grasp, the leader can rotate to his right side to execute the two kick steps, and then face his partner again on the ball–change steps. Or, the kick steps can be executed to either side, keeping the kick low with a pointed toe to avoid showing the sole of your shoes.

You can easily keep the tempo because something (either a step or another action) occurs on each underlying beat of the music with the delayed single swing's six-count pattern. For example, on a crowded dance floor, substituting a toe–heel drop is a useful variation because it takes less space (dig the toes or the ball of your foot on the first count, then drop the heel of that same foot for a weight change on the second count). Repeat your selected actions on both sides (counts 1, 2; 3, 4), and then do your ball–change (counts 5, 6).

### Leader

From a semiopen position, stand with your feet together and shift your weight onto your right foot. Moving your left foot slightly forward, dig the toes or ball of your left foot into the floor on count 1 and drop your left heel on count 2. Repeat on the other side to dig the toes or ball of your right foot, then drop onto your right heel. The ball–change is the same as described earlier for the single swing.

### Follower

From a semiopen position, stand with your feet together and shift your weight onto your left foot. Moving your right foot slightly forward, dig the toes or ball of your right foot on count 1 and drop your right heel on count 2. Repeat on the other side to dig the toes or ball of your left foot, then drop onto your left heel. The ball–change is the same as described earlier for the single swing.

Figure 8.5 shows the semiopen position footwork and timing cues for the toe–heel option used in the delayed single swing. A delayed single step means that you only make one weight change on counts 2 and 4.

## Figure 8.5　**TOE–HEEL DELAYED SINGLE SWING (MODERATE TEMPO)**

### Footwork Cues

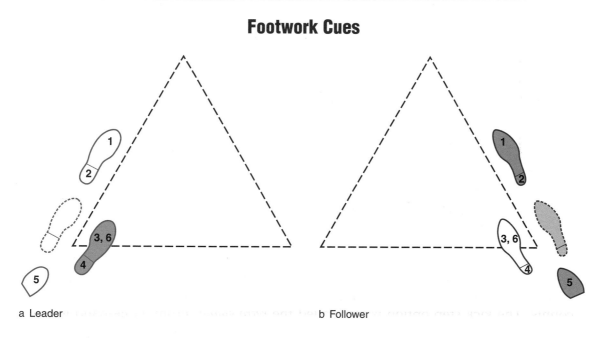

a Leader　　　　　　　　　　　　　　b Follower

***Leader***
Left toe/ball dig, left heel drop; right toe/ball dig, right heel drop; ball–change (left, right)

***Follower***
Right toe/ball dig, right heel drop; left toe/ball dig, left heel drop; ball–change (right, left)

*(continued)*

## Figure 8.5  TOE–HEEL DELAYED SINGLE SWING (MODERATE TEMPO) *(CONTINUED)*

### Timing Cues

| | |
|---|---|
| 4/4 time signature: | Four beats to a measure (group 1 1/2 measures) |
| Duration: | Each beat gets one count (total of six counts) |
| Total counts: | Six; 1, 2, 3, 4, 5, 6 |
| Rhythm: | Slow, slow, quick, quick |
| Weight changes: | Four (on counts 2, 4, 5, 6) |
| Direction of steps: | One-hand-joined position—side, side, backward, forward (to replace); Semiopen position—Forward, backward, backward, forward (to replace) |
| Foot positions: | One-hand-joined position—second, second, fifth; Semiopen position—fourth, fourth, fifth |

For both partners and in any position, add the characteristic upper-torso leans on both *slow, slow* rhythm cues. Let one shoulder dip slightly lower in the same direction in which you make your delayed single weight change (review figure 8.4, *a* and *b*). On the *quick, quick* (counts 5, 6), keep your torso more upright so that you can execute your ball–change steps under your center of gravity (review figure 8.4c). When making these two weight changes, you might think of marching in place instead of actually rocking your weight.

## Rhythmic Step Pattern for Triple Swing (Slow Tempo)

As mentioned earlier, the triple swing is synonymous with terms such as *triple-time swing, triple rhythm, triple step swing,* and the *East Coast swing.* It is typically used with slow swing music. The triple swing rhythmic step pattern is more difficult because you need to execute three weight changes within two beats of music—twice. However, a slow tempo gives you more time to execute these extra steps to each side.

### Leader

From a two-hands-joined position, stand with your feet together and shift your weight onto your right foot. This frees your left foot to move quickly. Execute three steps (a triple step) on each *slow;* step within two beats of music, using the cues *step, ball, step.* When you execute a triple step on each side of your body, the cues for the leader become *left, push, left* and *right, push, right.* This means that you take a step onto your left foot, put your weight only on the ball of your right foot as if you are pushing downward and backward on the floor, then step onto your left foot again. These three weight changes in the triple step should not be given equal timing. Because a triple step involves three weight changes in two counts, execute your left-side triple step weight changes on counts 1, &-2 or on 1, a-2 (using a rolling count). Now repeat a triple step on your right side on counts 3, &-4 or on 3, a-4 (using a rolling count), then add the ball–change steps (left, right weight changes on counts 5, 6, as previously described for the single swing).

### Follower

From a two-hands-joined position, stand with your feet together and shift your weight onto your left foot. This frees your right foot to move quickly. Execute three steps (a triple step) on each *slow* cue; step within two beats of music, using the cues *step, ball, step*. When you execute a triple step on each side of your body, the cues become *right, push, right* and *left, push, left*. Each triple should have three weight changes—one on each cue—for example, the right-side triple step on counts 1, &-2 or 1, a-2 (using a rolling count), and the left-side triple step on counts 3, &-4, or 3, a-4 (using a rolling count). Then add the ball–change steps (right, left) on counts 5, 6 as you did with the other swing rhythmic step patterns.

If you choose to start from a semiopen position, only the direction of the rhythmic step pattern changes to move forward and backward during the triple steps, respectively. Figure 8.6 shows the semiopen position footwork and timing cues for the triple swing rhythmic step pattern.

## Figure 8.6 RHYTHMIC STEP PATTERN FOR TRIPLE SWING (SLOW TEMPO)

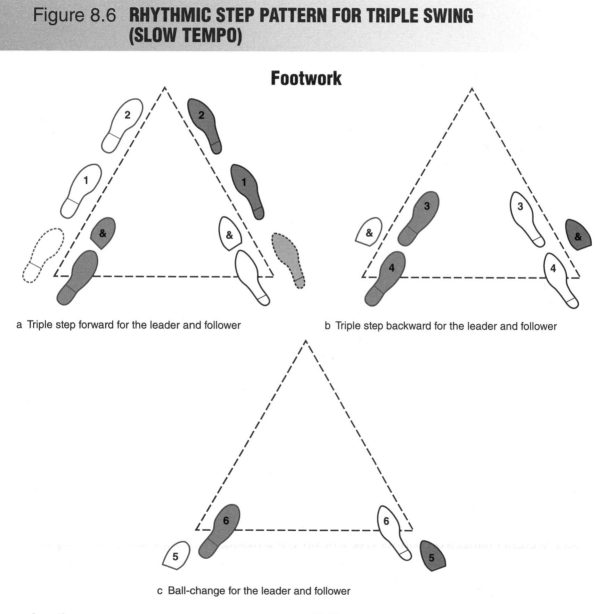

**Footwork**

a  Triple step forward for the leader and follower

b  Triple step backward for the leader and follower

c  Ball-change for the leader and follower

**Leader**
Triple step (left, right, left), triple step (right, left, right), ball–change (left, right)

**Follower**
Triple step (right, left, right), triple step (left, right, left), ball–change (right, left)

*(continued)*

## Figure 8.6 RHYTHMIC STEP PATTERN FOR TRIPLE SWING (SLOW TEMPO) *(CONTINUED)*

### Timing Cues

| | |
|---|---|
| 4/4 time signature: | Four beats to a measure (group 1 1/2 measures) |
| Duration: | Each beat gets one count (total of six counts) |
| Total counts: | Six; 1, &-2, 3, &-4, 5, 6; or 1, &-a-2, 3, &-a-4, 5, 6 |
| Rhythm: | Slow, slow, quick, quick |
| Weight changes: | Eight (on each whole count and on either the two & or the two *a* counts) |
| Direction of steps: | Two-hands-joined position—Side–together–side; side–together–side; backward, forward (to replace); |
| | Semiopen position—Triple step forward; triple step backward; backward, forward (to replace) |
| Foot positions: | Two-hands-joined position—second, third, second; second, third, second; fifth; fifth |
| | Semiopen position—fourth, third, fourth; fourth, third, fourth; fifth; fifth |

For both partners and in any position, add the characteristic upper torso leans on each *slow*. Let one shoulder dip slightly lower in the same direction as your triple steps (review figure 8.4, *a* and *b*). On the *quick, quick* (counts 5, 6), keep your torso more upright so that you can execute your ball–change steps under your center of gravity (review figure 8.4*c*). When making these two weight changes, you might think of marching in place instead of actually rocking your weight.

# DRILLS FOR SIX-COUNT SWING

The following drills help you practice the three different rhythmic step patterns associated with the three different tempos of swing music. Because each pattern is six counts, you may elect to execute any one of these rhythmic step patterns—even if your partner selects a different one! It is like one person taking the high road while the other person takes the low road; they both get to the same place. Thus, the directions are given in terms of the rhythm cues *slow, slow, quick, quick*. Again, you choose the specific rhythmic step pattern you would like to use. The drills introduce you to selected swing variations in three different partner positions (semiopen, one hand joined, and two hands joined). In addition, five transitions are covered because how you move from one partner position to another makes your dancing more fluid and prepares you for more complex moves later. For each drill, read the directions, and watch the video demonstrations on the enclosed DVD to see (a) how to execute the selected swing variations, and (b) how to combine them into short practice combinations. Then, practice until you can meet the Success Goal for each drill. You can look good doing a few things well! Use tracks 10, 11, and 12 to practice slow, moderate, and fast tempos, respectively.

# Drill 1
## Execution Challenge for Single Swing

Review figures 8.2 and 8.3 for the single swing rhythmic step pattern. Try this rhythmic step pattern by yourself, then try it with a partner. Start in a two-hands-joined position, then try the single swing from a semiopen position.

### TO DECREASE DIFFICULTY

- Without a partner, take a single step on each *slow, slow, quick, quick* cue and slightly bend your knee on the second count of each *slow* cue).
- Start with a slow tempo and gradually increase the tempo to match the music.

### TO INCREASE DIFFICULTY

- Add torso leans on the *slow* cues (review figure 8.4).
- Repeat the single swing to any fast-tempo swing music.

### *Success Goal*

Perform 10 consecutive repetitions of the single swing rhythmic step pattern without a partner. Then, continue with a partner for 2 minutes to swing music (use track 12). ___

### *Success Check*

- Rhythmic step pattern uses six counts. ___
- Step on count 1 and slightly bend that knee on count 2. ___
- Step on count 3 and slightly bend that knee on count 4. ___
- Ball–change steps on counts 5, 6. ___

# Drill 2
## Execution Challenge for Delayed Single Swing

Review the Keys to Success for the delayed single swing using the toe–heel actions on each *slow, slow* cue (see also figure 8.5). The following options are popular substitutions:

- Toe–heel, toe–heel, ball–change
- Tap step, tap step, ball–change
- Point step, point step, ball–change
- Kick step, kick step, ball–change

Try these optional actions by yourself to get the rhythm established. With a partner, start in a two-hands-joined position and try different actions. Choose your favorite!

*(continued)*

**Drill 2** *(continued)*

 **TO DECREASE DIFFICULTY**

- Repeat any one of the previous optional actions during the *slow, slow* cues.

- Without a partner, use verbal counts and match your actions to each count (i.e., do something on each whole count).

 **TO INCREASE DIFFICULTY**

- Randomly execute any two nonweight options during the *slow, slow* cues.

- Randomly execute each option above to moderate-tempo swing music.

## Success Goal

Perform 10 consecutive repetitions of the delayed single swing rhythmic step pattern without a partner. Then, continue with a partner for 2 minutes to moderate-tempo swing music (use track 11). ___

## Success Check

- Rhythmic step pattern uses a total of six counts. ___

- Any nonweight action (such as toe, tap, point, or kick) on count 1 and weight change on count 2. ___

- Repeat your selected nonweight action on count 3 and weight change on count 4. ___

- Ball–change steps on counts 5, 6. ___

# Drill 3
# Execution Challenge for Triple Swing

Review the Keys to Success (see figure 8.6) for the triple swing rhythmic step pattern. Try this step pattern by yourself to get the rhythm. Then, try it with a partner from a two-hands-joined position. Lastly, try it from either a closed or a semiopen position with your partner.

 **TO DECREASE DIFFICULTY**

- Without a partner, use verbal counts as you make a weight change not only on each count, but also on each & count.

- Face a partner without touching hands and slowly repeat the rhythmic step pattern and mirror actions in reverse, keeping your CPB over your left foot on a left-side triple or over your right foot on a right-side triple.

**TO INCREASE DIFFICULTY**

- Add a torso lean to each side during the triple steps.
- Repeat the basic pattern to any slow swing music.

## Success Goal

Perform 10 consecutive repetitions of the triple swing rhythmic step pattern without a partner. Then, continue for 2 minutes with a partner to slow swing music (use track 10). ___

## Success Check

- Rhythmic step pattern uses a total of six counts. ___
- Three weight changes (triple step) on counts 1-&-2. ___
- Three weight changes (triple step) on counts 3-&-4. ___
- Ball–change steps on counts 5, 6. ___

## Drill 4
# Match the Rhythmic Step Pattern to the Tempo

Ask a partner to play swing music without telling you the tempo ahead of time. Listen to the underlying beats and identify the tempo. Without a partner, try each of the swing's three rhythmic step patterns (single, delayed single, or triple) to the music selected. Decide which rhythmic step pattern best fits the selected music's tempo (slow, moderate, or fast). Remember that there is no one answer; rather, it is a matter of what feels most comfortable for you. Generally, each of the swing's rhythmic step patterns best fit a slightly different tempo, but you could use any one of the three rhythmic step patterns with any tempo. It can be a matter of how energetic you feel. Note that you may choose any one or all three of the swing's rhythmic step patterns to use with the variations and transitions that will be presented in drills 5 through 17.

**TO DECREASE DIFFICULTY**

- Ask a partner to announce the tempo, then you name and execute the rhythmic step pattern for that tempo.
- Start in a two-hands-joined position facing a partner to mirror each others' actions.
- Select only one tempo and its rhythmic step pattern at first, then gradually add another tempo, then another, and so on.

**TO INCREASE DIFFICULTY**

- Repeat this drill with different partners and a variety of swing music selections (randomly including three different tempos).
- Start in a semiopen position with a partner.

*(continued)*

Drill 4   *(continued)*

## Success Goal

Perform 2 minutes of continuous repetition of your selection from the swing's three rhythmic step patterns that best matches three different music selections (use tracks 10 through 12). ___

- With a slow tempo, try the triple swing rhythmic step pattern. ___
- With a moderate tempo, try the delayed single swing rhythmic step pattern. ___
- With a fast tempo, try the single swing rhythmic step pattern. ___

# Drill 5
# Arch-Out/Arch-In and Roll-Out/Roll-In Transitions

You have two transition options for moving from a closed to an open and back to a closed position: an arch-out/arch-in or a roll-out/roll-in. Both transitions are effective in moving from a semiopen position to a one-hand-joined position (the leader's left hand and the follower's right hand) and in returning to the semiopen position. One major difference in the roll-out and roll-in leads is to keep the hands at approximately waist height rather than lift them high, as in the arch-out and arch-in leads. In both transitions, each partner rotates either counterclockwise (CCW) or clockwise (CW) along an imaginary triangle on the floor.

## Arch-Out/Arch-In

To lead the arch-out, begin in a semiopen position with a partner and repeat the appropriate swing rhythmic step pattern at least twice. Then, at the end of any ball–change portion, the leader lifts his outside hand and arm, bringing both partners' outside arms up to form an arch. This indicates that a CW turn (an arch-out) for the follower is coming during the next repetition of the rhythmic step pattern. Both partners do the forward half of their rhythmic step pattern

(or *slow* on counts 1, 2) while the follower moves forward under the arch. On count 2, the leader presses with the heel of his right hand to guide the follower's CW 180-degree turn on her right foot.

Both partners continue their backward half of the rhythmic step pattern (or *slow* on counts 3-&-4) while facing each other in a one-hand-joined position; notice that the leader needs to move CCW into the spot that the follower vacated. On count 5, both partners pull their elbows and joined hands back in opposition (as if pulling on a rein). On count 6, the leader brings his left hand across his midline to his right side, lifting it high to form an arch. The leader can then loop his left hand over the head of the follower, who does a CCW turn (arch-in) under the raised hands during the next repetition of the rhythmic step pattern. Notice that the leader must now move CW back into his initial starting spot (on the left side of the imaginary triangle) on the first *slow*. This opens up the follower's initial starting spot (on the right side of the imaginary triangle) for her to move into during the second *slow* when the leader places his right hand on the follower's left shoulder blade to resume a closed position. Both partners are side by side in the semiopen position during the ball–change steps. This move can be viewed on the enclosed DVD.

## Roll-Out/Roll-In

To lead the roll-out, begin in a semiopen position with your partner. Repeat the appropriate rhythmic step pattern at least twice. At the end of the ball–change portion, the leader gently rotates his entire upper torso CCW (by twisting at the waist) to gently lead the follower along a curved path out toward the leader's left front diagonal. The leader can then move into the spot that the follower vacated (go to the right side of the imaginary triangle).

Then, at the end of any ball–change, the leader may signal the roll-in by gently pulling his left hand horizontally

toward his right side as he begins to move CW back to his initial starting position (left side of the imaginary triangle). At the end of the first *slow* count, the leader uses his left hand to trace a large J horizontally in the air at approximately waist height (starting at the top of the J). The cue word *J stroke* is used to signal that the follower should move toward the leader, then swivel on her right foot at the end of the first *slow* count to move into her starting position beside the leader (the leader is on the left side with his right hand on the follower's left shoulder blade and the follower on the right side of the imaginary triangle with her left hand on top of his right shoulder). Both partners execute both the second *slow* and the ball–change while stationary and in the semiopen position.

### TO DECREASE DIFFICULTY
- Practice only one transition option with a partner and use the same tempo.
- The leader can remain stationary (without rotating to the follower's location) on both transitions.

### TO INCREASE DIFFICULTY
- Experiment to mix and match these transitions. For example, try a roll-out and an arch-in, or an arch-out and a roll-in.
- Repeat this drill using the appropriate swing rhythmic step pattern to match at least three tempos (slow, moderate, or fast).

## Success Goal

Perform eight consecutive repetitions of each of the following combinations: two repetitions of the swing rhythmic step pattern followed by an arch-out/arch-in transition, and two repetitions of the swing rhythmic step pattern followed by a roll-out/roll-in transition. ___

## Success Check

- Four repetitions of the appropriate swing rhythmic step pattern are needed to complete each transition combination. ___
- The follower executes the turn (either CW or CCW) at the end of count 2 by swiveling on the ball of her right foot. Leaders need to avoid any tendency to signal the follower to go under the arch or to roll any earlier. ___

# Drill 6
# Clockwise and Counterclockwise Rotations

One of the characteristics of swing dancing is the constant rotation within a spot on the floor. It is fun to rotate with your partner. The challenge is to maintain your selected rhythmic step pattern. Together as a couple, you may rotate either CW or CCW. The degree of rotation on each swing rhythmic step pattern may also vary. For practice, just keep repeating the rhythmic step pattern in small increments of rotation until you have completed a 360-degree turn—or one rotation. However, the degree of rotation is up to the leader, who can use any amount of rotation necessary to avoid bumping into other couples or to more quickly transition into other variations.

## *Rotate Counterclockwise*

Start in a semiopen position with your partner and execute the appropriate rhythmic step pattern for a slow tempo. Just prior to the ball–change steps, the leader may open his left shoulder in order to rotate his chest and upper torso CCW. This CCW rotation can be as minimal as one eighth of a turn (see figure 8.7). Facing this new direction, execute the ball–change steps. Repeat until you've

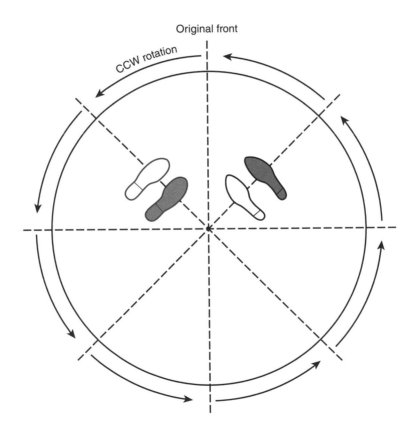

**Figure 8.7**   CCW rotation in the swing may rotate either more or less than one eighth of a turn with each rhythmic step pattern.

rotated 360 degrees back to where you started.

### Rotate Clockwise

Start in a semiopen position with your partner. Preceding to the ball–change portion of the swing rhythmic step pattern, the leader may bring his right shoulder back or rotate his chest and upper torso clockwise (see figure 8.8). Once facing the new direction, execute the rhythmic step pattern. Continue making these slight CW adjustments on each ball–change portion of the rhythmic step pattern until you have rotated 360 degrees back to your starting location.

Once you can execute each option separately, it is time to challenge yourself by putting them into a short combination. Start in a semiopen position with your partner and experiment with the following sample combinations using your preferred rhythmic step pattern for each basic:

- In-place basic, basics with CCW rotation, arch-out, and arch-in
- In-place basic, basics with CW rotation, arch-out, and arch-in
- In-place basic, basics with CCW rotation, roll-out, and roll-in
- In-place basic, basics with CW rotation, roll-out, and roll-in

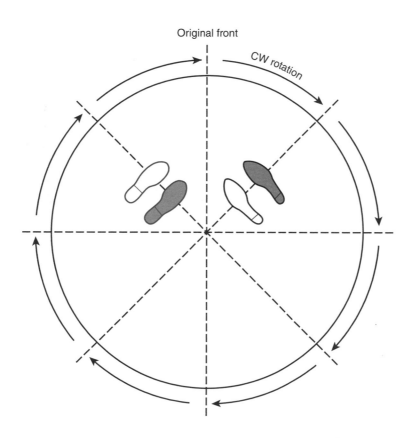

**Figure 8.8**   Clockwise rotation in the swing may rotate either more or less than one eighth of a turn with each rhythmic step pattern.

*(continued)*

**Drill 6** *(continued)*

### TO DECREASE DIFFICULTY

- Do multiple repetitions of the basic to gradually complete a 360-degree rotation.
- Select only one tempo and its appropriate rhythmic step pattern.
- Add as many repetitions of the rhythmic step pattern in place as you like before and after each 360-degree rotation.
- Alternate basic steps in place with basic steps using either CW or CCW rotations (i.e., leave out the transitions at the end of each of the combination examples).

### TO INCREASE DIFFICULTY

- Try to rotate on each portion of the swing rhythmic step pattern versus just prior to the ball–change steps.
- Experiment with the number of repetitions (e.g., try to complete a 360-degree rotation using only four rhythmic step patterns). What is the minimum number needed for you and your partner to rotate completely back to your starting location?
- Repeat this drill using the appropriate basic step for three tempos: slow, moderate, and fast.
- Vary or mix and match the order of the sample combinations to create your own combination.

## *Success Goal*

Execute at least three of the four sample combinations for 2 minutes, using the appropriate swing rhythmic step pattern for the tempo selected. ___

## *Success Check*

- Keep the upper torso and frame firm during rotation leads. ___
- Think of moving your center to face the new direction. ___

# Drill 7
# Change of Position

Start (and end) in a two-hands-joined position facing your partner. Do your selected swing rhythmic step pattern while in this position, executing the *slow* steps to each side. A change of position is literally moving 180 degrees to exchange places with your partner. Be aware that the amount of rotation may be either slightly more or slightly less than 180 degrees; it is up to the leader and the momentum established. Both partners need to use small steps. The direction cues for your change-of-position steps will be *forward, side,* then remain facing your partner to do the ball–change steps on counts 5, 6. Regardless of which of the three swing rhythmic step patterns you choose to use, there is a swivel at the end of the first *slow,* on count 2. Each partner's footwork is described next.

## Leader

Take the left-foot steps forward and slightly outside the follower's right foot, which brings your right hips closer together. It helps to open your arms low to the sides on count 1 of this first *slow.* Keep your hands and arms horizontally at waist level. The wider that you extend your arms out to the sides (at waist level), the more you facilitate the rotation needed to swivel at the end of the first *slow.* To lead the swivel, keep your left hand firm and pull back with your right hand and shoulder. Keep your weight on the ball of your left foot during the swivel and make a CW half turn on count 2 to face your partner. Take the second *slow* with your right foot to your right side and bring your joined hands back to center. Remain facing your partner on the ball–change steps (left, right).

## Follower

Take right-foot steps forward and slightly toward your left front diagonal (stepping outside your partner's left foot). Your right hip should be closer to the leader's right hip on this first *slow.* Swivel on the ball of your right foot CW a half turn on count 2. Face your partner to take your left foot steps (on the second *slow*) to the side. Then do your ball–change steps (right, left) while facing your partner (and still in the two-hands-joined position).

### TO DECREASE DIFFICULTY

- Use only one tempo and the corresponding basic until the combination becomes more automatic.
- Repeat two or more repetitions of the rhythmic step pattern preceding a change of position.

### TO INCREASE DIFFICULTY

- Do only one repetition of the rhythmic step pattern, then a change of position.
- Try two or more changes of position in a row.

## Success Goal

Alternate the swing rhythmic step pattern with a two-hand change of position to music for 2 minutes. ___

## Success Check

- Continuously repeat the swing rhythmic step pattern appropriate for the selected tempo. ___
- Avoid getting too far apart. ___
- Directions are *forward, side, back, replace.* ___

# Drill 8
# Single Under

Start in a one-hand-joined position facing your partner. The lead for the single under is the same as for the arch-in transition with one exception: The leader must exchange places, in a 180-degree switch, with the follower (versus remaining stationary as he did for the arch-in transition).

## *Leader*

After any ball–change, bring your left hand across your midline toward your right shoulder. Then, lift it high to make a small CCW loop over the follower's head (see figure 8.9a). To end the turn, lower your hand and keep your elbow bent approximately 90 degrees (see figure 8.9b). Throughout the follower's left inside turn, face your partner and rotate 180 degrees clockwise at the end of count 2. Face each other to execute the second *slow* and the ball–change (see figure 8.9c). During the turn, the leader keeps his fingers pointing downward and the follower loosely cups her hand around the leader's fingers (maintaining contact without gripping tightly).

## *Follower*

The follower's footwork for the single under is the same as that used with the arch-in transition. On the first *slow,* travel forward and spin 180 degrees CCW on the ball of your right foot at the end of count 2. Face your partner to execute both the second *slow* and the ball–change steps.

a Leader's left hand lifted

b Leader's left hand lowers at the end of the CCW turn

c Face partner to do ball–change

**Figure 8.9**　Single under.

Once you can execute the single under and distinguish it from the arch-in transition, it is helpful to combine what you know so far. Start in a semiopen position and do the following three-lead combination: an arch-out transition, a single under, and an arch-in transition.

You should end in a semiopen position. The leader must be ready to either switch places with his partner and remain in a one-hand-joined position or remain stationary and bring his partner back to the semiopen position.

### TO DECREASE DIFFICULTY

- Use only one tempo and the corresponding swing rhythmic step pattern until the combination becomes more automatic.

- Repeat each part in isolation, gradually linking them.

### TO INCREASE DIFFICULTY

- Vary the number of consecutive single under repetitions (e.g., try two, three, four, or more consecutive leads).

- Vary the tempo and use the appropriate swing basic for the tempo selected, whether slow, moderate, or fast.

- Lengthen the combination by adding either CCW or CW rotation preceding the arch-out.

## *Success Goal*

Perform eight consecutive repetitions of this three-lead combination with correct timing. ___

## *Success Check*

- Continuously repeat the rhythmic step pattern appropriate for the selected tempo. ___

- Avoid getting too far apart. ___

# Drill 9
# Double Under

The double under swing variation has sometimes been called a *she–he turn* because of the timing of the turns—she goes, then he goes. To execute the double under, proceed as if you are doing a single under (see figure 8.10*a*), except that the leader turns CCW under the arched hands and arms during the second *slow* (see figure 8.10*b*). The follower's part remains the same whether she is doing the arch-in, inside left turn, single under, or double under. To avoid hitting heads in the middle, make sure

that the follower's turn is completed (on counts 1 and 2 of the first *slow*) before the leader turns under his left arm (on counts 3 and 4 of the second *slow*). Both partners end up switching positions 180 degrees and facing each other for the ball–change steps.

Again, you can challenge yourself by putting the double under in a practice combination. Start with the combination from the previous drill and add any number of repetitions of the double under after the single under. After

*(continued)*

**Drill 9** *(continued)*

leading the double under, the leader has at least three options: (1) to immediately lead another double under, (2) to lead a single under, or (3) to lead the arch-in transition back into the semiopen position. Try each of these three options after a double under with your partner at least four times to slow music.

**a** Follower's CCW underarm turn on the first slow

**b** Leader's CCW underarm turn on the second slow

**Figure 8.10** Double under.

### TO DECREASE DIFFICULTY

- Practice each of the three options after a double under separately.
- Alternate one single under with a double under using any number of basics in between.

### TO INCREASE DIFFICULTY

- Vary the tempo and use the appropriate swing rhythmic step pattern for the tempo selected, whether slow, moderate, or fast.
- Create your own combinations to include the double under.

## Success Goal

Perform four repetitions of each of the three options after a double under. ___

- The timing order should be *she–he* for the double under turns corresponding to the first two *slows.* ___
- Face your partner on the ball–change steps. __
- The leader lifts his left hand toward his right shoulder on count 6 of any swing basic step in order to nonverbally signal that an inside left turn is coming. ___
- The leader's lead for a double under starts with an inside left turn or single under.___

# Drill 10
# Brush

The brush is a fancy, behind-the-back pass for the leader from a one-hand-joined position. It ends up with an awkward hand grasp that is easily adjusted by leading immediately into either a single or a double under. This adjustment will soon become automatic.

## Leader

To set up the brush, the leader needs to transfer the follower's right hand from his left to his right hand (see figure 8.11*a*) on any second *slow* (counts 3 and 4). Both partners continue the basic on count 5. On count 6, as the leader finishes the ball–change and shifts his weight forward, he also rotates his wrist CCW, as if turning a doorknob. During the *slow* forward, the leader passes the follower on her right side (see figure 8.11*b*) as he

lowers his right hand to pass her hand from his right to his left hand. The leader's pass needs to be low, approximately at hip level, to avoid bending the elbows and hitting the follower on his turn (see figure 8.11*c*). Then both partners face each other for the second *slow* and the ball–change steps with a backhand grasp (see figure 8.11*d*). To return to a normal grasp, the leader has two immediate options—to lead either a single under or a double under.

## Follower

The follower uses the same footwork as she did with the change of position. To start the brush step, the follower does the basic swing rhythm in place as the leader changes to a right-to-right hand grasp. During the ball–change, the leader will

*(continued)*

**Drill 10** *(continued)*

start to turn CCW with his right hand low, preparing to change hands behind his back. The follower steps forward onto her right foot on the first *slow*. She continues to do a CW half turn to face the leader and step onto her left foot on the second *slow*. She does the ball–change steps in place facing the leader and in a one-hand-joined position. The follower needs to be ready for the next lead, which is likely to be a single under lead to get the hand grasp back to a normal position.

**a** Right-to-right hand grasp

**b** Brush right shoulders to lead

**c** Follower turns CW; leader turns CCW

**d** Ball–change

**Figure 8.11**  Brush step.

### TO DECREASE DIFFICULTY

- Without using any footwork, slowly execute only the hand changes in the brush step, including the changing sides with your partner.
- Use only one selected tempo and corresponding rhythmic step pattern.

### TO INCREASE DIFFICULTY

- Vary the tempo and use the appropriate swing rhythmic step pattern for the tempo selected, whether slow, moderate, or fast.
- At the end of a single under, the leader may switch to a right-to-right hand grasp so as to go immediately into the brush without another basic step in place.
- From the right-to-right hand grasp, the leader may lift his right arm for the follower to turn CCW on the first *slow* preceding his low hand pass behind his back on the second *slow.*
- Include the brush in a longer combination. For example, starting in semiopen position, do either a CCW or a CW rotation, an arch-out, a single under, a brush step, a double under, and a roll-in.

## *Success Goal*

Perform four repetitions of each option (either a single or a double under) immediately after a brush step. ___

## *Success Check*

- Set up with a right-to-right hand-shake grip. ___
- The leader must keep his behind-the-back hand pass low (without sharply bending his elbows). ___
- Avoid getting too far apart. ___
- Switch positions with your partner during the brush step. ___

# Drill 11
# Belt Loop

The belt loop is sometimes called a *waist slide.* It starts from a one-hand-joined position. As in the brush step, this variation also ends with the hands in an awkward position, yet it is easily adjusted by immediately leading either a single or a double under.

## *Leader*

After any ball–change, the leader may bring his right hand and arm over the top of the grasped hands. On the *slow,* the leader turns CCW, placing his left hand at his belt loop on the right side of his

*(continued)*

Drill 11 *(continued)*

waist and releasing his partner's hand. On the next *slow,* he continues with a half turn and grasps her right hand again on the left side of his waist with his left hand. Thus, the leader's left hand is used throughout this variation. The ball–change is executed in a one-hand-joined position. The leader then immediately leads either a single or a double under to adjust the hand position.

## Follower

On the two *slow* cues, the follower remains facing the leader while switching locations 180 degrees—like she did in the brush step. The difference on the first *slow* is that the leader places the follower's right hand at the right side of his waist, just above the belt area, and releases it. On the second *slow,* the follower continues with a CW half turn as she keeps contact with the leader by lightly sliding her right hand across the leader's back. The leader will pick up the follower's right hand on the left side of his waist, as both partners face each other to do the ball–change.

### TO DECREASE DIFFICULTY
- Practice the waist slide portion without footwork.
- Use only one swing tempo at first.

### TO INCREASE DIFFICULTY
- In random order, substitute the belt loop for the brush step.
- Vary the tempo and use the appropriate swing rhythmic step pattern for the tempo selected, whether slow, moderate, or fast.
- Do a belt loop, a single under with a hand change to a right-to-right hand grasp, then lead a brush step.

## Success Goal

Perform four repetitions of each option (either a single or a double under) immediately after a belt loop. ___

## Success Check

- The leader turns CCW, initially rolling into his own left arm, releasing, then grasping again with his left hand. ___
- Remember to switch places with your partner. ___

# Drill 12
# Shoulder Touches

The shoulder touches are an extended variation of the six-count swing rhythmic step pattern. It is sometimes called a *sprinkler* because it resembles a revolving lawn sprinkler that alternates the flow of the water in one direction and another. In this case, the timing is extended to be eight counts, or four *slow* steps—using four alternating shoulder touches with each getting two counts. Both partners rotate CW.

## Leader

The shoulder touches are executed from a right-to-right hand grasp. How can you get there? From a one-hand-joined position, the leader starts with a side step on the first *slow*. On the second *slow*, the leader passes the follower's right hand from his left hand into his right hand, then both finish with the ball change. Or, using another option to get to this position, the leader may choose to lead a single under and pass (her right hand to his right hand) on the second *slow,* then finish with the ball change. For the next eight counts, execute four *slows* alternating your left foot, right foot, left foot, and right foot. On the first and third *slow* cues, the leader moves forward and touches the follower's right shoulder or upper back with his left hand. On the second and fourth *slow* cues the follower moves forward and touches the leader's right shoulder or upper back.

To end these alternating shoulder touches, resume the rhythmic step pattern and lead a single under turn with a hand change at the end. The leader signals a single under turn for the follower by lifting his right hand and making a CCW loop over the follower's head on the first *slow*. On his second *slow*, the leader passes her right hand immediately back into his left hand. Do the ball–change steps facing the follower.

## Follower

On the first *slow*, the leader's actions cause you to open your left shoulder beyond normal, and he will touch your left shoulder or upper back with his left hand. On the second *slow*, the leader's actions will rotate you clockwise such that you will be standing behind him and able to touch his right shoulder or upper back with your left hand. These alternating shoulder touches may be repeated any even number of times, which repeats the *slow* cues until the leader signals something else. With this drill, you will execute four *slows* during the shoulder touches (each getting two counts), then the leader lifts his right hand high enough for you to do a CCW single turn, then face the leader both on the second *slow* and on the ball–change (right, left).

### TO DECREASE DIFFICULTY

- Position yourself with a partner to try alternating shoulder touches without any footwork. Freeze each position for clarity.
- Maintain the six-count basic rhythm on the shoulder touches by doing only two shoulder touches, then a CCW turn for the follower as the leader does his ball-change steps.

### TO INCREASE DIFFICULTY

- After the follower's CCW turn the leader may lead a brush step (to pass behind his back on the second *slow* and get to the follower's right hand in his left hand), face on the ball–change, then lead a single under.
- The leader may lead any even number of shoulder touches preceding the CCW turn. For example, try six or eight *slow* steps preceding the CCW turn.
- The shoulder touches are easier to execute using either single swing or triple swing basics—try both!

*(continued)*

Drill 12  *(continued)*

## Success Goal

Alternate any number of repetitions of the swing rhythmic step pattern with four shoulder touches and a single under with a hand change for 2 minutes. ___

- Right-to-right hand grasp sets up the shoulder touches. ___
- Travel forward on each *slow* to alternately touch your partner's shoulder or upper back with your left hand. ___
- The leader touches on the first and third *slow* steps. ___
- The follower touches on the second and fourth *slow* steps. ___
- End the shoulder touches with a single under and the leader's hand change (six counts). ___

# Drill 13
# Tuck and Spin

The tuck and spin, or tuck turn, includes a CW, 360-degree turn on one foot for the follower. It is a fun variation that requires a firm arm position for both the leader and the follower.

## Leader

The tuck-and-spin variation starts from a right-to-right hand grasp. So, after a single under or on a basic step, pass the follower's right hand into your right hand with your palm facing upward. Finish your basic step. On the first *slow,* tuck or bring your right elbow in close to your right side, keep the elbow bent 90 degrees, and hold it firmly in place. Think of pulling your right elbow back until your right hand is by your waist, then push your forearm and hand forward and release your grasp to lead the spin. On the second *slow,* grasp the follower's right hand with your left hand at the end of her spin. Both of you do the ball–change facing each other in a one-hand-joined position.

## Follower

The different hand position that the leader uses will prompt you to have your right palm downward. On the tuck, keep your elbow bent 90 degrees and lean your weight into the leader's hand and keep your right hand and arm firm. When the leader pushes his right forearm and hand forward, keep your weight on the ball of your right foot and spin clockwise on count 2 (or in between the two *slow* steps). Make sure that your entire body turns, rather than just your right arm moving backward. Then face your partner to finish the basic step.

### TO DECREASE DIFFICULTY

- Without a partner, the follower may face a wall, lean into the wall with her right hand, then push against the wall to spin clockwise on the ball of her right foot. Notice that there is a rotation from a slight CCW direction to a CW direction, which is an example of Newton's law of action–reaction.

- Without a partner, the leader may practice rotating his shoulders slightly clockwise as he steps onto his left foot, then rotate his shoulders CCW (bringing his left shoulder back) for his spin on the ball of his left foot.

### TO INCREASE DIFFICULTY

- As an option, the leader may also spin CCW on the ball of his left foot on count 2 (at the end of the first *slow* and the same time as the follower's spin).

- The tuck-and-spin variation is easier to execute using either single swing or triple swing basics—try both!

## *Success Goal*

Alternate swing basic steps and the tuck and spin, either with only the follower spinning or with both spinning, for 2 minutes. ___

## *Success Check*

- On the tuck, the leader keeps his right hand firmly at or slightly in front of his waist. ___

- Both partners keep their elbows bent 90 degrees on the tuck. ___

- On the spin, the follower needs to have a firm right arm and to transfer the momentum to her body for the CW spin on the ball of her right foot. ___

- The leader may spin CCW on the ball of his left foot simultaneously with the follower's spin. ___

# Drill 14
# Wrap and Unwrap

The wrap and unwrap basically reverses the order of the arch-out and arch-in transitions, except that two hands are held throughout. Begin in a two-hands-joined position facing your partner. The leader remains stationary and brings the follower to his right side (for the wrap), then back to the facing position again (for the unwrap). It takes a minimum of one swing basic step to get into the wrap position and one swing basic step to unwrap. The number of basic steps executed in the wrap position is optional.

*(continued)*

**Drill 14** *(continued)*

### Leader

From a two-hands-joined position, the lead for the wrap is given on any ball–change and is twofold. While keeping his right hand low at his right side, the leader also lifts his left hand toward his right shoulder and circles CCW above the follower's head (see figure 8.12*a*). These actions both turn the follower 180 degrees CCW and place her on the leader's right side, yet slightly in front (see figure 8.12*b*). Finish with the second *slow* and ball–change steps in the wrap position.

The lead to unwrap is given on any ball–change. The leader needs to lift his left hand to form an arch for the follower to go under (see figure 8.12*c*). He may also gently press on his partner's right side with the inside wrist of his right hand to guide her under the arch. Continue to hold both hands with your partner to end up in a two-hands-joined position. Finish the second *slow* and ball–change steps in this position.

### Follower

The follower's footwork is the same as for a single under, except that both hands are held and she ends up standing on the right side of the leader (review figure 8.12*b*). Both partners remain in the wrap position to execute the second *slow* and the ball–change steps.

To unwrap, the follower goes under the arch, turning CW 180 degrees on the first slow of the next basic step forward. Remain facing your partner to finish the swing basic step.

**a** Leader's left arm is lifted with his right arm low at his right side

**b** Follower in wrap position

**c** Leader lifts hands to form an arch to unwrap the follower

**Figure 8.12** Wrap (to leader's right side) and unwrap.

## TO DECREASE DIFFICULTY

- Take as many basic steps before leading the wrap as needed to establish the tempo with your partner.
- It is easier to use only one swing basic to wrap, then one swing basic to unwrap.
- An easy transition to a one-hand-joined position is for the leader to release his right hand during the unwrap.

## TO INCREASE DIFFICULTY

- Add basic steps when in the wrap position.
- Experiment with either a CCW or a CW basic step rotation while in the wrap position.
- The leader can extend his left hand low, and bring his right hand toward his left shoulder and loop CW over the follower's head to a wrap position on the left side of the leader, then arch out.

## Success Goal

Alternate swing basic steps and the wrap and unwrap for 2 minutes. ___

## Success Check

- Both partners' hands are held throughout. ___
- The follower is on the right side and slightly in front of the leader when in the wrap position. ___
- The leader extends his right hand to his right side, then lifts his left hand CCW over the follower's head to lead into the wrap. ___
- The leader lifts his left hand to form an arch, and gently presses with his inside right wrist to lead the unwrap. ___

# Drill 15
# Row Step

The row step is a fun variation that takes advantage of centrifugal force and uses a two-hands-joined position. Because this step involves spinning first on one foot and then the other, it is typically done with single swing basics, even if you are dancing to slow or moderate tempos. Once the row step is over, resume whatever swing basic step is most appropriate for the music's tempo.

Stand facing your partner and imagine a small circle on the floor that connects your feet. Label this circle like a clock and notice that each partner's 12 o'clock is in the direction that the partner's midline is facing. Imagine that you

*(continued)*

**Drill 15** *(continued)*

are standing at 6 o'clock and your partner is positioned at 12 o'clock. Grasp both hands with your partner. At the end of any ball–change, the leader may rotate CCW approximately 45 degrees. On the first *slow,* with both partners facing a diagonal, step forward toward your partner's right side, yet still on the imaginary circle connecting your feet. Spin on the ball of that foot approximately 180 degrees to face your partner's left side and make a weight change either by bringing your feet together or by stepping behind your other foot (on the second *slow*). Continue the rotation

to face your partner with your shoulder square to execute the ball–change.

The hands and arms are positioned at shoulder level for the two *slow* steps, then back to a two-hands-joined position for the ball–change. If you imagine a bow-and-arrow type pull, then the leader pulls his left hand back with his right arm extended during the first *slow* (see figure 8.13a). For the second *slow,* the leader pulls his right hand back with his left arm extended (see figure 8.13b). Resume a two-hands-joined position for the ball–change (see figure 8.13c).

**a** Right shoulders together (Slow)

**b** Left shoulders together (Slow)

**c** Shoulders square (Ball–change)

**Figure 8.13** Row step.

Notice that the bow-and-arrow lead for the row step is executed at shoulder height, which distinguishes it from a half-rotation turn (or change of position with arms extended at waist height). Both partners need to keep both arms flexible, yet firm enough to provide sufficient resistance for the proper lead. Avoid *spaghetti arms* here! Your arms and shoulders need to act together so that a gentle push or pull on your hand will cause your entire upper torso (and not just your arms) to rotate.

### TO DECREASE DIFFICULTY

- Bring your feet together on the second *slow*.
- Practice just the arm positions, then add the footwork.

### TO INCREASE DIFFICULTY

- Try two consecutive repetitions of the row step.
- Experiment with more rotation during the row step by the leader crossing his right foot behind his left foot on the second *slow*.
- Alternate the row step with a wrap and unwrap.

## Success Goal

Alternate swing basic steps and the row step (using the single swing rhythmic step pattern) for 2 minutes. ___

## Success Check

- Align right shoulders (and hips) close together, left shoulders (and hips) close together, then shoulders square. ___
- Step diagonally, bring your feet together (or step behind), and ball–change. ___
- Experience some momentum or revolution with your partner. ___

# Drill 16
# Double Cross

The double cross can be done by itself or immediately after any number of row steps. It is executed from a two-hands-joined position. The double cross ends in and thus becomes another transition to get into a handshake grip (right-to-right hand position). It is easiest to use a single swing rhythmic step pattern during the double cross variation.

Start in a two-hands-joined position with your partner. At the end of any ball–change, the leader may lift both hands high to form two arches. The leader keeps the hands high as both partners make a CCW quarter turn, then the leader lowers his right hand behind his partner's head and his left hand behind his own head during the first *slow*. On the CW quarter turn back to face each other, the leader releases both hands, yet keeps his right arm parallel and on top of the follower's right shoulder during

*(continued)*

**Drill 16** *(continued)*

the second *slow*. The leader then slides his hands down to grasp right hand to right hand on the ball–change.

After you finish a double cross, you are in a perfect position for the leader to lead a brush step, which is typically followed by either a single or a double under. This move can be viewed on the enclosed DVD.

### TO DECREASE DIFFICULTY

- Hold or freeze each position with your partner for at least two counts to clarify the actions needed (e.g., lift to form two arches, CCW quarter turn, lower arms behind head, CW quarter turn back to partner, and slide apart to re-grasp). Extend the number of counts to 8 or 10 total counts.
- Eliminate footwork on the first two *slow* portions; instead, focus on positioning your body to face to your left side, then toward your partner. Continue with your ball–change.
- Use a single swing rhythmic step pattern, regardless of the tempo of the music.

### TO INCREASE DIFFICULTY

- Combine the row step with the double cross.
- Combine the double cross with at least five other variations covered so far.

## Success Goal

Alternate swing basic steps and the double cross immediately combined with a brush step and either a single or a double under for 2 minutes. ___

## Success Check

- Move in unison with your partner into each position. ___
- Face your left side on the first *slow* cue. ___
- Face your partner on the second *slow* cue. ___
- Slide apart to a right-to-right hand grasp on the ball–change. ___
- Use a single swing rhythmic step pattern on the double cross. ___

# Drill 17
# On Your Own: Creating Swing Combinations

You may have noticed that swing variations can be categorized according to the dance position from which they are executed. Three dance positions have been used: semiopen position, one-hand-joined position, and two-hands-joined position. Thus, grouping by position is one way of helping you recall the swing variations covered in this book.

Challenge yourself by creating swing combinations that include any two or more variations from each of the three positions with appropriate transitions as follows:

| | |
|---|---|
| **Semiopen position variations** | • **Rhythmic step patterns in place (single, delayed single, or triple swing; each of these swing patterns has six counts)**<br>• **Swing patterns rotating CCW**<br>• **Swing patterns rotating CW** |
| **One-hand-joined position variations** | • **Single under**<br>• **Double under**<br>• **Brush step**<br>• **Belt loop**<br>• **Shoulder touches**<br>• **Tuck and spin** |
| **Two-hands-joined position variations** | • **Change of position**<br>• **Wrap and unwrap**<br>• **Row step**<br>• **Double cross** |
| **Transitions** | • **Arch-out and arch-in**<br>• **Roll-out and roll-in**<br>• **Release one hand during unwrap** |

You may place them in any order and use any number of repetitions of each. Select the variations that you do best, and remember to add styling with upper-torso leans on the two *slow* steps. Practice your sequence to the tempo of your choice. Repeat your selected sequence three times in a row. Rehearse with your partner until you feel comfortable enough either to imagine that you are performing before an audience or to demonstrate your selected sequence for others to watch.

## TO DECREASE DIFFICULTY

- Start in the order listed (i.e., from semiopen position), and add two variations from either the one-hand-joined or the two-hands-joined position, then transition back to the semiopen position again.
- Review the sample combinations from the previous drills to give yourself a starting place to solve this challenge.

## TO INCREASE DIFFICULTY

- Vary the tempo and use the appropriate swing rhythmic step pattern for the tempo selected, whether slow, moderate, or fast.
- Practice with a variety of partners.

*(continued)*

Drill 17  *(continued)*

### Success Goal

Perform three consecutive repetitions of your favorite sequence combining at least two variations from each of three partner positions, including an appropriate transition___

### Success Check

- Maintain your selected swing rhythmic step pattern. ___
- Keep transitions and variations smoothly connected. ___
- Make a list of your favorite combinations for future reference. ___
- Thank your partner after you are finished dancing together. ___

# SUCCESS SUMMARY FOR SIX-COUNT SWING

The swing is a popular, energetic dance. It offers three different rhythmic step patterns to choose from that are based on the tempo of the music (fast, moderate, or slow). Either or both partners may elect to do any one particular rhythmic step pattern at the same time, depending on your preference because the basic swing rhythm uses six counts, cued as *slow, slow, quick, quick*. Each *slow* gets two counts. Each *quick* gets one count. The variations for the swing are categorized according to the specific partner position in which they occur (semiopen, one-hand-joined, or two-hands-joined position). Many variations and multiple combinations are possible with the swing. Styling for the swing includes a slight knee bend and upper torso lean to each side on the *slow, slow* cues, then upright, vertical posture on the *quick, quick* cues. The swing constantly revolves, which makes it a fun dance!

# Foxtrot

## *Dancing Regally*

The foxtrot is an American dance that was introduced in 1913 or 1914. It has many variations. The foxtrot got its name from Harry Fox, a musical comedy star who performed a fast, trotting step to ragtime music in a Ziegfeld musical. As the result of a publicity stunt, Oscar Duryea, who was a star nightclub performer, was hired to teach this step to the public. However, the original version was too exhausting, so it was modified to alternate four walking steps with eight quick running steps.

Later, Vernon and Irene Castle and other professional dancers helped shape the foxtrot into a smooth, graceful dance. An erect posture and stationary torso and arm movements lend elegance as the partners move around the floor counterclockwise. Imagine Fred Astaire and Ginger Rogers fluidly dancing in many of the early 20th century musical films. They were doing the foxtrot.

Famous dance instructor Arthur Murray created another variation of the foxtrot, called the *magic step.* Mr. Murray and his wife, Katherine used a six-count combination of slow and quick beats (the magic step) in several surprising ways. The magic step is one of two popular dance rhythms used in foxtrot today. It uses a *slow, slow, quick, quick* six-count rhythmic step pattern simply known today as *basic rhythm.*

A second popular dance rhythm used in the foxtrot is a *slow, quick, quick* four-count rhythmic step pattern, which is typically used in a box step, thus it is called *box rhythm.* The 4/4 time foxtrot music is the type of music played most frequently during an evening of ballroom social dancing. Primarily, the foxtrot is danced in a closed position, which was scandalous at one time because of the leader's right hand touching the follower's back. However, the popularity of the foxtrot and its engaging music has helped it to become a favorite smooth dance style for dancers of all ages.

## RHYTHMIC STEP PATTERNS FOR FOXTROT

Foxtrot music accents counts 2 and 4 as does swing music. Thus, the foxtrot has a jazzy quality that is reflected when one foot briefly closes beside the other foot on counts 2 and 4. You'll soon see how both of the foxtrot dance rhythms reflect these accents. This section first describes the box rhythm because it corresponds to one measure of 4/4 time music. It also provides many stationary variations that are useful for beginner-level dancers. Then it describes the basic rhythm, which corresponds to one and a half measures of 4/4 time music. It provides many progressive variations that are useful for traveling in the LOD, which is the ultimate goal in foxtrot—whenever another couple is not blocking your path! You cannot predict the floor traffic, so you need to be prepared for any situation by being able to execute both foxtrot dance rhythms and their variations.

## Four-Count (Box) Rhythm (Slow, Quick, Quick)

The box rhythm may be executed forward, backward, diagonally, or turning, making it a versatile step. Imagine a box shape on the floor, then divide it in half along the diagonal. It takes two repetitions of this *slow, quick, quick* rhythmic pattern, or two half-boxes, or two measures, to complete a full box step.

Although the term *box step* implies a square, its shape actually becomes more rectangular. The forward and backward steps of the box should extend approximately 18 inches (45 cm; or, longer than your side step), and the side steps should be approximately the width of your own shoulders. The leader starts with the left foot to execute the forward half of the box while the follower starts with the right foot to execute the backward half of the box. The follower both mirrors and reverses the leader's part. When the leader moves forward, the follower moves backward, and vice versa.

Throughout the following descriptions, two terms often get confused. Note that *together* means bringing the feet together with a weight change, whereas *close* means bringing the feet together with no weight change.

### Leader

To execute the forward half-box, bend your right (standing) knee, push off to extend your left leg forward, and step onto your left foot (and shift your weight) on count 1. For styling on count 2, you may bring the ball of your right foot beside the ball of your left foot to brush it, but do not shift your weight. Then continue moving your right foot directly sideways (notice that your right foot traces a 90-degree angle along the floor). On count 3, step to your right side onto your right foot (your side step should be approximately the width of your shoulders). On count 4, bring your left foot beside your right to bring your feet together and transfer your weight onto your left foot. Then reverse these actions to execute the backward half-box (see follower's footwork, which starts with the backward half-box). An alternative is to continue to travel forward on the second half-box. You'll then be executing half-box progressions forward.

### Follower

To execute the backward half-box, start with your right foot. For momentum, bend the knee of your left (standing) leg, push off to extend your right leg backward, and step onto the ball of your right foot on count 1. For styling on count 2, you may bring the ball of your left foot beside the ball of your right foot to brush it, but do not shift your weight. Then continue moving your left leg directly sideways to step (on count 3) onto your left foot (both feet should be approximately shoulder-width apart). On count 4, bring your right foot beside your left to bring your feet together and transfer your weight onto your right foot. Then execute the forward half-box (see leader's footwork, which starts with the forward half-box). An alternative is to continue to travel backward on the second half-box. This alternative starts the half-box progressions backward for the follower.

Figure 9.1 shows the various ways you might organize the counts and footwork for the foxtrot four-count, or box, rhythm. Some cues will be more helpful to you than others. Select those cues that most help you retain how to execute both the foxtrot box step and the half-box progression step.

### Figure 9.1 FOUR-COUNT (BOX) RHYTHMIC STEP PATTERN FOR FOXTROT

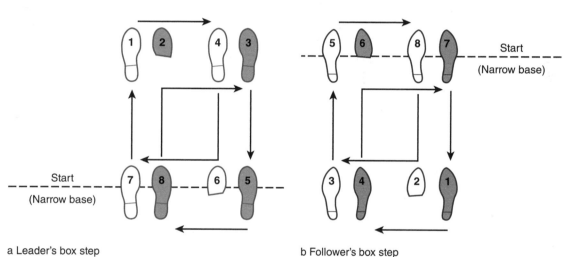

**Footwork Cues**

a Leader's box step

b Follower's box step

### Box Step

**Leader**
Left forward, (brush right), right side, left together; right backward, (brush left), left side, right together

**Follower**
Right backward, (brush left), left side, right together; left forward, (brush right), right side, left together

*(continued)*

## Figure 9.1 FOUR-COUNT (BOX) RHYTHMIC STEP PATTERN FOR FOXTROT *(CONTINUED)*

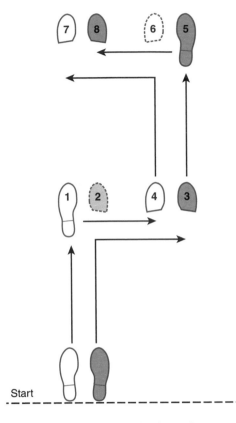

c Leader's half-box progression forward

d Follower's half-box progression forward

### *Half-Box Progression*

**Leader**

Left forward, (brush right), right side, left together; right forward, (brush left), left side, right together

**Follower**

Right backward, (brush left), left side, right together; left backward, (brush right), right side, left together

## Timing Cues

| | |
|---|---|
| 4/4 time signature: | Four beats to a measure (group two measures) |
| Duration: | Each beat gets one count (total of eight counts) |
| Rhythm: | Slow, quick, quick; slow, quick, quick |
| Counts: | 1-2, 3, 4; 5-6, 7, 8; or 1-2, 3, 4; 2-2, 3, 4 |
| Weight changes: | Six (in two measures; on counts 1, 3, 4 and 5, 7, 8) |
| Direction of steps: | Box step—Forward, brush, side, in place; backward, brush, side, in place |
| | Half-box progression—Forward, brush, side, in place; forward, brush, side, in place (backwards for follower) |
| Foot positions: | Fourth (brush in first), second, first; fourth (brush in first), second, first |

# Six-Count (Basic) Rhythm (Slow, Slow, Quick, Quick)

The basic rhythm in foxtrot gives you a lot of traveling options. The leader starts with the left foot while the follower starts with the right foot. After one repetition of the six-count basic rhythm, each partner's original starting foot is free again.

### Leader

Stand in correct body alignment with your feet in a narrow base (feet parallel in first position and no more than two to three inches apart). To extend your reach to approximately 18 to 24 inches (45-60 cm), bend your right knee, push off, reach forward, and transfer your weight (heel–ball–toe) onto your left foot on count 1. Bring your right foot forward and brush the ball of that foot beside your left foot on count 2. Bend your left knee, push off, reach forward, and transfer your weight (heel–ball–toe) onto your right foot on count 3. Bring your left foot forward and brush the ball of that foot beside your right foot on count 4. On count 5, take a shoulder-width side step to your left onto your left foot. On count 6, bring your feet together and transfer your weight onto your right foot.

### Follower

Stand in correct body alignment with your feet in a narrow base (feet parallel in first position and no more than 3 in, or 7 cm, apart). To match the extension of your partner's leg reach, bend your left knee, push off, extend your right leg backward, and transfer your weight (toe–ball-heel) onto your right foot on count 1. Continue your left foot backward to brush the ball of that foot beside your right foot on count 2. Bend your right knee, push off, reach backward, and transfer your weight (toe–ball–heel) onto your left foot on count 3. Bring your right foot backward and brush the ball of that foot beside your left foot on count 4. On count 5, take a shoulder-width side step to your right onto your right foot. On count 6, bring your feet together and transfer your weight onto your left foot.

Figure 9.2 shows the various ways you might organize the counts and footwork for the foxtrot six-count, or basic, rhythm. Some cues will be more helpful to you than others. Select those cues that most help you retain how to execute this rhythmic step pattern.

## Figure 9.2 SIX-COUNT (BASIC) RHYTHMIC STEP PATTERN FOR FOXTROT

### Footwork Cues

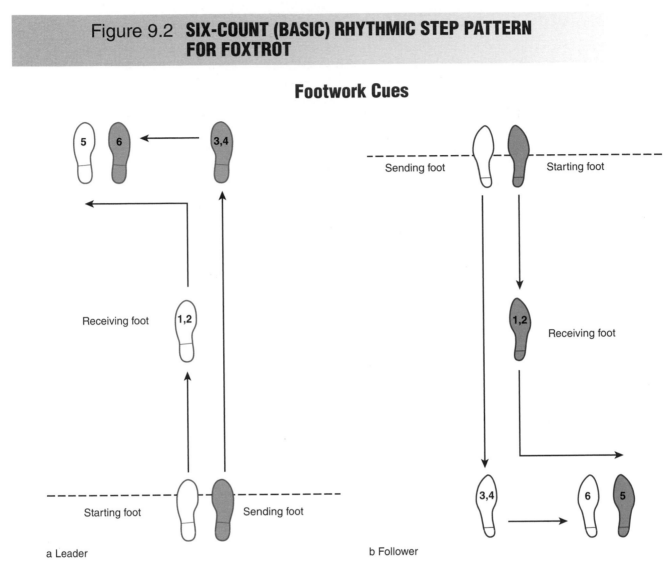

a Leader

b Follower

**Leader**
Left forward (& brush), right forward (& brush), left (side), right (together)

**Follower**
Right backward (& brush), left backward (& brush), right (side), left (together)

### Timing Cues

| | |
|---|---|
| 4/4 time signature: | Four beats to a measure (group 1 1/2 measures) |
| Duration: | Each beat gets one count (six total counts) |
| Counts: | 1-2, 3-4, 5, 6 |
| Rhythm: | Slow, Slow, Quick, Quick |
| Weight changes: | Four (on counts 1, 3, 5, 6) |
| Direction of steps: | Leader—Forward (& brush), forward (& brush), left side, in place |
| | Follower—Backward (& brush), backward (& brush), right side, in place |
| Foot positions: | Fourth (pass through first on brush), fourth (pass through first on brush), second, first |

# DRILLS FOR FOXTROT

The following drills help you practice both foxtrot dance rhythms. These rhythms are to be interspersed as they are needed to either help you remain stationary or travel. Each *slow* cue gets two counts and one weight change in the foxtrot (as in the single swing), except that the foxtrot ultimately travels in the LOD on the *slow* steps. The *quick* steps get one count and one weight change each. For each drill, read the directions, and watch the video demonstrations on the enclosed DVD to see (a) how to execute the selected foxtrot variations, and (b) how to combine them into short practice combinations. Then, practice until you can meet the Success Goal for each drill. Use track 13 for foxtrot music.

## Drill 1
## Lengthening Your Stride (Bend and Send)

Because the smoothness of the foxtrot depends so much on the long, reaching step with each *slow step,* it helps to practice how to modify your regular walking step to achieve the proper length. The actual reaching length varies depending on your height and your leg length, but it should be longer than your regular walking stride. The purpose of this drill is to identify your walking stride as opposed to your reaching stride.

To start this drill, place your heels on a line and stand with your feet 2 or 3 inches (5-7 cm) apart. Ask a partner to put one end of a yardstick (or meterstick) beside you and perpendicular to the line your heels are touching. Take one regular walking step forward, transfer your weight forward onto the ball of your foot, and freeze your position. Use the yardstick (or meterstick) to measure the distance from your starting heel position to the tip of the big toe of your front foot. Record this measurement.

Now place your heels back on the starting line and modify your previous actions by shifting your weight onto one foot. Bend your supporting knee and push off against the floor with the ball of the sending foot. Reach forward with your receiving foot, take one step forward, and freeze your position. Use the yardstick (or meterstick) to measure your stride length, or where the tip of the big toe of your front foot ends. Record this measurement. Compare the two measurements just taken. Which is longer? The second one should be at least 2 inches (5 cm) longer than the regular walking step. When you lower your CPB by bending one leg and push back with the ball of that foot, it sends your other foot forward and lengthens your stride. Try a series of *slow* steps forward and aim for a *bend and send* on each step. Watch for any tendency to hesitate or pause between each step. Travel in a counterclockwise direction around the perimeter of the room (in the line of dance, or LOD).

*(continued)*

Drill 1 *(continued)*

 **TO DECREASE DIFFICULTY**

- Face a partner and match your facing palms. Experiment with taking a step, first without and then with a knee bend, preceding your *slow* step. Notice that a knee bend will give you more connection with your partner (lowering your center), making it easier to start in unison.

- Step forward such that the front of your heel hits the floor first rather than the back of your heel. This will help you shift your weight over the receiving foot.

**TO INCREASE DIFFICULTY**

- Face a partner matching palms and feel the momentum of your bend-and-send shift on each forward step in the LOD. Switch sides with your partner to experience this lead.

- Match palms with your partner to repeat the six-count basic rhythm in the LOD.

## Success Goal

Become aware of the lengthening effect that a knee bend and a push-off add to your reach on consecutive *slow* forward steps in the LOD. ___

## Success Check

- Keep your center over the foot and leg that bear your weight. ___

- Bend the knee of your sending foot to lower your CPB prior to taking a step. ___

- Connect with the floor by pushing down and in the direction opposite to your intended direction (e.g., push down and back with one foot to move the other foot forward). This provides more momentum to go in the desired direction. ___

# Drill 2
# Execution Challenges for Box Rhythm

You have two options within the box rhythm: a box step, or a half-box progression. The first option is a good choice when forward movement is restricted, whereas the second option is a good choice when there is room to travel.

## Box Step

Imagine the outline of a rectangle drawn on the floor. Without music or a partner, step in each corner of this rectangle. Notice that you will need to step with one foot either forward or backward (along the length of the rectangle), then make two weight changes (along the width of the rectangle). Review figure 9.1 as necessary for the specific footwork and timing cues. Practice starting with either the forward or the backward half-box. Notice that a different foot starts each half box. Try this with a partner in closed position.

## Half-Box Progression

For the half-box progression, repeat the first half box forward as you did with the box step. However, if no other couples are immediately in front of you and your partner, then the leader may choose to continue forward on the second half box. Try this with a partner in closed position.

### TO DECREASE DIFFICULTY

- Either imagine or place tape or string on the floor to outline a rectangle, then follow this floor shape as you execute the box step.

- Match an action with each underlying beat such that you do a *forward, brush, side, together* or a *backward, brush, side, together* pattern, matching an action with each beat within each four-count measure. This alternative gives you a head start on styling your free foot in order to move through your base of support.

### TO INCREASE DIFFICULTY

- Execute each of the box rhythm options to slow foxtrot music (use track 13).

- Combine two box rhythm options, such as two box steps and four half-box progressions.

## Success Goal

Perform the four-count box rhythm, executing box steps, then half-box progressions, for 2 minutes with a partner and music. ___

## Success Check

- Width of the rectangle should be no wider than your shoulders. ___

- Length of the rectangle should have a long stride (remember to bend and send on the *slow*). ___

- Take two counts for the *slow*; step and brush the free foot along the length of the rectangle. ___

- Take one count for each *quick, quick* along the width of the rectangle. ___

# Drill 3
# Execution Challenge for Basic Rhythm

The timing in the six-count, or basic, rhythm alternates two *slows* and two *quicks* within six total counts of music. This basic step combines two reaching steps with a small side step (review figure 9.2). Try the basic six-count rhythm with a partner in a closed position and travel in the LOD. Remember to bend and send on each *slow* in order to increase your stride length and to add a brush on counts 2 and 4 to improve your balance and styling. Be aware that like swing, foxtrot music accents counts 2 and 4. In foxtrot, your brush occurs on the upbeats within each measure— on counts 2 and 4, matching the music. Your feet should close briefly in first foot position on these brush actions.

**TO DECREASE DIFFICULTY**

- Gradually increase the tempo of the counts until you are up to the tempo of the slow music selected.
- Face your partner and grasp two hands, keeping the hands in the center as you repeat this drill so that you can feel the momentum of each knee bend (and lowering of your CPB) before reaching and stepping on counts 1 and 3.

**TO INCREASE DIFFICULTY**

- Repeat the drill with a variety of partners.
- Combine two box steps and four basic rhythm steps.

## *Success Goal*

Execute the six-count basic rhythm in the LOD with a partner and music. ___

## *Success Check*

- Keep a narrow base on forward or backward steps (feet 2-3 in, or 5-7 cm, apart).___
- Lower your CPB to bend your supporting knee before stepping on counts 1 and 3 in order to keep the momentum moving forward. ___
- Close your feet briefly when you brush your free foot on counts 2 and 4 (with no weight change). ___

# Drill 4
# Alternate Two Rhythms

When you are first learning a new step, it is helpful to do a minimum of two repetitions of any step before switching to something new. The purpose behind this rule is to make a combination that is both easy to remember (if you are the leader) and easy to recognize (if you are the follower). Because the foxtrot has two different dance rhythms, you need to be able to easily move from one to the other. This drill will help you alternate between four-count box rhythm and six-count basic rhythm. Start in closed position with a partner and try the following sample combinations:

- Two box steps and two basic rhythm steps
- Two basic rhythm steps and four half-box progression steps

After you can do each of the previous combinations without music, try it to slow foxtrot music.

## TO DECREASE DIFFICULTY

- Repeat each basic step as many times as needed to plan ahead for the next move.
- Start from a two-hands-joined position to do this drill.

## TO INCREASE DIFFICULTY

- Vary both the order and the number of repetitions of each dance rhythm.
- Use fewer repetitions, which can be more difficult because the leader must plan ahead.

## Success Goal

Execute the sample combinations to music for 2 minutes.___

## Success Check

- Avoid watching either your own or someone else's feet. ___
- Keep your eyes level and stand tall. ___
- Notice that the box rhythm is a stationary option, while the basic rhythm option is a traveling option. ___

# Drill 5
# Cross Step

The cross step uses two half-boxes and two measures of music. It is a transition between a closed position and a promenade position (both partners face their extended arms with their bodies forming a V). This transition is more challenging because it requires isolation such that your hands and arms remain stationary while your torso and lower body angle 45 degrees. To get an idea, stand facing a wall without a partner. Place your hands against the wall at about shoulder height. Position your weight over the balls of your feet and twist your feet such that your toes, knees, and hips alternately face either your right hand or your left hand.

You don't need to be extremely flexible; you only need to rotate from your hips 45 degrees to either side, or 90 degrees total. The most common error is to move your arms. The second most common error is to rotate too far to the side (beyond 45 degrees). Practice this subtle lower-body rotation alone, then with a partner in a two-hands-joined position.

The first half-box is modified to become a transition into a promenade position, which is also called an *open twinkle*. The second half-box uses a crossover step to transition back to a closed position (see figure 9.3).

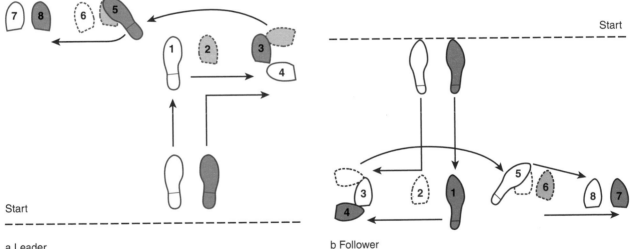

a Leader

b Follower

**Figure 9.3** Cross step footwork and counts (*a*) for the leader, and (*b*) for the follower.

## *Leader*

From a closed position, start to execute a forward half-box. Step forward with your left foot on count 1, then brush to close your right foot beside the left on count 2. On count 3, step to your right side onto your right foot. On count 4, keep your weight on the ball of your right foot to swivel and rotate the hips, legs, and feet counterclockwise (CCW) approximately 45 degrees as you bring

your left foot beside the right foot (feet together) to be in a promenade position. On the second half-box, step with your right foot crossing over your left foot on count 1. On count 2, swivel on the ball of your right foot clockwise (CW) to face the follower and brush with the left foot (closing the feet). On count 3, step onto your left foot to your left side. On count 4, bring your feet together (with a weight change onto the right foot).

## Follower

On the first half-box, step back with the right foot on count 1, and brush to close the left foot beside the right foot on count 2. Step to the left side onto the left foot on count 3, then swivel CW on the ball of the left foot, and bring the feet together (making a weight change onto the right foot) on count 4. In the promenade position, step with the left foot crossing over the right foot on count 1. On count 2, swivel on the ball of her left foot CCW to face the leader and brush with the right foot (to close the feet briefly). On count 3, step onto your right foot to your right side. On count 4, bring your feet together (making a weight change onto her left foot).

### TO DECREASE DIFFICULTY

- Place your hands on a wall at approximately shoulder height. Keep your weight on the balls of your feet as you practice the entire cross step in place without a partner.
- Repeat the drill at least twice before changing to something different.

### TO INCREASE DIFFICULTY

- Repeat the cross step only once, then combine it with any other step covered so far.
- Practice to a variety of tempos.

## Success Goal

Perform 10 correct hip rotations first without a partner, then with a partner and music, alternating the box step with a cross step. ___

## Success Check

*First Half-Box*
- Leader: Forward (left foot), brush (right foot), side (right foot and swivel CCW), together (left foot). ___
- Follower: Backward (right foot), brush (left foot) side (left foot and swivel CW), together (right foot). ___
- Angle the lower body 45 degrees with the leader's right side and the follower's left side closer together to form a V when in the promenade position. ___

*Second Half-Box*
- Inside feet (leader's right and follower's left) cross on first weight change (on the *slow*), then swivel. ___
- Square up your shoulders (to be parallel) with your partner on the side step and bring the feet together to resume the closed position (on the *quick, quick*). ___

# Drill 6
# Left Box Turn

A left box turn rotates CCW and is a variation of the box step. For each half-box taken, a degree of upper body rotation is initiated preceding the *slow* step, then the *side, together* steps are executed. This process of rotating slightly with each half-box gradually achieves a left box turn. How much rotation is done with any half-box is optional. Figure 9.4, *a* and *b,* shows one example in which the leader may execute a left box turn with four half-boxes (and making a quarter turn to face a new wall on each half-box, for a total of 16 counts). In contrast with the left box turn done with three counts per quarter turn in the waltz, the foxtrot has four counts per quarter turn. The leader starts with his left foot and his left front diagonal direction. The follower starts with her right foot and her right back diagonal direction.

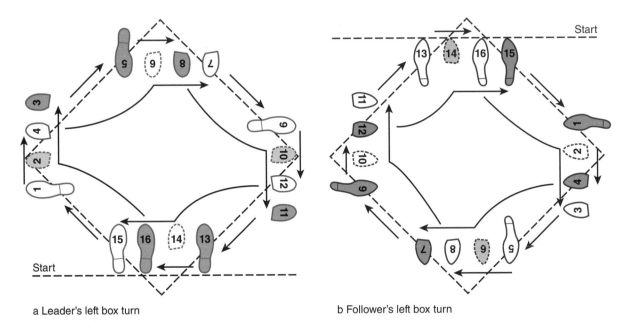

a Leader's left box turn

b Follower's left box turn

**Figure 9.4**　Left box turn footwork for the foxtrot (16 total counts).

## Leader

The lead occurs just before the downbeat of a measure and before executing a forward half-box. The lead consists of a slight CCW rotation of the upper torso while keeping the chest and shoulders firmly connected with the arms (maintaining a frame). This upper torso rotation facilitates an outward-angled left foot position on each forward half-box and an inward-angled right foot position on each backward half-box. When a quarter-turn rotation is desired with each half-box, then the foot placements occur along a 45-degree angle (either the left front diagonal or the right back diagonal). Continue the CCW momentum while executing the backward half-box. Alternately repeat the forward and backward half-boxes. To signal that the left box turn is over, you must firmly keep your upper torso in a closed dance position and avoid any momentum tendencies to continue the CCW rotation.

## Follower

Starting with a backward half-box, be aware of the upper torso rotation lead just before taking the first step. This signals you to angle the toes of your right foot slightly inward and along your right-back diagonal rather than stepping straight backward. Then the *side, together* steps are finished as usual. As the CCW momentum continues, you should be aware of the natural toes-out position, or angle of your left foot, just before executing a forward half-box. Continue rotating CCW as you alternately repeat backward and forward half-boxes until the leader stops rotating his upper torso.

### TO DECREASE DIFFICULTY

- Do a forward half-box and angle to rotate on the backward half-box only, then later you can angle on each half-box.
- Reduce the amount of rotation on each half-box so that you gradually turn CCW, slowly rotating a few degrees preceding each half-box.

### TO INCREASE DIFFICULTY

- Try two consecutive left box turns.
- Combine any variation covered so far with a left box turn.

## Success Goal

Alternate two box steps with a left box turn for 2 minutes. ___

## Success Check

- Rotate frame CCW to initiate a quarter turn with each half-box, using a total of four half-boxes and four measures to complete a 360-degree turn. ___
- Maintain frame in the closed position. ___
- Keep the box rhythm in tempo with the music. ___

# Drill 7
# Rock Step

The rock step is a stationary variation of the basic six-count rhythm in foxtrot. It requires a shift of weight in two directions: forward and backward. Each weight shift gets two counts, then the *side, together* steps each get two more counts (see figure 9.5, *a* and *b*). Remain in a closed position for this variation. After a few trials, notice that multiple repetitions of the basic rock step move both you and your partner toward the leader's left side.

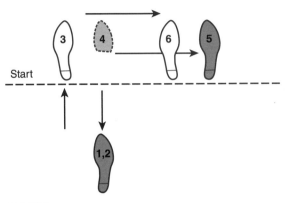

a Leader

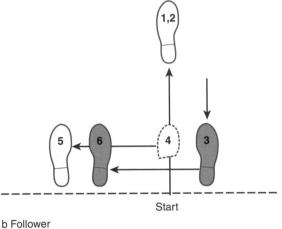

b Follower

**Figure 9.5** Rock step footwork and counts *(a)* for the leader and *(b)* for the follower.

## Leader

Step forward with your left foot on count 1. Either keep your feet in a parallel fourth position or draw up your right foot by sliding it just above the floor and placing the ball of your right foot on the floor to touch or tap it on count 2. Repeat in the opposite direction, stepping backward onto your right foot and either keeping your feet in a parallel fourth position or drawing your left foot beside your right foot to touch the floor. Finish by stepping sideways onto your left foot and bringing your right foot beside your left foot, shifting your weight onto your right foot.

On the first *slow*, the lead for the rock step requires a firm right hand position to stop the forward momentum on count 2. You then pull gently toward your midline to shift, or rock, your weight backward on the second *slow*. Keep the upper torso and arms firm as you move toward your left side to signal the *side, together* steps.

## Follower

Start with a backward step onto your right foot on count 1. Become aware that the leader is limiting further backward motion so that you may either keep your feet in a parallel fourth position or have time to touch your left foot beside your right foot during count 2. The leader will then shift directions to pull you slightly toward him. On the second *slow*, reverse your actions to step forward onto your left foot and either keep your feet in a parallel fourth position or touch with your right foot on count 4. The last two counts occur as you step sideways with your right foot, then bring your feet together and shift your weight onto your left foot.

### TO DECREASE DIFFICULTY

- Practice without a partner.
- Keep your feet in a forward–backward stride (fourth position) and keep your CPB between both feet as you shift from one foot to the other on each *slow* step.

### TO INCREASE DIFFICULTY

- When executing more than approximately four repetitions of this variation—or when you run out of space to move sideways—start to gradually rotate CCW (see the next drill, which expands on this strategy).
- As another option, the leader may rock back with his left foot, then forward on his right foot and *stride, together.*
- Combine this variation with any other variation that you know so far.

## Success Goal

Alternate the basic rhythm in the LOD with the rock step to slow music for 2 minutes. ___

## Success Check

- Use either fourth foot position or fourth and first foot positions on each of the two *slow* steps. ___
- Keep side steps no wider than the width of your own shoulders.___
- Maintain a firm frame throughout. ___

# Drill 8
# Left Rock Turn

Once you are comfortable with the rock step, then adding a CCW rotation is a very useful variation. The amount of rotation may vary from a gradual rotation to a quarter-turn rotation (or more, once you get really good at it) on each repetition of the six-count basic rhythm. If you decide to make quarter turns, you can use the walls of the room as location references (see figure 9.6, *a* and *b*). With each quarter turn, face a new wall; four walls equals a full turn.

### Leader

Step forward on count 1 of your first *slow* and either keep your feet in fourth position or briefly bring your right foot beside your left foot on count 2. During your second *slow*, the timing of the lead needs to take advantage of the momentum as you shift back along a right-back diagonal onto your right foot on count 3. On count 4, briefly bring your left foot beside your right foot and swivel on the ball of your right foot to make a CCW or left quarter turn. Finish with your normal *side, together* steps on counts 5, 6 to your left side. Repeat this six-count left rock turn four times to complete a 360-degree turn.

### Follower

Step backward on count 1 of the first *slow* and either maintain fourth position

*(continued)*

**Drill 8** *(continued)*

or bring your left foot beside your right foot on count 2. During your second *slow*, step forward along a left-front diagonal and keep your weight on the ball of your left foot on count 3. On count 4, briefly bring your right foot beside your left foot and swivel on that foot to make a CCW or left quarter turn. Continue with your normal *side, together* steps on counts 5, 6 to your right side. Repeat this six-count left rock turn four times to complete a 360-degree turn.

As another option, try a right rock turn for another variation of the six-count

basic rhythm that also permits you to remain in one spot instead of travel. In this case, the leader steps backward with his left foot on the first *slow,* then forward along a right-front diagonal with his right foot on the second *slow* and swivels on the ball of his right foot as he rotates with his right shoulder back to make a CW or right quarter turn. Keep the frame firm to do the *side, together* steps on counts 5, 6. The follower does the mirror reverse. The leader may execute four quarter turns for a full right rock turn.

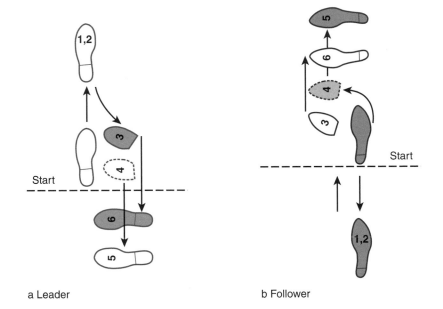

a Leader                                    b Follower

**Figure 9.6**    Left rock turn footwork and counts *(a)* for the leader and *(b)* for the follower.

## TO DECREASE DIFFICULTY

- On the second *slow* of the left rock turn, slightly angle the foot toward the direction of the turn; the leader's right toes angle inward and the follower's left toes angle outward.
- Without a partner, execute the left rock turn and use your own momentum (left shoulder goes back) to rotate CCW approximately 90 degrees on each quarter turn

## TO INCREASE DIFFICULTY

- Do only one or two quarter-turn rotations.
- Execute the six-count basic rhythm along the length of the room, then do one left-rock quarter-turn rotation to square or turn the corner when you get to each corner of the room.
- Alternate four left rock turns (four quarter turns) with four right rock turns (four quarter turns).

## Success Goal

Alternate two rock steps with a left rock turn to music for 2 minutes. ___

- Make sure that your closed position includes your feet being offset from your partner's instead of standing toe-to-toe with your partner. ___
- Maintain a firm frame throughout. ___
- Use the momentum of changing directions to facilitate either the CCW or CW rotation. ___

# Drill 9
# Sway Step

Another variation of the rock step is to transfer your weight from side to side. When you let your CPB move over your supporting foot as you shift from one foot to the other, you are doing the sway step. Either verbally or mentally use the cues *side, touch; side, touch; side, together* as you execute this six-count variation. The sway step is executed from a closed dance position. For styling, let your upper body slightly lean to each side on the two *slow* cues, then resume a neutral, upright posture for the ball–change steps. For practice, repeat the sway step at least twice before leading another variation.

## Leader

Step to your left side with your left foot on the first *slow* and touch your right foot beside your left (without changing weight). Repeat to the opposite side by stepping to your right with your right foot on the second *slow* and touching your left foot beside your right (without changing weight). If you keep your frame firm and move your entire body to the side, it will be easy for the follower to recognize the lead. In addition, you may gently press with the heel of your right hand before moving to your left side, then gently pull with your right hand's fingers before moving to your right side. Finish the *quick, quick* steps with the normal *side, together* steps (changing weight from your left foot to your right foot on both counts 5 and 6, respectively). Notice that this variation takes you to your left side. Thus, after so many repetitions, you may not have room to continue to your left. You can then alternate this variation with other variations that you know.

## Follower

Step to your right side with your right foot on the first *slow* and touch your left foot beside your right foot without changing weight. Repeat to the opposite side by stepping to your left with your left foot on the second *slow* and touching your right foot beside your left foot without changing weight. Take your regular *side, together* steps to finish this six-count variation. Notice that this variation takes you to your right side.

*(continued)*

Drill 9   *(continued)*

**TO DECREASE DIFFICULTY**

- Stand with your feet approximately shoulder-width apart and shift from one foot to the other to get the rhythm—two counts or beats per side or per weight change (without the touch).

- Practice the sway steps without a partner, then repeat the sway steps with a partner in a two-hands-joined position.

**TO INCREASE DIFFICULTY**

- Leaders may execute only one repetition of the sway step prior to leading another variation of your choice.

- Leaders may experiment with a slow, CCW rotation by angling the upper torso approximately 45 degrees before taking the first *slow* step.

- Leaders may also experiment with a slow, CW rotation by angling the upper torso approximately 45 degrees before taking the second *slow* step.

## *Success Goal*

Alternate the rock step with the sway step for 2 minutes. ___

## *Success Check*

- Keep your side steps approximately the width of your own shoulders. ___

- Tap or touch your foot by placing the ball of your free foot beside the instep of your weighted foot on counts 2 and 4. ___

- Let your upper torso sway (or lean slightly) to each side on the *slow* cues. ___

# Drill 10
# Promenade, or Conversation Step

The promenade, or conversation step, is a popular six-count basic rhythm variation that starts in a closed position and moves to a promenade, or semiopen, position. The promenade position permits a conversation to occur between partners as they travel in the LOD.

## *Leader*

From a closed position facing the LOD, use an open twinkle transition to get to the promenade position. The open twinkle was also used in the waltz, but the timing is different because the foxtrot's box rhythm has four counts instead of three. Thus, you take a forward step with your left foot on *slow* and rotate your torso toward the diagonal front wall. With your right foot, step toward the diagonal front wall on the first *quick*. On the second *quick*, bring your feet together as you step on your left foot. When in the promenade position, your extended left arm and hand should be pointing toward the LOD and your upper torso is rotated CW approximately 45 degrees.

In the promenade position, take two walks (left, right), one on each *slow, slow* cue, traveling in the LOD. The two *quick, quick* steps (left, right) are executed while facing your partner and moving sideways toward the LOD during the *side, together* steps. Repeat the promenade step at least twice, then you can remain in closed position and rotate the upper torso CCW to face the LOD again.

## *Follower*

The open twinkle transition uses four counts in the foxtrot. On the first *slow*, the follower steps backward with the right foot. In response to the leader's upper body rotation, you take your first *quick* step with your left foot stepping diagonally back, keeping your weight on the ball of your left foot so you can swivel CW on the ball of your left foot (at the end of count 3) to face the LOD and be on the right side of the leader. Step onto your left foot with feet together on count 4 (the second *quick* cue).

In the promenade position, take two walking steps (right, left) toward the LOD, one step on each *slow, slow* cue. Rotate CCW to face the leader to do *side, together* steps (right, left). Repeat the promenade step again. On any *side, together* steps, the leader may rotate his upper torso CCW to resume a closed position facing the LOD.

## TO DECREASE DIFFICULTY

- Without using any footwork or a partner, hold your arms in closed position, keep your weight on the balls of your feet, and swivel your toes to face your extended hand (leader's left, follower's right). This lower-body rotation places you in a correct promenade position.

- Without a partner, hold your arms in promenade position and walk through the promenade steps, being aware that your extended hand remains towards the LOD.

- Start in promenade position and execute consecutive promenade steps to travel in the LOD.

## TO INCREASE DIFFICULTY

- In promenade position, add a CW underarm turn for the follower between the two *slow* cues.

- Experiment with a CW underarm turn for the follower during the two *quicks*.

- Combine this variation with any other variation that you know so far.

*(continued)*

Drill 10  *(continued)*

## *Success Goal*

Alternate an open twinkle with two promenade or conversation steps for 2 minutes. ___

- Keep your frame (arms and shoulders) firm.___
- Rotate lower body (hips, knees, and toes) to face the extended hands when in promenade position.___
- In promenade position, take two *slow* steps forward in the LOD.
  ___
- Swivel to face your partner during the *quick, quick* side–together steps in closed position. ___

# Drill 11
# Right Box Turn

A right box turn rotates CW when the leader's right foot is free. However, because the leader starts with his left foot, a half-box needs to be taken first. Think of four quarter turns sandwiched between two half-boxes for a total of six half-boxes. Remain in closed position during the right box turn. It is a useful option when you need to remain stationary or in one spot.

## *Leader*

- *First half-box:* Execute a forward half-box, while facing the LOD.
- *Second half-box:* Rotate your frame to face the diagonal right front as you step onto your right foot, briefly brush your left foot beside your right, and step *left, right,* on your *side, together* steps (for the first quarter turn). The leader is facing the outside wall.
- *Third half-box:* The leader again rotates his frame CW as he

extends his left foot diagonally back, briefly brush his right foot beside his left foot, then steps *right, left* on his *side, together* step (for the second quarter turn). The leader is now facing the rear LOD.

- *Fourth half-box:* Repeat actions starting with the leader's right foot as used with the second half-box to rotate the leader a quarter turn to face the center of the room.
- *Fifth half-box:* Repeat actions starting with the leader's left foot as used in the third half-box to rotate the leader a quarter turn to face the LOD.
- *Sixth half-box:* The leader's right foot is now free to execute a forward half-box progression.

## Follower

- *First half-box:* Execute a backward half-box.

- *Second half-box:* Step diagonally back onto your left foot, briefly brush your right foot beside your left, and step *right, left* on your *side, together* steps for the first quarter turn. The follower is now facing the center of the room.

- *Third half-box:* Extend the right foot diagonally forward, briefly brush the left foot beside the right foot, then step *left, right* on your *side, together* step for the second quarter turn. The follower is now facing the LOD.

- *Fourth half-box:* Step diagonally back with your left foot, briefly brush your right foot beside your left, rotate a CW quarter turn, and step *right, left* on your *side, together* steps. The follower is now facing the outside wall.

- *Fifth half-box:* Step with your right foot diagonally forward to rotate a CW quarter turn and have your back toward the LOD.

- *Sixth half-box:* Your left foot is now free to execute a backward half-box progression.

As a traveling option, combine two CCW quarter turns, then two CW quarter turns. From a closed position, the leader needs to step diagonally forward with his left foot (one half-box for the first CCW quarter turn), diagonally backward with his right foot (one half-box for the second CCW quarter turn), then reverse directions to move CW by stepping diagonally backward with his left foot (one half-box for the third quarter turn), and continue CW to step diagonally forward with his right foot (one half-box for the fourth quarter-turn rotation). The follower does the mirror reverse.

## TO DECREASE DIFFICULTY

- Without a partner, practice the right box turn making sure you step on the diagonal and angle your foot in the direction of the turn on the first *slow* of each half-box quarter turn.

- Hold your partner's shoulders to keep them parallel as you slowly walk through the right box turn.

## TO INCREASE DIFFICULTY

- Add on the traveling option after the right box turn in the previous sequence.

- Combine the right box turn with any two variations covered so far.

## Success Goal

Alternate two box steps with a right box turn for 2 minutes. ___

## Success Check

- Use a total of six half-boxes to complete the right box turn.___

- Maintain a constant tempo throughout. ___

# Drill 12
# Weave Step

The weave step is a variation that uses an open twinkle and three crossover steps for a total of four half-boxes. In the weave step, the outside arms open to each side when in the promenade position. Avoid opening the arms and rotating the shoulders beyond 45 degrees (see figure 9.7, *a-d*).

**a** Half-box to open outside arms in promenade position

**b** Cross inside feet and open outside arms on second half-box

**c** Cross inside feet and open outside arms on third half-box

**d** Cross inside feet and resume closed position on fourth half-box

**Figure 9.7** Weave step.

## Leader

Start in a closed position with your partner. Execute a forward half-box, using an open twinkle to rotate to the promenade position as you also release your left hand so that both partners' hands and arms are open to your left side (extending your left hand and the follower's right hand). Both partners cross over with their inside feet (your right and follower's left) to execute the second half-box and rotate to face your right side on the *side, together* steps, opening the outside arms (extending your right hand and the follower's left hand). On the third half-box, both partners cross over with the inside feet (your left and follower's right) and rotate to your left side during the *side, together* steps, again opening the outside arms. On the fourth half-box, both partners cross over with the inside feet (your right and follower's left), and you face each other to resume a closed position on the *side, together* steps.

## Follower

During the three crossover steps, hold your arms in frame without dropping your elbows, then the leader may alternately reach under either your right or left arm to place the heel of one hand on that shoulder blade and gently press with his fingertips, which signals you to open to the opposite side.

## TO DECREASE DIFFICULTY

- Without a partner, stand facing a wall with your hands placed at shoulder height. Press into the wall with your hands to keep your upper torso stationary and swivel your toes to face the side. Then do consecutive crossover steps using your inside foot (closest to the wall) on each half-box to get an idea of the importance of the swivel in executing the weave step easily.

- As an alternative, the leader may not open his outside arm in promenade position during the first half-box. He does release his right hand at the end of the second half-box to open the arms. He just brings his left hand across his midline on the third half-box, and resumes a closed position on the fourth half-box.

## TO INCREASE DIFFICULTY

- Alternately combine the weave step with any other variation that you know so far.

- Experiment with creating combinations of any three variations that include the weave step.

*(continued)*

Drill 12 *(continued)*

## Success Goal

Alternate two box steps with the weave step for 2 minutes. ___

- Keep your weight over the balls of your feet on the *side, together* steps of each half-box in order to swivel prior to each of the three crossover steps. ___

- The weave step uses a total of four half-boxes, or 16 counts. ___

- Keep your outside (free) arm gently curved, in front of your own shoulders, and symmetrical with your partner's open arm position. ___

# Drill 13
# Rollovers

Rollovers are a fun way to progress in the LOD and might be considered a traveling weave step. In this variation, the leader brings the follower to his right side and releases his left hand so that both open up facing the LOD. The person on the left side then moves across in front of the person on the right (by rolling over to the opposite side) while the person on the right does a half-box in place. In this drill, an open twinkle sets up the side-by-side open-arms position, the leader rolls over, the follower rolls over, then both resume a closed position.

## Leader

Start in a closed dance position. During the first half-box, execute an open twinkle and release your left hand as both partners face the LOD (the leader is on the left, while the follower is on the right). Avoid opening shoulders beyond a 45-degree angle so that your shoulders can form a V position when standing side by side.

On the second half-box, the leader's right foot is now free to step along his right front diagonal, facing his partner and ending up on the right-hand side. As the leader rolls over, he releases his right hand and places his left hand on the follower's right shoulder blade. On the third half-box, the leader remains in one location to execute his half-box while it is the follower's turn to roll over in front of the leader. Whenever the follower rolls across, the leader may stop the rollovers, which may be on the third (or fifth, or seventh, and so forth) half-box. To end the rollovers, the leader slides his left hand down the follower's right arm to grasp hands in promenade position. On the fourth half-box, the leader rotates his torso and frame CCW to bring the follower back into a closed position as he does a forward half-box progression.

## Follower

At the end of the first half-box's *quick,* swivel 180 degrees clockwise on the ball of your left foot to open toward the LOD. On the second *quick,* bring your feet together and extend your right hand and arm, keeping it curved and symmetrical to match the leader's open left arm. On the second half-box, execute your steps in place as the leader moves from your left to your right side. Then, on the third half-box, your right foot is free to step across along the right front diagonal and roll over from the leader's left to his right side. To end the rollovers, the leader will slide down your right arm to grasp your hand in promenade position on the third half-box. Then on the fourth half-box, angle your left foot as you step along the diagonal left front to rotate CCW to face the leader and resume a closed position.

## TO DECREASE DIFFICULTY

- With a partner and no specific footwork, walk through the body positioning needed to complete the rollovers.
- Use a total of only four half-boxes: (1) to get the follower to the right-hand side, (2) for the leader to roll over, (3) for the follower to move in front and to a promenade position, and (4) to resume a closed position.

## TO INCREASE DIFFICULTY

- Do any even number of half-box repetitions to extend the rollovers, for example, with the leader sliding down the follower's arm on the fifth, or seventh, half-box in order to resume a closed position during the sixth, or eighth, half-box.
- Combine the rollovers with any other variation that you know so far, such as the half-box progressions.

## Success Goal

Alternate two box steps with the rollovers for 2 minutes. ___

## Success Check

- The person on the left side moves along a diagonal when rolling over and switching places. ___
- Open up toward the LOD with bodies forming a V during the rollovers. ___
- The leader rolls over on the even-numbered half-boxes; in other words, he rolls over on the second, fourth, sixth, and so on. ___
- The follower rolls over on the odd-numbered half-boxes; in other words, she rolls over on the third, fifth, seventh, and so on. ___
- The leader's last half-box is taken as a forward half-box progression. ___

# Drill 14
# Parallel Forward and Backward Basics

The six-count basic rhythm is used in the parallel forward and backward variation. It is sometimes called the *outside parallels* because each partner steps outside the other partner's feet. This variation permits the leader to travel both forward and backward. It also introduces a modification of the closed position, which includes both right and left parallel partner positions. The forward–backward (or backward–forward) direction change occurs on the *quick, quick* steps.

## Leader

Start in a closed position. As you take two *slows* forward, step slightly along your diagonal left front in order to move up beside your partner so that she is on your right side (and your right shoulders are almost touching in a right parallel position). On the *quick, quick* steps, lead a half turn CW by pulling back with the heel of your right hand toward your midline and rotating your shoulders and frame clockwise. You'll end up facing the rear line of dance (RLOD) with the follower on your left side, which is a left parallel position. Take two walking steps backward on the *slow, slow,* then rotate a half turn CCW on the *quick, quick* steps to face the LOD again. Continue alternating this six-count basic rhythm traveling forward two steps, then in place during the CW half turn, and traveling backward two steps, then in place during the CCW half turn. You may resume a closed position facing the LOD at the end of any even-numbered repetitions of the six-count basic rhythm.

## Follower

Your movements are the mirror reverse. Take two *slow* steps backward. Notice that the leader has moved beside you on your right-hand side. In place, rotate a half turn CW to face the LOD as you execute the *quick, quick* steps. The leader will now be on your left-hand side. Execute two walks forward (on the *slow, slow*), and rotate a half turn CCW to face the RLOD as you take your *quick, quick* steps while in a right parallel position with your partner. To end this combination, the leader will remain facing you to resume a closed position.

**TO DECREASE DIFFICULTY**

- Without any footwork, practice just the arm switch needed to rotate or pivot a half turn CW, then CCW. Notice that the leader always remains on the inside (closest to the center), while the follower always remains on the outside (closest to the wall).

- From a closed position, the leader needs to take longer strides and the follower needs to take shorter strides in order to move to a right parallel position by the end of the second *slow.*

**TO INCREASE DIFFICULTY**

- Vary the tempo and the number of repetitions.
- Alternate this variation with any other variation that you know so far.

## Success Goal

Alternate the six-count basic rhythm with parallel forward and backward basic steps for 2 minutes. ___

## Success Check

- Keep your shoulders parallel to your partner's shoulders on the two *slow* steps of each basic rhythm.__

- Keep your weight on the balls of your feet and use small steps during the half turn on the *quick, quick* steps. ___

# Drill 15
# Zigzag

The zigzag variation, which is named because of the zigzag path that you follow, is another traveling option that alternates two repetitions of the six-count basic rhythm and two directions. Start in closed position with the leader facing the forward diagonal wall (or his diagonal right front direction). The leader takes two *slow* forward steps in this diagonal direction. The *side, together* steps need to be small steps taken while facing the outside wall (i.e., the leader's left shoulder is toward the LOD). On the second repetition, the leader rotates to face the back diagonal wall direction as he takes two *slow* steps backward in the forward diagonal center direction. Again, the leader's *side, together* steps need to be small steps taken while facing the outside wall (with his left shoulder toward the LOD).

It takes either a minimum of 12 counts for the zigzag variation, or any even-numbered repetitions of the basic rhythm may be used. It is easier to take your two *slow* steps outside your partner's feet, or you may step in between your partner's feet on the two *slow* steps of each six-count basic rhythm. Either way is acceptable. The follower does the mirror reverse. Remember that both partners need to lightly brush the free foot (in order to briefly collect the free leg under the body) on counts 2 and 4 of each execution of the six-count basic rhythm.

## TO DECREASE DIFFICULTY

- Do two or more repetitions of the zigzag, stepping outside partner's feet.

- Execute the zigzag along the length of the room, then execute a left rock turn to turn the corner prior to travel along the ends of the room.

## TO INCREASE DIFFICULTY

- Vary the number of repetitions of the zigzag with a minimum of two before leading another variation.

- Combine the zigzag with half-box progression steps, using the box rhythm to travel in the LOD.

*(continued)*

**Drill 15** *(continued)*

## Success Goal

Alternate the six-count basic rhythm with the zigzag variation for 2 minutes. ___

- The leader starts facing the forward diagonal wall. ___
- The follower starts facing the rear diagonal center. ___
- Both partners travel in the LOD by stepping on the diagonals during the *slow, slow* steps, then *side, together* on the *quick, quick* steps. ___
- The leader alternately angles his shoulders to face the forward diagonal wall on his forward steps, to face the outside wall on the *quick, quick* steps, and to face the diagonal right back on his backward steps. ___

# Drill 16
# Waterfall Mixer

If you ever have the opportunity, join in a mixer that focuses on changing partners in a random way. For example, the popular waterfall mixer (see figure 9.8) starts with the dancers forming two lines on each side of the room (leaders on one side, followers on the other), then coming toward each other at the top of the room, which is usually on the end where the music is located. The first person in each line walks to meet the other in the center. They introduce themselves, then dance down the middle of the floor. Foxtrot music is usually played, but sometimes waltz music is played too. At the other end of the room, they thank each other and walk back to start over again with a new partner. When the first row gets a third of the way down the middle of the floor (approximately two basics), the next row should be ready to start, and so on. More than one couple may dance down the middle at a time, depending on the space available.

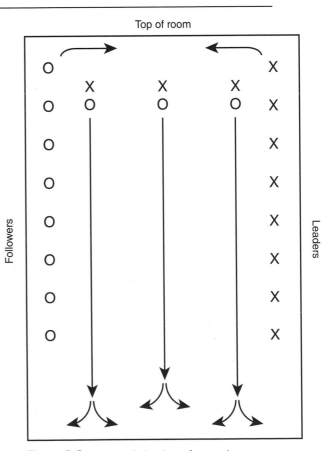

**Figure 9.8** Waterfall mixer formation.

**TO DECREASE DIFFICULTY**

- Use basic steps that travel down the floor.
- Adjust your moves to fit your partner's skill level, such that you don't show off with complicated moves or embarrass your partner.

**TO INCREASE DIFFICULTY**

- Vary the foxtrot dance rhythms, as possible, when you travel down the center of the floor.
- Increase the tempo.

## *Success Goal*

Dancing with different partners while traveling down the center of the room to the selected music for 2 minutes. ___

## *Success Check*

- Introduce yourself to each new partner. ___
- Thank each partner after dancing down the center of the room. ___
- Avoid criticizing your partner. ___
- Graciously dance with each person you meet as the two lines randomly join together. ___

# Drill 17
# On Your Own: Intermixing Foxtrot Rhythms

Once you are comfortable with the selected variations covered so far, experiment with combining them so that you don't have to think about what you want to do after each individual variation. The previous drills helped you practice short combinations of two or three foxtrot variations that flow naturally together. Now, it is time to challenge yourself to link any four or more four-count variations, or six-count variations, and to intersperse these two foxtrot dance rhythms. When selecting your foxtrot variations, use the following chart.

| | |
|---|---|
| **Four-count box rhythm variations** | • Box step<br>• Half-box progression (forward and backward)<br>• Cross step<br>• Box turn (left and right)<br>• Weave step<br>• Rollovers |
| **Six-count basic rhythm variations** | • Basic step<br>• Rock step<br>• Rock turn (left and right)<br>• Sway step<br>• Promenade, or conversation step<br>• Parallel forward and backward basics<br>• Zigzag |

*(continued)*

**Drill 17** *(continued)*

The leader has the option of doing either foxtrot dance rhythm separately or inter-mixing these two rhythms. Have fun identifying your favorite combinations.

### TO DECREASE DIFFICULTY

- Combine any three variations in short sequences to help remember them.
- Use a slow tempo.

### TO INCREASE DIFFICULTY

- Create a sequence of four variations by combining any two variations from each of the two foxtrot dance rhythms.
- Use a variety of tempos.
- Switch partners frequently.

### Success Goal

Link any four or more variations together first using only box rhythm, then using only basic rhythm, and finally alternating box and basic rhythms. ___

### Success Check

- Make smooth transitions from one partner position to the next, as appropriate for your selected combination. ___
- Maintain the tempo and flow throughout. ___
- Make a list of your favorite three combinations for future reference. ___

---

# SUCCESS SUMMARY FOR FOXTROT

The foxtrot is one of the most popular dances on the social dance floor. It is a smooth dance that is associated with high-society poise and glamour, especially in the movies. It has two dance rhythms: a four-count, or box, rhythm, and a six-count, or basic, rhythm. The foxtrot is danced to 4/4 time music that has accents on counts 2 and 4 giving it a swing-like quality. Each *slow* step in the foxtrot gets two counts, while each *quick* step gets one count. In the foxtrot, the closed position is used the majority of the time; however, it is helpful to know how to make the transition to the promenade, or semiopen, position and back to closed position again. The right and left parallel partner positions are also used in selected foxtrot variations. The foxtrot uses long, gliding steps with the goal of traveling in the LOD whenever the traffic permits.

STEP

# 10

# Polka

## *Having Fun*

The polka originated as a Czech peasant dance. The *hop, step, close, step* of the polka can be found in English country dances and in German and Polish folk dances. The Czech word *pulka* for *half step* refers to the quick shift of weight from one foot to the other. Polka dancing was originally done by the "working people" and soon evolved into a vivacious couple dance in the early nineteenth century. It was refined by dance masters and introduced to the ballrooms of Prague in 1835, then to the ballrooms in Paris in 1840. During this time frame, dancing was considered important for the socially prominent. Cellarius, a famous French dancing master, stated the following about the polka: "What young man is there, although formerly most opposed to dancing, whom the polka has not snatched from his apathy to acquire, willy-nilly, a talent suddenly become indispensable?"* The attraction of the polka to men and women resulted in what was called *polkamania*. In both England and the United States, the waltz and polka became *the* dances to do, gradually replacing the contredance and cotillion by the middle of the 19th century. The polka brought with it other popular dances, such as the gallop, or *galoppade*. It consisted of a series of rapid chassés around the room with an occasional turn. It was a favorite final dance of the evening that was done to fast polka music. Selected polka variations today include gallop steps.

With the introduction of ragtime, jazz, and newer dances of the early 20th century, the polka declined a bit. However, after World War II, the polka was adopted by Polish immigrants to the United States as their *national* dance in 1945. Additional enthusiasm for the polka came from other Americans, who followed Lawrence Welk (a famous band leader with his popular dance music on television) and other postwar bands. Polka music is happy and robust. A variety of styles of the polka exist, from a light, springy quality reflecting its Polish roots to a heavy and forceful quality reflecting its German roots. You'll also find that country-western dancers eliminate the hop and use more of a shuffle on the triple steps and add a lilt that makes the polka enjoyable to do both for fun and in competitions. Because the polka is so vigorous, you will need to build up your stamina to last the entire length of a song—and ultimately an evening's worth of polkas and other dances!

*Stephenson, R. and J. Iaccarino. 1980. New York: Doubleday & Company, Inc., 18.

# RHYTHMIC STEP PATTERN FOR POLKA

The rhythmic step pattern for the polka uses two counts, or one measure of 2/4 time music. However, you need to repeat the rhythmic step pattern on both sides, so there are a total of four counts before your starting foot is free again. Thus, many dancers find it helpful to count in sets of four counts (merging two measures) and to treat the music as 4/4 time.

Characteristic of the polka is a hop that is combined with a triple step and can be cued *hop, step, ball, step*—all within two beats of music. The hop is a rise off the floor and a landing on the same foot. The triple step has three weight changes. At first, the polka may seem difficult, because you must perform more actions than with any other basic step and you must do it very quickly. The timing of four actions (1 hop + 3 weight changes) corresponds to the counts *&-1-&-2*.

From a stationary start with your weight on your nonstarting foot, three actions need to be executed preceding the downbeat in order to incorporate the hop: a knee bend and push off the floor, a slight rise in the air, and a landing on that same foot with a soft knee. The knee bend and push-down in order to rise up is an application of Newton's Third Law of motion: Every action has an equal and opposite reaction. It is important to do two things: Bend your knee to absorb the force of the landing, and time the landing to occur on the cue *&*. Sometimes you can give yourself more time to use the cues *&-a* and land on the *a*. You only have half a count in which to execute the hop. Then the triple step's three weight changes are executed. If it is too difficult for you to hop on the first execution of the basic polka rhythm, you may want to eliminate the first hop and start with the triple step and then add the modified hop preceding the downbeat of your second triple step. Once started, these actions become continuous movements; the hop is modified to the timing of a skip with a triple step.

## Leader

From an inside-hands-joined position, start with your weight on your right foot. To execute the hop, bend your right knee, push off the floor to rise high enough to bring the ball of your right foot slightly off the floor, and land on your right foot. Keep these actions in a vertical plane; avoid traveling forward. To start the triple step, step forward onto your left foot on count 1. Position the ball of your right foot beside the instep of your left foot and push downward and backward on the *&* count. Step forward onto your left foot again on count 2. Repeat these actions on the other side by landing the hop on your left foot and executing the triple step with your right foot.

## Follower

From an inside-hands-joined position, start with your weight on your left foot. To execute the hop, bend your left knee, push off the floor to rise high enough to bring the ball of your left foot slightly off the floor, and land on your left foot. Keep these actions in a vertical plane; avoid traveling forward and instead use a *down, up, down* motion. To start the triple step, step forward with your right foot on count 1. Position the ball of your left foot beside the instep of your right foot and push downward and backward on the *&* count. Step forward onto your right foot again on count 2. Repeat these actions on the other side by landing the hop on your right foot and executing the triple with your left foot.

Notice that one foot is always in front of the other foot during the triple step, which is also called *keeping one foot in the lead* or *in front*. Keep your CPB over your working foot (your left foot, during the triple executed on your left side, or your right foot during the triple executed on your right side). Figure 10.1 shows the various ways that you might organize the counts and footwork cues for the polka rhythmic step pattern. Some cues may be more helpful than others. Select those cues that most help you retain how to execute both sides of the rhythmic step pattern for the polka.

## Figure 10.1    RHYTHMIC STEP PATTERN FOR POLKA

### Footwork Cues

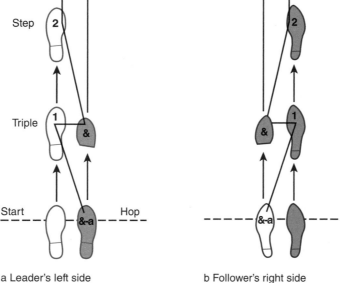

a Leader's left side          b Follower's right side

*Leader*
Hop (bend, rise, and land on right foot), triple step (left, right, left); hop (bend, rise, land on left foot), triple step (right, left, right)

*Follower*
Hop (bend, rise, and land on left foot), triple step (right, left, right); hop (bend, rise, land on right foot), triple step (left, right, left)

### Timing Cues

| | |
|---|---|
| 2/4 time signature: | Two beats to a measure (group two measures) |
| Duration: | Each beat gets one count (total of four counts) |
| Rhythm strategy: | Hop with three steps in two beats of music |
| Counts: | Four; &-1-&-2; &-3-&-4; or &-1-&-2; &-2-&-2 |
| Weight changes: | Hop (on one foot), three (on triple); Hop (on one foot), three (on triple) |
| Direction of steps: | Leader—In place, forward, forward, forward; in place, forward, forward, forward |
| | Follower—In place, backward, backward, backward; in place, backward, backward, backward |
| Foot positions: | One foot, fourth, third, fourth; one foot, fourth, third, fourth |
| Floor contact: | Hop, flat, ball, flat; hop, flat, ball, flat |

# DRILLS FOR POLKA

The polka is fast paced and fun to do. It is challenging at first because you need to execute four actions within two beats of music—on each side of your body! It is helpful to start with slow counts and slow polka music; try track 14 on the enclosed DVD. Once you get the rhythmic step pattern at a slow tempo, try a moderate or fast tempo; try track 15 on the enclosed DVD. Use the following drills to guide your practices. For each drill, read the directions, and watch the video demonstrations on the enclosed DVD to see (a) how to execute the selected polka variations, and (b) how to combine them into short practice combinations. Then, practice until you can meet the Success Goal for each drill. It's time to polka!

## Drill 1
## Execution Challenge for the Polka

Because you combine a hop and a triple step in the polka's rhythmic step pattern, it is helpful to practice each part separately, then put them together. Thus, use slow counts to give yourself enough time to execute each part. Try each of the following parts without a partner or music until it becomes automatic.

a. *The hop:* A hop begins and lands on the same foot. It is executed in a vertical plane; you should not travel forward, or you'll lose your balance. Stand with all your weight on one leg. Bend that knee and push off the floor to spring into the air just high enough that the ball of your foot comes slightly off the floor. Land on the same foot that you started with, and bend that knee to absorb the force of your landing. Thus, one knee should bend, straighten, and bend again during the execution of each hop. Try executing only a hop on one foot. Then combine a step and a hop. On each hop, you should remain in one location; that is, keep the hop in a vertical plane (using *down, up,*

*down* actions). On each step, move forward or backward.

b. *The triple step:* You've combined three weight changes to perform a triple step in the triple swing. Try executing a series of triple steps. For example try four triple steps forward, then four triple steps backward. Notice that it takes two repetitions of the triple step, or four counts, before your starting foot is free to begin again.

c. *The polka rhythmic step pattern:* Combine a hop with a triple step to do consecutive polka steps in the LOD, which is counterclockwise around the room. Make sure that you are blending each part into one continuous motion (review figure 10.1). Notice that the third step of each triple step becomes the foot that you hop on. Also, notice that the timing of the hop now becomes a skip because the hop is executed within only a half count; you land on count *&*, preceding the downbeat, or count 1. Can you execute the polka steps both forward and backward by yourself? Then, try the polka steps with a partner in a two-hands-joined position and travel in the LOD.

The leader hops on his right foot and starts the triple step with his left foot, while the follower hops on her left foot and starts the triple step with her right foot.

### TO DECREASE DIFFICULTY

- Gradually speed up the tempo until you can land on one foot and bring your free foot forward to step on count 1, combining a hop and a step and using the timing of a skip.

- Eliminate the hop on the very first basic step and start with the triple step on the downbeat. Then add the hop at the end of each triple step thereafter. Or, use all triples steps.

### TO INCREASE DIFFICULTY

- Add slow polka music (use track 14).
- Change partners frequently.

## Success Goal

Correctly execute the polka rhythmic step pattern as follows: (a) combining four triple steps forward and four triple steps backward without a partner, and (b) moving in the LOD with a partner in a two-hands-joined position, for 2 minutes.

___

## Success Check

- Use a *down, up, down* motion to both initiate and absorb the landing force on the first & count with each hop. ___

- On counts *1-&-2,* one foot alternately stays in the lead on any one side of the body with each triple step. ___

- After the hop, bring your free foot forward to be ready to execute the triple step. ___

# Drill 2
# Polka in Promenade Position

The polka rhythmic step pattern may be executed from a promenade, or semiopen, position with a partner. Stand beside a partner with the leader on the left and the follower on the right. Rotate your shoulders and upper torso by bringing your outside shoulder forward approximately 45 degrees toward your partner. Place your hands in the promenade position. Shift your weight onto your inside foot (closest to your partner). Execute the polka rhythmic step pattern while maintaining this position. Both partners repeat the hop and triple step of the rhythmic step pattern first with their outside feet, then with their inside feet.

*(continued)*

Drill 2   (continued)

**TO DECREASE DIFFICULTY**

- Gradually increase the tempo from counts to slow polka music.
- Stand beside a partner and repeat the drill without touching.

**TO INCREASE DIFFICULTY**

- Repeat the drill and follow a curved, CCW path around the perimeter of the room.
- Vary the tempo of the music.

## Success Goal

Execute the polka rhythmic step pattern with a partner in a promenade position to slow music for 2 minutes. ___

## Success Check

- Take small steps on the triple steps. ___
- Keep one foot in the lead on each triple step. ___
- Keep your upper torso and arms stationary. ___
- Coordinate your actions such that both outside feet, then both inside feet, move in unison when in promenade position. ___

# Drill 3
# Polka From an Inside-Hands-Joined Position

Stand beside a partner such that the leader is on the left side, the follower is on the right side, and both are facing the same direction. Join inside hands and put your free hand on your hip. Stand with your weight on your inside leg (the one closest to your partner). Slowly go through each part of the polka's rhythmic step pattern. In unison, hop on your inside foot, bring your outside foot forward, and execute a triple step starting with your outside leg (the one farther away from your partner). Reverse these actions starting with your outside foot to hop, then execute a triple step forward starting with your inside foot.

It is fun to relate to your partner by rotating your outside shoulder forward 45 degrees during your triple step with your outside foot, then rotating your inside shoulder forward 45 degrees during your triple step with your inside foot. You'll be looking at your partner, then away from your partner. The inside-joined hands naturally swing back as you face inward (see figure 10.2a), then swing forward as you face outward (see figure 10.2b). The hands swing to waist or shoulder height only. Also be aware of a tendency to overrotate your shoulders to literally face or turn your back to your partner. Try to align your shoulders to be facing either toward the diagonal wall or the diagonal center. Keep your toes facing the LOD as your execute the polka steps.

a                      b

**Figure 10.2** Polka inside arm swing *(a)* backward on the first triple step with outside feet, and *(b)* forward on the second triple step with inside feet.

## TO DECREASE DIFFICULTY

- Place both hands on your hips and twist your upper body without moving your lower body. This isolation drill is good practice for the styling needed in doing the polka steps from an inside-hands-joined position.
- Eliminate the arm swings.

## TO INCREASE DIFFICULTY

- Travel in the LOD.
- Use faster music.

## *Success Goal*

Execute the polka rhythmic step pattern from an inside-hands-joined position to slow music for 2 minutes. ___

## *Success Check*

- On the triple steps, partners use their outside feet, then their inside feet in unison.___
- Rotate the outside shoulder 45 degrees forward with the outside foot's forward triple step, then the inside shoulder forward for the inside foot's forward triple step. ___
- Inside arms swing back on the first triple step, then forward on the second triple step.___

## Drill 4
# Transition Leads Connecting Inside-Hands-Joined and Promenade Positions

If you start the polka rhythmic step pattern from an inside-hands-joined position, how do you lead into the promenade position? One easy transition takes advantage of the natural swinging motion of the inside hands. It is described by its actions such that the leader places the joined hands onto his shoulder to make the transition to a promenade position. From the promenade position, an easy way to make the transition back to the inside-hands-joined position is to slide apart. It is also helpful to break down the polka rhythmic step pattern of four counts into two subparts as the polka steps are repeated on each side of the body with each side getting two counts. The following transitions use four polka basics, each getting two counts, or two polka rhythmic step patterns.

### Hand-to-Shoulder Transition Leads

Technically, any time the inside hands and arms swing back and you step with your outside foot, the lead may be given for this transition. For example, execute two polka basics, one with the outside feet, then another basic with the inside feet with a partner and let your inside arms swing backward and forward. With the outside feet on the third polka basic, swing arms back as usual, except the leader now places the follower's joined hand on top of his right shoulder (see figure 10.3a). On the fourth forward polka basic, the leader releases his right hand, places it just below the follower's left shoulder blade (see figure 10.3b), and extends his outside (left) arm and hand forward so that the follower can put her right hand on top to grasp hands (see figure 10.3c). Continue basics in promenade with your partner.

**a** Leader's hand to his right shoulder on basic with outside feet

**b** Leader's right hand on follower's back on basic with inside feet

**c** Promenade position on basic with outside feet

**Figure 10.3** Hand-to-shoulder transition leads.

## Slide-Apart Transition Leads

Once in the promenade position, the leader may make the transition back to the inside-hands-joined position whenever both partners' outside feet are executing the basic step. For example, take two basics to establish a tempo with your partner in promenade position (see figure 10.4a). On the third basic, the leader releases his left hand grasp (see figure 10.4b). On the fourth basic, the leader begins to move apart as he slides his right hand with the palm up under the follower's arm until both can grasp inside hands (see figure 10.4c). On the fifth basic, both partners may again place their outside hands on their hips and let their joined hands swing back (see figure 10.4d). Continue basics with inside-hands joined with your partner.

**a** Two basics in promenade position

**b** Basic with outside feet and release left hand

**c** Basic with inside feet and slide to hands

**d** Basic with outside feet and inside-joined arms swing back

**Figure 10.4** Slide-apart transition leads.

*(continued)*

**Drill 4** *(continued)*

 **TO DECREASE DIFFICULTY**

- Without footwork, practice only the hand positions on each transition.
- Practice to a slow count, gradually increasing the tempo until you can move to slow polka music.

 **TO INCREASE DIFFICULTY**

- Practice with different partners and different tempos.
- Do four basics in promenade, and four basics with each of the previous transitions to create a short sequence that you can repeat.

## Success Goal

Execute polka basics while transitioning from an inside-hands-joined position to a promenade position and back to an inside-hands-joined position for 2 minutes. ___

## Success Check

- When swinging inside hands, keep outside hands on hips. ___
- Lead the hand-to-shoulder transition during a basic step with outside feet and when hands swing back. ___
- Keep extended arms firm when in the promenade position to establish a frame with your partner. ___
- Lead the slide-apart transition during a basic step with the outside feet and take another basic step with the inside feet to join the inside hands. ___

# Drill 5
# Polka in Closed Position

A third partner position from which you can execute the polka basic steps is from a closed position. The leader faces the LOD, and the follower faces the leader with her back to the LOD. Thus, the leader moves forward while the follower moves backward. It is a bit more difficult to travel backward when executing the basic step. The main difference occurs on the triple steps. When moving backward, the follower's right foot is still in front, but the reference point becomes the heel of the foot rather than the toe. You can identify the direction of travel by extending an imaginary line from her heel toward the LOD.

To avoid stepping on your partner's feet in this closed position, the leader needs to start with his feet on either side of the follower's right foot, keeping her on his right side. In addition, the leader can angle his left shoulder forward slightly as he executes the basic step starting with his left foot. On his second basic step starting with his right foot, the leader needs to angle his right shoulder slightly forward. Both partners travel in the LOD; however, the rotation of the leader's shoulders signals to the follower which side to execute her basic step.

### TO DECREASE DIFFICULTY
- Gradually increase the tempo from slow counts to slow music.
- Modify the dance position to a two-hands-joined position, which will give each partner more room to move.

### TO INCREASE DIFFICULTY
- Use a faster tempo or faster music.
- Change partners frequently.
- Face a partner without touching hands and repeat the rhythmic step pattern in the LOD. Maintain a constant distance between each other.

## Success Goal

Execute polka basics in closed position with a partner to music for 2 minutes. ___

## Success Check

- Leader's left shoulder is angled forward during his left foot's triple, and his right shoulder is angled forward during his right foot's triple step. ___
- Avoid rotating shoulders beyond the diagonals (rotate 45 degrees or less). ___
- Follower's right shoulder is back during her right foot's triple step, and her left shoulder is back during her left foot's triple step. ___
- Keep the frame firm. ___

# Drill 6
# Transition Leads Connecting Closed and Promenade Positions

To make smooth transitions from a closed to a promenade position and back again, it is helpful to group at least eight basic steps, or 16 counts. The leader remains facing the LOD throughout these transitions. The follower starts with her back to the LOD, then rotates to face the LOD, then turns to face her partner again.

### Rotate Frame CW to Promenade

From a closed position, the leader may signal a transition to promenade at the end of any even-numbered basic step. For example, partners take two basic steps; on the second one, the leader

*(continued)*

Drill 6 *(continued)*

gradually rotates his entire upper torso and arms clockwise (CW) until his left hand is pointed toward the LOD, which brings the follower to the leader's right side. There is no need to rush this transition. Take two full basic steps, or four counts, to transition to promenade position. Thus, at the end of count 4 the follower should be ready to pivot CW 180 degrees on the ball of her left foot until she faces the LOD. The leader can gently press with the heel of his right hand to open the follower's right shoulder. Now both partners are in a promenade position to repeat the basic step.

## Rotate Frame CCW to Closed

From a promenade position, the leader may signal a transition to closed position at the end of any even-numbered basic step. For example, partners take two basic steps and at the end of the second one, the leader gradually rotates his entire upper torso and arms CCW to bring the follower into closed position again. On count 4 the follower should be ready to pivot CCW 180 degrees on the ball of her left foot to face her partner again.

### TO DECREASE DIFFICULTY
- Practice to counts, then to slow polka music (use track 14).
- Practice each transition separately.

### TO INCREASE DIFFICULTY
- Do any even number of basic steps before leading these transitions.
- Use the appropriate transitions to connect three partner positions while doing basic steps.

## Success Goal

Execute polka basics while transitioning from a closed position to a promenade position and back to a closed position for 2 minutes. ___

## Success Check
- The lead may be given at the end of any even-numbered basic step. ___
- The follower pivots on the ball of her left foot, either CW or CCW, on count 4. ___

# Drill 7
# Couple's Polka Turn

The couple's polka turn is fun to do and represents one of the most popular polka variations. Do at least two basic steps to set the tempo and connect with your partner in closed position (see figure 10.5a).

The lead for the couples' turn is twofold. The leader lowers and angles his extended left hand and arm below his waist at the same time that he raises his right elbow a few inches (cm). This downward angle of the leader's left hand and a firm right hand signals to the follower that the couple's polka turn is coming— and that the leader will be moving in front. By keeping his right hand firmly on his partner's left shoulder blade, it is a signal for the follower to execute her third basic step in place. On the third basic step, the leader moves ahead of the follower (see figure 10.5b). On the hop preceding the fourth basic step, both partners rotate clockwise a half turn. Now it is the leader's turn to execute the basic step in place. He signals the follower to move ahead toward the LOD by angling the arms from high to low toward the LOD (see figure 10.5c). Notice that you need to execute at least two more basic steps to resume a closed position.

**a** Two basics in closed position

**b** Leader moves in front on counts 1-&-2

**c** Follower moves in front on counts 3-&-4

**Figure 10.5** Clockwise couple's polka turn.

## TO DECREASE DIFFICULTY

- Focus your eyes toward the LOD during the *triple step* portion of the basic step.
- Practice the footwork without a partner using a very slow count.
- Add more basic steps in between each couple's turn.

## TO INCREASE DIFFICULTY

- Experiment with two or more consecutive couple's turns without any basic steps between them.
- Use a variety of polka music tempos.

## Success Goal

Alternate two polka basics forward (in closed position) and two polka basics for the CW couple's turn to slow polka music for 2 minutes. ___

## Success Check

- Notice that the basic steps are executed in sets of four or eight counts. ___
- The leader moves across and in front on the first triple step, then he brings the follower around on the second triple step. ___

# Drill 8
# Underarm Turn

An underarm turn is a variation that permits the follower to rotate 360 degrees via two half-turns. It is easy to lead an underarm turn from any of the three dance positions you know so far.

## From a Closed Position

For practice, the underarm turn takes a total of four basics. Do two basics and transition to a promenade position after count *4* as the leader simultaneously lifts his left hand to make an arch. The leader maintains contact with the follower's upper back to guide the follower's triple step facing the LOD on counts *5-and-6*, then she pivots 180 degrees CW on the ball of her right foot on count *6* to face the leader. On the fourth basic (counts *7-&-8*), the follower does a backward basic and resumes a closed dance position.

## From an Inside-Hands-Joined Position

For practice, the underarm turn takes a total of four basics. Do three basics, letting your inside hands naturally swing backward, forward, then backward,

respectively (see figure 10.6*a*). On the fourth basic, as the hands swing forward, the leader lifts his hand above the follower's head, extends two fingers for the follower to cup her hand around, and makes a small circular CW motion above her head. These actions lead the follower into a turn on the fourth basic (see figure 10.6*b*). Gradually let the arms swing backward on the next triple step with both outside feet (see figure 10.6*c*).

## From a Promenade Position

For practice, the underarm turn takes a total of four basics or eight counts. Do two basics to connect with your partner and the music. On the third one, the leader lifts his left hand to form an arch, while he keeps his right hand on the follower's left shoulder blade. This signals and guides the follower to execute her third basic forward with a CW half turn, or pivot, on her right foot on count *6*. The follower does a backward basic with a CW half turn on her left foot on count *8*. After the follower completes her turn, the leader lowers his left hand and resumes a promenade position.

**TO DECREASE DIFFICULTY**

- Without a partner, do a triple step forward with your right foot and make a CW half-turn on count 2, then do a triple step backward and make a CW half-turn on count 4.
- With a partner, slowly move through the body facings for the follower's underarm turn, then add footwork with a slow count.

**TO INCREASE DIFFICULTY**

- Do a continuous polka sequence with an underarm turn in each of the previous positions.
- Lead two turns in a row: The leader starts the turn by lifting his left hand, the follower does the turns, and the leader stops each turn by lowering his left hand.

**a** Inside arms swing back with outside feet    **b** Follower turns CW with inside feet

**c** Inside arms swing back with outside feet

**Figure 10.6** Underarm turn lead from the inside-hands-joined position.

## Success Goal

Execute polka basics with the underarm turn in each of three partner positions to slow polka music. ___

## Success Check

- The follower's pivots occur at the end of counts *2* or *4*. ___
- Take your time to execute a pivot at the end of each triple step. You don't need to rush. ___

# Drill 9
# Front-to-Front and Back-to-Back Half Turns

This variation is executed from an inside-hands-joined position and uses two basics and two pivots to complete a full turn (CW for the leader and CCW for the follower). For practice, take two basics to get connected with your partner and to let your inside hands swing naturally to the back, then to the front. On the next one, the leader faces the follower and grasps her right hand with his left hand, which modifies the basic to be *side, together, side* (and in a front-to-front position). Pivot a half turn on the next hop (the leader turns CW while the follower turns CCW). Do a *side, together, side* basic progression in this back-to-back position as the leader reaches back (and toward the LOD) with his right hand and palm up. The follower places her left hand in the leader's open palm. Repeat these actions twice for eight counts and two full turns. Pivot a half turn on the next hop to return to the inside-hands-joined position again and place your free hand on your hip.

### ▣ TO DECREASE DIFFICULTY
- Eliminate the back-to-back turn portion by executing four basics in the following directions: side, backward, side, forward. Face your partner on the first basic and grasp both hands (*side, together, side*). The leader releases his right hand and brings his left hand through the middle to face the RLOD as both do the second basic backward. The leader brings his left hand through the middle again to face his partner and grasp two hands to do the third basic (*side, together, side*). The leader releases his left hand and brings his right hand through the middle to face the LOD for the fourth basic forward.
- Use a slow tempo.

### ▣ TO INCREASE DIFFICULTY
- Try more than two consecutive repetitions of this variation.
- Create a combination linking this variation with at least one other variation that you know so far.

## *Success Goal*

Execute the polka basics from an inside-hands-joined position with front-to-front and back-to-back half turns to slow polka music for 2 minutes. ___

## Success Check

- Pivot a half turn on the *hop*. ___
- Modify the triple steps to be more of a slide or *side, together, side* when facing either front-to-front or back-to-back. ___
- Make a hand change on each basic, first when facing your partner, then when facing away from your partner. ___
- Look at your partner when facing front-to-front. ___

# Drill 10
# Gallops

Gallops are a popular variation from a promenade position. They are typically executed in eight counts. The rhythm for the gallops is *1, &-2, &-3, &-4, &-5, &-6, &-7-&-8.* Start with the leader's left foot and the follower's right foot. For the first six whole counts, step onto your lead foot, then bring your feet together with a weight change on the & cues. Keep the outside foot in the lead for six counts. To end the gallops, hop on your outside foot on the & cue and bring your inside foot forward, then do a polka basic on counts *7-&-8* with your inside foot (the leader's right foot and the follower's left foot). Try the gallops in the LOD whenever you have enough room to travel forward.

### TO DECREASE DIFFICULTY

- Execute the gallops by yourself to a slow count, gradually increasing the tempo to match slow polka music.
- Stand beside a partner without touching, try the gallops and be aware of the outside feet in the lead for six counts, then a polka basic with the inside feet.

### TO INCREASE DIFFICULTY

- Do two consecutive gallop variations without any basics in between.
- Gallop four times in promenade position with your outside feet, do a half-turn and continue with four more gallops with your inside feet, looking over the leader's right shoulder and the follower's left shoulder. Resume a promenade position on the next hop.

## *Success Goal*

Alternate four polka basics in promenade with the gallops variation to slow polka music for 2 minutes. ___

## *Success Check*

- Step, together (gallop) six times, then execute a polka basic (with inside feet).___
- Make a weight change on each rhythm cue. ___
- Make sure that you have enough room to execute the gallop variation. ___
- Maintain a V position with your partner's shoulders on the gallops instead of facing with your shoulders parallel. ___

## Drill 11
# Swivels, or Twists

The swivels, also called *twists*, variation combines two basic steps with four swivel steps. Each swivel gets one count, so the variation takes a total of eight counts. The swivels result from a twisting action on the ball of the sending foot as the receiving foot crosses in front. For styling, look at your partner when both outside feet swivel, then look in the LOD when both inside feet swivel.

### *Leader*

From a promenade position, execute at least two basics. At the end of the second one, hold your upper torso and arms very firm as you swivel on the ball of your right foot to angle toward your partner. This allows you to bring the left foot in front (see figure 10.7a). Then you swivel on the left foot and bring the right foot in front (see figure 10.7b). These two swivel-and-forward actions are repeated for a total of four swivels, one on each of four counts.

### *Follower*

After any two basics in promenade position, swivel on the ball of your left foot to angle toward your partner. This allows you to bring your right foot in front (review figure 10.7a). Swivel on your right foot and bring your left foot in front (review figure 10.7b). Repeat these two swivel-and-forward actions for a total of four swivels or twists, one on each of four counts.

a                                                    b

**Figure 10.7** Swivels, or twists, alternately position both partner's (a) outside feet forward, then (b) inside feet forward.

### TO DECREASE DIFFICULTY

- Without a partner, place your hands against a wall, lean into the wall, and practice swiveling your back foot and bringing the other foot in front, or crossing, on each whole count.
- Do four or more polka basics before executing the twist combination.

### TO INCREASE DIFFICULTY

- Experiment with either four or eight twists.
- Execute the twists with at least one other variation that you know so far.

## Success Goal

Alternate polka basics in promenade with four swivels to slow polka music for 2 minutes. ___

## Success Check

- Keep your knees slightly bent during the swivels. ___
- The arm and upper torso remains stationary while the lower body twists. ___
- Maintain a promenade position for two basic steps and four swivels. ___

# Drill 12
# Transition Leads Connecting Closed and Sweetheart Positions

Another partner position used in the polka is the sweetheart position. From a closed position, this transition groups six basics (two counts each, or a total of 12 counts) to make the transition to the sweetheart position. The leader remains facing the LOD while the follower makes 1 1/2 turns to face the LOD. The turns for the follower are divided into three half turns, which help with balance.

## Left Hand Arch and Hand-Change Leads

In closed position, take at least two basics to establish a tempo with your partner (see figure 10.8a). On the third basic, the leader lifts his left hand and arm to form an arch and presses with the heel of his right hand while keeping his right hand on the follower's upper back. This signals the follower to pivot 180 degrees CW on the ball of her left foot to face the LOD and execute her third basic starting with her right foot while facing the LOD (see figure 10.8b). At the end of count 6 of the third basic, the follower pivots 180 degrees clockwise on the ball of her right foot to face her partner as the leader transfers her hand from his left to his right hand (see figure 10.8c). Traveling backward, the follower executes her fourth basic. At the end of count 8 of the fourth basic, the leader continues with a

*(continued)*

### Drill 12 *(continued)*

small, CW, circular motion above the follower's head to signal her to do another 180-degree CW pivot on the ball of her left foot to face the LOD again (see figure 10.8*d*). As the follower's left hand passes the leader's left hand, he may grasp it.

Remember to position your hands just in front of the follower's shoulders and equidistant from her shoulders. Continue with two more basics (counts 9-&-10 and counts 11-&-12) while in the sweetheart position.

**a** Two basics in closed position

**b** Third basic with follower's half turn to face the LOD

**c** Fourth basic with follower's half turn to face the leader with a hand change

**d** Fifth basic with half turn to face LOD in sweetheart position

**Figure 10.8** Polka transition leads from the closed to the sweetheart position.

## *Right Hand CCW Loop and Hand-Change Leads*

The following transition uses eight counts or four basics to transition from the sweetheart position back to closed position. Take at least two basics in the sweetheart position. At the end of any second basic step (count 4), the follower's weight is on her left foot. The leader needs to time the lift of his right hand over the top of the follower's head to coincide with count 4, when the follower may pivot CCW on the ball of her left foot to face the leader again. The leader finishes the transition by placing the follower's right hand into his left hand and resuming a closed position.

### TO DECREASE DIFFICULTY

- Use a slow tempo, gradually moving from counts without music to practicing with music.
- Without any footwork, go through the timing of the hand and arm positions with your partner.

### TO INCREASE DIFFICULTY

- Practice with different partners.
- From a sweetheart position, the leader may keep his right hand above the follower's head to signal three half turns back to closed position. After two half turns, he changes hands and lowers them to resume a closed position.

## *Success Goal*

Execute 2 minutes of polka basics while transitioning from closed to sweetheart position, then back to closed position again. ___

## *Success Check*

- The follower should be approximately a half step in front of the leader when in the sweetheart position. ___
- The follower makes three CW half turns at the end of her triple step on counts 4, 6, and 8 to get to sweetheart position. ___
- The leader makes a hand change both into and out of the sweetheart position. ___

# Drill 13
# Around-the-World Variation

In the around-the-world polka variation, the leader is considered the *world* and the follower moves around him. For practice, this drill uses eight basics—four to set up and four to complete the around-the-world variation. The drill starts and ends in a sweetheart position. Both partners hold both hands throughout, using fingertip pressure.

Execute three forward polka basics in the sweetheart position (see figure 10.9*a*). On the fourth basic, the leader lowers his right hand and lifts his left hand over the follower's head to signal a half turn such that the follower is facing the reverse LOD (see figure 10.9*b*). The leader continues to bring his left hand over his own head and his right hand up by his right shoulder on the fifth basic, then places the follower's right arm behind his own head on the sixth basic. At this point, the follower should be halfway around and on the leader's left-hand side (see figure 10.9*c*). The leader continues to pull gently with his left hand and lifts his right hand over his own head and over the follower's head (see figure 10.9*d*) in order to bring the follower in front of him (on the seventh basic). On the eighth basic, the leader's right hand forms an arch for the follower to face the leader and move back to sweetheart position (see figure 10.9*e*).

## TO DECREASE DIFFICULTY

- Practice the leads without any footwork. Freeze and check each position.
- The leader may move slightly to one side or the other to decrease the distance that the follower needs to travel around him.

## TO INCREASE DIFFICULTY

- Start in a closed position and transition to the sweetheart position to execute the around-the-world variation, then transition back to closed position.
- Try only two basics before leading the around-the-world variation.

## Success Goal

Alternate four polka basics in sweetheart position with four basics to execute the around-the-world variation to slow polka music. ___

## Success Check

- The leader executes four basics in place, taking small steps. ___
- The follower starts to move clockwise around the leader on the fifth basic. ___
- On the sixth basic, the follower should be on the leader's left side. ___
- Take two more basics to get back to sweetheart position. ___
- The follower faces the leader as she continues the clockwise rotation. ___

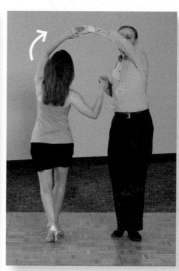

**a** Three basics in sweetheart position

**b** Follower's CW half turn on the fourth polka basic

**c** Fifth and sixth polka basics to bring follower to leader's left side

**d** Seventh polka basic to pull with leader's left hand and right hand over follower's head

**e** Continue into sweetheart position on eighth polka basic

**Figure 10.9** Around-the-world variation executed within eight polka basics from a sweetheart position.

# Drill 14
# Reverse Around-the-World Variation

The reverse around-the-world variation takes four basics for the leader to bring the follower around him in a CCW direction. Start in a sweetheart position (see figure 10.10a) and do four basics to connect with your partner and the tempo. Then, the leader executes his next four basics in place as he gives the following leads, for a total of eight basics.

From the sweetheart position, the leader gently pulls in a CCW direction with both hands as he brings his right hand over the follower's head on the fifth basic and slightly lowers his left hand (see figure 10.10b). Then he continues his gentle CCW pull, placing his right hand (and the follower's right arm) over and behind his own head. His left arm extends from his left shoulder, with the follower now on his left-hand side (on the sixth basic, which is shown in figure 10.10c). As the leader continues to pull in a CCW direction with his right hand, he lifts up with his left hand over both his own head and the follower's head on the seventh basic, as shown in figure 10.10d. The leader continues to pull with his right hand as the follower goes under his left-hand arch (see figure 10.10e). Finish the follower's turn back to the sweetheart position on the eighth basic (see figure 10.10f).

### TO DECREASE DIFFICULTY
- Practice the arm leads without any footwork. Freeze and check your positions.
- Use an even number of polka basics preceding the reverse around-the-world variation.

### TO INCREASE DIFFICULTY
- Try this variation with different partners.
- Add the transition from closed to sweetheart position, then lead the reverse around-the-world variation and transition back to closed position.
- Combine the around-the-world variation with the reverse around-the-world variation.

## Success Goal

Alternate four polka basics in the sweetheart position with four polka basics to execute the reverse around-the-world variations to slow polka music for 2 minutes. ___

## Success Check

- The leader needs to take small steps in place. ___
- The follower needs to be on the leader's left side after two basics.___
- The follower needs to face the leader as she is lead in the CCW rotation.___
- Use fingertip pressure to correct with your partner.___

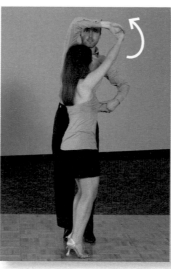

a Four basics in sweetheart position

b Leader's right hand pulls CCW on fifth basic

c Follower on leader's left side on sixth basic

d Leader pulls with his right hand as he lifts his left hand over his own head

e Leader continues pulling with his right hand as follower turns CCW on seventh basic

f Back to sweetheart position on eighth basic

**Figure 10.10** Reverse around-the-world variation executed within eight polka basics from a sweetheart position.

# Drill 15
# On Your Own: Combining Three Polka Positions

Your challenge with the polka is to select one variation from at least three partner positions to create your own combinations using variations from each position covered in this book, as in the following chart. Review the previous transition drills for connecting these positions if necessary.

*(continued)*

Drill 15 *(continued)*

| Inside-hands-joined position | • Polka basics<br>• Underarm turn<br>• Front-to-front, back-to-back half turns |
|---|---|
| Promenade position | • Polka basics<br>• Underarm turn<br>• Gallops<br>• Swivels, or twists |
| Closed Position | • Polka basics<br>• Underarm turn<br>• Couple's turn |
| Sweetheart Position | • Polka basics<br>• Around-the-world variation<br>• Reverse around-the-world variation |

### TO DECREASE DIFFICULTY

- Put together three combinations linking at least three variations from at least two partner positions using any number of polka basic steps.
- Write down your favorite combinations and refer to them as needed.

### TO INCREASE DIFFICULTY

- Put together one long combination linking at least six variations and four partner positions.
- Practice with a variety of partners.

## *Success Goal*

Perform four different combinations linking at least three variations from at least three different partner positions. ___

## *Success Check*

- Make transitions smooth and fluid. ___
- Maintain a constant tempo as appropriate to the music selected. ___
- Keep your CPB over your working foot, especially on the triple steps. ___

# SUCCESS SUMMARY FOR POLKA

The polka is a lively dance that is just plain fun to do. The basic step is challenging because it combines a hop and a triple step that must be executed quickly to match the music tempo and repeated on both sides of the body. It takes four beats or counts before your starting foot is free again. You have many transition options, and you can use several partner positions. One transition option is from an inside-hands-joined position to a promenade and back to an inside-hands-joined position. Another transition option is from a closed position to a promenade position and back to closed position again. Once you can transition between partner positions, you can add turns and other variations that are characteristic of the polka. Smooth transitions make you look good! For added styling, place your free hand on your hip. Remember that the polka rhythmic step pattern uses four counts, or two measures of 2/4 time music. Thus, the variations also group a minimum of four counts. Keep building up your endurance for dancing the polka!

# Cha-Cha

## *Being Flirtatious*

The cha-cha is one of the most popular Latin dances. It was originally called the *cha-cha-cha* in Cuba during the mid-1950s to reflect the three quick steps used in the footwork and the calypso sounds heard in the music. Finding "cha-cha-cha" cumbersome to say, however, Americans shortened the name to *cha-cha*. The Latin influence on the cha-cha means it alternates between smooth and staccato movements, requiring coordination and control and a blending of other dances. In particular, it slows down the timing yet still breaks on count 2, as in the mambo, and it adds a modified triple step from the swing. A break step is a change of direction using a rocking motion, such as stepping forward and backward or backward and forward. Some even refer to the cha-cha as a *triple mambo* because of the combining of the break step with three small steps to the side. The cha-cha is done to 4/4 time music with four beats to a measure, each beat getting one count, and two measures of music grouped together before your starting foot is free again.

The cha-cha is also characterized by Cuban motion in that the upper body remains level while the lower body moves. Cuban motion results from alternately bending one knee as you straighten the other—the hips only *appear* to do all the work! The leg bearing the weight has a straight knee, whereas the non-weight-bearing leg is positioned with a bent knee, which results in a delayed weight change. It takes a lot of practice to achieve proper Cuban motion.

The styling for the cha-cha is flirtatious. For instance, on turns you might look at your partner out of the corners of your eyes as you turn your head slightly to tease and challenge your partner to follow or look at you. Another way to give the illusion of a challenge is to alternately follow your partner's forward and backward movements—one advances and the other retreats. Thus, you seem to be connected, but you are actually approximately 2 feet (0.6 m) apart and facing each other in the shine position.

Another unique styling of the cha-cha is the addition of hand movements, or *talking* with your hands. Initially, you can talk with your hands by keeping your elbows bent 90 degrees and fairly close to your sides, but allowing them to move approximately 45 degrees either forward or backward from your shoulder joints. Then let your forearms, wrists, and hands rotate freely with the flow of your movements.

# RHYTHMIC STEP PATTERN FOR CHA-CHA

The rhythmic step pattern for cha-cha combines a break step (two weight changes in two counts to execute a change of direction that propels the body in a new direction on each step) with a triple step (three weight changes in two counts) that is executed twice for a total of eight counts. The break step is an agility move that alternates a forward-to-backward or a backward-to-forward direction change. The triple step is called the *cha-cha-cha* steps. The downbeat in cha-cha music occurs on count 1, or the first beat of each four-beat measure, while the break step occurs on counts 2, 3. The styling of *breaking on count two* fits the music best, which changed in the 1980s. A common way to count the cha-cha rhythmic step pattern starts with the break step as follows: *2, 3, 4, &-1*. Because it takes two measures, or eight counts, and two repetitions of the cha-cha rhythmic step pattern before your starting foot is free again, you may count each measure using the cues *2, 3, 4-&-1; 2, 3, 4-&-1*. Or, alternatively, you may count two measures of music together as follows: *2, 3, 4, &-5, 6, 7, 8, &-1* which places the forward break step and replace step on counts 2, 3, and the backward break step and replace step on counts 6, 7. Either method of counting the two measures is acceptable.

The *cha-cha-cha* steps (triple step) may be executed while traveling to either the right or the left side or in a forward or in a backward direction. When you move to the side, you are following an H-shaped floor path (see figure 11.1). This floor path is very versatile for sideward travel and offers many variation options. Thus, the basic H floor path is considered home base for executing the cha-cha rhythmic step pattern. Come back to the basic H floor path after doing selected cha-cha variations that will be covered in the drills.

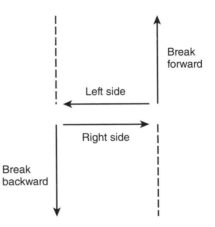

**Figure 11.1**  Basic H floor path represents home base for cha-cha.

Both partners execute the cha-cha rhythmic step pattern by splitting it into two halves defined by the direction of the break steps: a forward half basic includes a forward break step, and a backward half basic includes a backward break step. The follower does the mirror reverse. For example, when the leader is breaking forward, then the follower is breaking backward. And, when the leader travels to his left side on the cha-cha-cha steps, the follower is executing them to her right side, and vice versa. Each direction for the break step is described separately. Each half basic takes one measure.

### Forward Half Basic

Your left foot should be free to initiate the forward break portion of the cha-cha rhythmic step pattern that completes half of the basic H floor path. For the first weight change on count 2, place your left foot forward and shift your weight onto that foot. For the second weight change on count 3, shift your weight back onto your right foot using a replace step by lifting and lowering that foot in its original location. Throughout the break step weight changes, keep your upper torso centered above both feet, rather than letting your upper torso move beyond your base of support. Your left foot is now free to execute a triple step (stepping left, right, left) on counts 4-&-1 as you move either to your left side, or backward, on the *cha-cha-cha* steps.

### Backward Half Basic

Your right foot should be free to initiate the backward break portion of the cha-cha rhythmic step pattern that completes half of the basic H-shaped floor path. For the first weight change on count 2, place the ball of your right foot slightly behind the heel of your left foot and transfer your weight onto *only* the ball of your right foot yet place your whole foot on the floor as you slightly lift your left foot off the floor. On the second weight change on count 3, transfer your weight forward onto your left foot, replacing your weight and keeping that foot in its original location. As you execute the backward break step, you need to keep your upper torso centered above both feet, much like an agility drill so that you can quickly shift your weight, or like marching in place. Now your right foot is free to execute a triple step (right, left, right) on counts 4-&-1 as you move either to your right side, or forward, on the *cha-cha-cha* steps.

The rhythmic step pattern for the cha-cha may be initiated from a shine position, a one- or two-hands-joined position, or a closed position. Figure 11.2 shows various ways that you might organize the counts and footwork for repeating the eight-count cha-cha rhythmic step pattern. Some cues will be more helpful to you than others. Select those cues that most help you retain how to execute each half of the rhythmic step pattern whether traveling to the side, or alternating forward and backward, on the triple step. Notice that the forward half basic always starts with your left foot (and a forward break), while the backward half basic always starts with your right foot (and a backward break).

## Figure 11.2   RHYTHMIC STEP PATTERN FOR CHA-CHA

### Footwork Cues

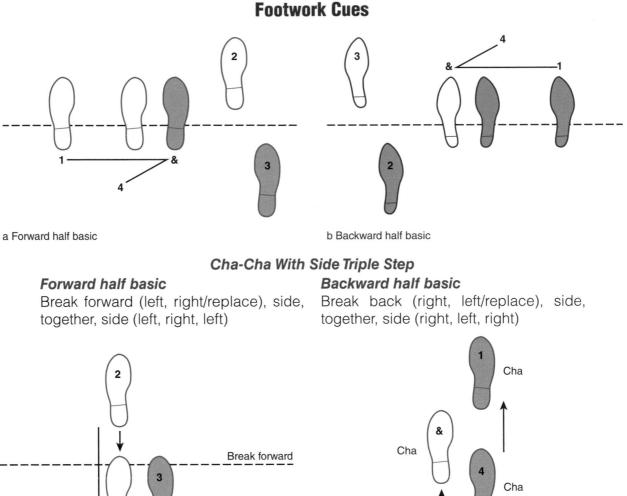

a Forward half basic

b Backward half basic

### Cha-Cha With Side Triple Step

**Forward half basic**
Break forward (left, right/replace), side, together, side (left, right, left)

**Backward half basic**
Break back (right, left/replace), side, together, side (right, left, right)

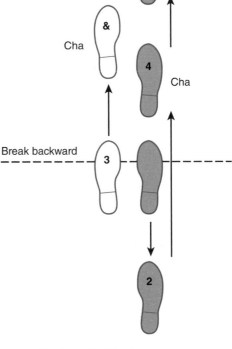

c Forward half basic

d Backward half basic

### Cha-Cha With Forward/Backward Triple Step

**Forward half basic**
Break forward (left, right/replace), back, back, back (left, right, left)

**Backward half basic**
Break back (right, left/replace), forward, forward, forward (right, left, right)

## Timing Cues

| | |
|---|---|
| 4/4 time signature: | Four beats to a measure (group two measures) |
| Duration: | Each beat gets one count (total of eight counts) |
| Rhythm: | Quick, quick, triple step; quick, quick, triple step |
| Counts: | Either 2, 3, 4-&-5, 6, 7, 8-&-1 (breaks occur on counts 2, 3 and on counts 6, 7); or 2, 3, 4-&-1; 2, 3, 4-&-1 (break occurs on counts 2, 3 for each half) |
| Weight changes: | 10 (on each cue) |
| Direction of steps: | Break—Forward, backward/replace; or backward, forward/replace |
| | Triple step—Back-back-back, or forward-forward-forward; left side, or right side |
| Foot positions: | Cha-cha with side triple step—Fourth, fourth, second, first, second; Fourth, fourth, second, first, second |
| | Cha-cha with forward/backward triple step—Fourth, fourth, fourth, first (or fifth), fourth; Fourth, fourth, fourth, first (or fifth), fourth |
| Floor contact: | Ball–flat, ball–flat, ball–flat, ball, ball–flat; Ball–flat, ball–flat, ball–flat, ball, ball–flat |

## STARTING OPTIONS

As noted earlier, each half of the cha-cha rhythmic step pattern is often described with the break that occurs on counts 2, 3 (and on counts 6, 7, if grouping two measures). What happens on count 1? How can you start the rhythmic step pattern for the cha-cha to best match the music? Three common options are described next. Try each and select the one you like best; all work fine! Each option includes an action (or nonaction) that may be used on count 1 as follows: (1) a side step with your normal starting foot (i.e., the leader's left foot and the follower's right foot), (2) a hold (i.e., a wait or a freeze) for one count, then break with your normal starting foot, or (3) a step sideways or shifting of weight onto your nonstarting foot (i.e., the leader's right foot and the follower's left foot), then break with your normal starting foot. Each option is described in more detail as follows.

### Starting Option 1

In the first starting option, use your normal starting foot to take a preparatory side step on the downbeat (or count 1 of the four-beat measure), then do a break step. That is, the leader steps to his left side with his left foot, and the follower steps to her right side with her right foot on the downbeat. The leader's right foot is then free, and he can break backward from this position. At the same time, the follower's left foot is free, and she can break forward from this position. You also need to consider when to begin this starter option. In order to match the eight-count rhythmic step pattern to the music that has miniphrases of eight beats, you need to begin on count 5 (and the leader breaks back on count 6). All you need to do is to mentally count *1, 2, 3, 4* (one measure), then begin moving on the second measure. This ensures that the leader always breaks forward on count 2 and backward on count 6. However, there are no dance police on the dance floor, so you can choose to break on count 2 by counting each half of the basic step progression if that option is easiest for you for you.

### Starting Option 2

A second starting option is to hold (not move) on count 1, so that the leader's left foot is free to do a forward break on count 2 (and the follower's right foot is free to do a backward break). Notice that once you get started, the third *cha* step occurs on the downbeat (first count of each measure), so it may help to imagine that the preparatory side step (whether it is a weight shift or a hold) coincides with the last *cha*. So, mentally count *5, 6, 7, 8, 1,* and do the leader's forward break on count 2.

### Starting Option 3

A third starting option is to step or shift your weight onto the side with your nonstarting foot. In this option, the leader steps (shifts weight) from his left foot onto his right foot to his right side on count 1. Then, he continues with a forward break (starting on count 2). The follower shifts her weight from her right foot to her left foot, and she continues with a backward break on count 2. This option can be cumbersome when dancing with a partner who is not used to starting with the opposite foot. However, it achieves the goal of permitting the leader to break forward on count 2 and backward on count 6. Most dancers choose starting option 1.

# DRILLS FOR CHA-CHA

The cha-cha is a Latin dance done to 4/4 time music. It contrasts slow and sustained with quick and staccato actions during the break step and the triple step, respectively. The rhythmic step pattern for the cha-cha combines a break step on counts 2, 3, with a triple step on counts 4, &-1. It is repeated twice before your starting foot is free again. The triple step may be executed to either side or in a forward or in a backward direction. For each drill, read the directions, and watch the video demonstrations on the enclosed DVD to see (a) how to execute the selected cha-cha variations, and (b) how to combine them into short practice combinations. Then, practice until you can meet the Success Goal for each drill. Use track 16 to practice your cha-cha moves.

## Drill 1
## Execution Challenge for the Cha-Cha

The rhythmic step pattern for the cha-cha is composed of a break step and a triple step executed twice. Remember that the break step takes two counts and is a way to change directions quickly, shifting weight either forward to backward or backward to forward. The triple step includes three weight changes in two beats of music. The triple step may be executed either to the right or left side or forward or backward (review figure 11.2, *a-d*). After each forward break (starting with your left foot), your left foot is free to do a triple step either to your left side, or moving backward. After each backward break (starting with your right foot), your right foot is free to do a triple step either to your right side, or moving forward. Stand facing a partner in shine position, approximately an arm's length apart.

Choose one of the three starting options for count 1 so that you can coordinate the break steps to coincide with counts 2, 3 and 6, 7, when counting two measures together. Try the cha-cha rhythmic step pattern first to slow counts, then with music. For practice, combine the four different directions by executing the cha-cha rhythmic step pattern in the H floor path twice (for 16 counts), then in a forward and backward direction twice (for 16 counts).

## TO DECREASE DIFFICULTY

- Face a partner with fingertips and palms touching (halfway between the two of you) and use multiple repetitions of the rhythmic step pattern.

- Select or imagine the desired floor path (either an H floor path or a straight line on the floor) that you can follow while repeating this drill.

- Ask an observer to give you feedback on how precisely you move in the four directions. It should be easy for an observer to identify in which direction you are traveling. Avoid traveling on a diagonal at this point.

## TO INCREASE DIFFICULTY

- Review foot positions for more precise execution.
- Repeat the drill using a closed dance position.

## Success Goal

For 2 minutes, alternately execute the cha-cha rhythmic step pattern (a) following an H floor path, then (b) moving in a forward or backward direction. ___

## Success Check

- A forward break shifts weight forward onto the left foot on count 2, then back onto the ball of the right foot on count 3. ___

- A backward break shifts weight backward onto the ball of the right foot on count 6, then forward onto the left foot on count 7. ___

- Triple step uses three weight changes in two beats of music. ___

- Each triple step occurs on either counts 4-&-1 (per measure) or counts 4-&-5 and 8-&-1 (two measures together). ___

## Drill 2
# Leads Into and From Shine Position

The shine position is a featured position in the cha-cha; it lets the dancers *shine*, or express their personality, when not holding hands. The elbows are primarily at a 90-degree angle, which places the hands in front of the body. Thus, whenever the leader chooses to close up and resume another dance position, he can find the follower's hands. This drill alternates a two-hands-joined position (see figure 11.3) with a shine position. Notice that the leader's thumbs are under the follower's palms and his fingers are on top, when using a two-hands-joined position in cha-cha. Later, this modification is automatically used with the leader's left hand when moving from a closed position. Execute the cha-cha rhythmic step pattern while traveling in a forward/backward direction to experience how to connect two different dance positions.

**Figure 11.3**  Modified two-hands-joined position hand grasp for the cha-cha.

### *Release Both Hands*

From a two-hands-joined position, the leader may release both hands to get into a shine position. It is easy to take advantage of the momentum during your forward and backward direction changes to make your transition. Thus, after any backward break, the leader can release both hands and take smaller steps on his forward triple step to let the follower get farther away (or open up the space between them) to be in a shine position.

### *Resume Partner Contact*

The leader also has many options for resuming contact with the follower from a shine position. For example, after any backward break, the leader can simply travel farther on his forward triple step to close up the space between him and his partner and resume a two-hands-joined position.

## TO DECREASE DIFFICULTY

- Practice each position option separately.
- Use a slow tempo.

## TO INCREASE DIFFICULTY

- Alternately transition from a shine position to a closed position.
- Change partners frequently.

### Success Goal

Perform 10 smoothly executed transitions alternating a two-hands-joined position and a shine position. ___

### Success Check

- Keep the elbows at about a 90-degree angle when separated from your partner and not holding hands (in shine position). ___
- The leader releases his hand grasps to transition to shine position. ___
- The leader moves forward and closer to the follower on the triple step to grasp two hands.

  ___
- Group a minimum of two measures (8 counts) before moving into another position. ___

## Drill 3
## Add Styling

In the shine position, imagine that horizontal strings are connecting the two of you at your shoulders, hips, and ankles. As one moves either forward or backward, the other automatically follows in unison. This invisible connection helps you to move fluidly with your partner and also presents you both with the challenge of following the other's directional changes.

Once you can move as a unit with a partner, experiment with *talking* with your hands: Keep your elbows at approximately 90-degree angles, but let them move forward and backward approximately 45 degrees in either direction from your shoulder joints. It is natural for one arm to swing forward as the other swings backward. Notice that these arm actions are opposite of the leg or foot actions; your right elbow and forearm swing forward when your left foot is forward and your left elbow and forearm swing forward when your right foot is forward. As you become more comfortable with repeating the basic step pattern, you'll soon find that your forearms, wrists, and hands rotate freely as you execute your movements. Have fun with it.

*(continued)*

Drill 3  *(continued)*

### TO DECREASE DIFFICULTY

- Practice your footwork and timing without a partner.
- Mentally count the rhythm (2, 3, 4-&-1) during each measure of cha-cha music to match your actions to the tempo of the music.

### TO INCREASE DIFFICULTY

- Use a variety of cha-cha music selections with different tempos.
- In closed position, use an H-shaped floor path, then transition to a shine position and forward/backward triple steps after the leader's forward break step. Do a minimum of eight counts in each position.

## Success Goal

Execute the cha-cha rhythmic step pattern while in shine position (executing triple steps in a forward/backward direction) with at least two partners using slow cha-cha music. ___

## Success Check

- Bend the elbows approximately 90 degrees. ___
- Let the wrists, hands, and forearms rotate freely to gesture as you move. ___
- Fluid movements connect with the music. ___
- Maintain the rhythm. ___

# Drill 4
# Chase

Both of the following variations in the shine position exemplify the teasing and flirting with the eyes that are characteristic of the cha-cha, because you continue to look over your shoulder toward your partner as long as you can on each turn. The half-chase variation involves a minimum of two half-turns (eight counts), and the full chase involves a full turn (four counts).

Both variations involve a follow-the-leader challenge such that the leader does a variation and then the follower must repeat that same variation. Both partners do the same footwork, except the follower executes the variation four counts later. This alternating process continues until the leader stops turning and remains facing front and his partner, which nonverbally signals that the chase is over.

## Half Chase

As its name implies, the half chase involves a half turn. The half chase starts with the leader's forward half basic. As usual, he steps forward onto his left foot on count 2 to start his forward break step. He pivots clockwise (CW) 180 degrees on the balls of his feet before transferring his weight onto his right foot on count 3. The leader has his back to his partner as he travels forward to execute his *cha-cha-cha* steps on counts 4-&-1.

To face his partner again, the leader steps forward with his right foot on count 2. He pivots 180 degrees CCW on the balls of both feet and shifts his weight forward onto the ball of his left foot on count 3. The leader then continues traveling forward with his triple step on counts 4-&-1. After eight counts, the leader's left foot is free again, and he has two options: to continue the half chase or to end it. If the leader decides to continue the half chase, the follower will see his back. If he decides to end the variation, the follower will be facing her partner again.

## Full Chase

The full chase is similar to the half chase, except that a full turn occurs. To execute the full turn, repeat the half chase directions on counts 2 and 3. However, on counts 4-&-1, continue to rotate clockwise during your small *cha-cha-cha* steps by rotating your toes slightly clockwise with each step to complete another 180-degree turn (see figure 11.4). The leader completes his full turn, after which it is the follower's turn to complete her full turn.

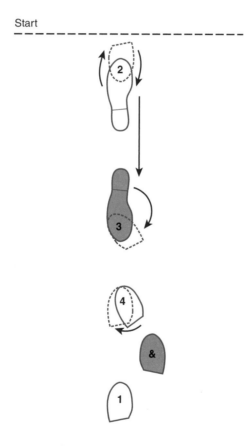

**Figure 11.4** Foot positions on the full chase turn.

*(continued)*

Drill 4   *(continued)*

### TO DECREASE DIFFICULTY

- Execute the turns without a partner. On the half chase, imagine opening and shutting a door to help you remember which way to turn. On the full chase, continue all the way around.
- Face a partner, do basic steps, and slowly go through the half chase, starting the pivot when the leader's left foot is free. The follower starts her pivot when her left foot is free.

### TO INCREASE DIFFICULTY

- The leader may randomly alternate half and full chases.
- Experiment with a double chase (by executing a double turn). Make a half turn on counts 2 and 3, then complete a 1 1/2 turn on counts 4-&-1 so as to face your partner again.

## Success Goal

Alternate cha-cha basics in shine position with (a) four half chases, then (b) a full chase to slow cha-cha music for 2 minutes. ___

## Success Check

- Shift your weight on each break step whether executing a half or a full chase. ___
- Orient the directions of the half turns according to your own midline. Imagine that your midline initially faces 12 o'clock. Thus, during the half chase, alternately turn CW (from 12 o'clock to 6 o'clock) and CCW (from 6 o'clock back to 12 o'clock). ___

# Drill 5
# Cross and Hop Variation

From a shine position, this variation may be executed on any forward half basic. Either partner may initiate this variation while the other does the backward half basic. Cross your left foot over your right foot and shift your weight onto your left foot on count 2. Cross your right foot over your left foot and shift your weight onto your right on count 3. On the & before count 4, add a hop in the backward direction with your right foot. Then continue traveling backward with your *cha-cha-cha* steps (left, right, left).

### TO DECREASE DIFFICULTY

- Match each position with a cue, *cross left, cross right, hop, cha-cha-cha,* giving the hop a half beat, or an & cue.
- Leave out the hop.

## TO INCREASE DIFFICULTY

- During the hop, accent it by lifting your arms to form a diagonal line, with your left arm placed high above your head and your right arm placed below your waist.
- Randomly alternate any of the chase variations with the cross and hop variation.

### Success Goal

Perform eight repetitions of the cross and hop to slow cha-cha music. ___

### Success Check

- Start this variation with your left foot, while your partner does a backward half basic. ___
- To execute the hop, bend your right knee, push off, and land on your right foot. ___
- This variation takes four total counts. ___

# Drill 6
# Closed Position to a Two-Hands-Joined Position

In the cha-cha, the closed position may be modified slightly for styling. If you choose to add this modification, then bend the arms of your joined hands at the elbow and bring them closer together in the center space between you until your forearms almost touch. Even if you don't elect to use this modification, notice the distance between you and your partner when in a closed position. Imagine a centerline or wall is separating you. Most of the leads in the cha-cha initiate from this centerline. Each partner has one half of the shared space. Avoid moving your hands either beyond or behind the centerline that indicates your half of the partner position. Start in closed position with your partner for the following transitions.

basic steps to establish a tempo with your partner. After any backward break step with the right foot, as the leader shifts his weight forward onto his left foot, he may press gently through the palm of his left hand into the follower's right hand. If the center hands are kept in the same location, then the follower is signaled to take a larger back step (at the end of her forward break step). At the same time, the leader also needs to release his right hand. These actions signal the follower to move, or *float,* away as both continue with a triple step to the side and into a two-hands-joined position. Continue the cha-cha rhythmic step pattern using the basic H floor path and the two-hands-joined position.

### Float Away

Following the basic H-shaped floor path (with the triple to the side), take some

### Close Up

To resume a closed position, the leader may use the same backward break step

*(continued)*

**Drill 6** *(continued)*

and hand pressure to signal that he is going to move closer to the follower during his right side *cha-cha-cha* steps. The leader also releases his right hand and prepares to put it on the follower's left shoulder blade during his right side triple step. This signals the follower to lift her left elbow to put her hand on the leader's right shoulder. Both continue the cha-cha rhythmic step pattern in a closed position.

### TO DECREASE DIFFICULTY

- Keep your elbows and hands in front of your shoulders so that you can take advantage of your body's weight shift from backward to forward during any backward break step.
- Remember to maintain your frame in each position.

### TO INCREASE DIFFICULTY

- Float away to a one-hand-joined position (his left, her right) as you follow the H-shaped floor path, then close up to resume to a closed position.
- Add an underarm turn from a one-hand-joined position. The leader may lift his left hand to make an arch during his left side *cha-cha-cha* steps so that the follower can prepare to execute an underarm turn by angling her right foot outward on count 1. On count 2, the follower does a pivot turn starting with her left foot to the side wall (see figure 11.5a). She pivots and shifts her weight from her left onto her right foot to face the opposite side on count 3 (see figure 11.5b), then she continues the CW turn to face her partner as both execute the side triple step (alternating with her left, right, left foot).

**a** Arch lead with follower's left foot to start the pivot

**b** Shift onto the follower's right foot during the pivot

**Figure 11.5** Follower's underarm turn during the leader's backward break step.

## Success Goal

Perform 10 smoothly executed transitions from closed position to a two-hands-joined position and back to closed position again. ___

# Drill 7
# First Position Break Steps

From a two-hands-joined position, this variation alternates between second position (where feet are approximately shoulder-width apart) and a first position (where feet are together). On count 1, the leader steps to his left with his left foot to be in a second foot position. The follower steps to her right onto her right foot on count 1. On counts 2, 3, bring your feet together (with a weight change), and remain in first foot position as you make a second weight change onto your other foot. These two break steps are taken in place for two counts: The leader steps right, left while the follower steps left, right. Then, do a side triple step on counts 4-&-1. Repeat the first position breaks with your *feet, together* actions on the other side on counts 2, 3, then a side triple step.

**TO DECREASE DIFFICULTY**

- Without a partner, practice foot positions to clearly distinguish between second position and first position.
- Bring the feet together on counts 2, 3 and on the & of the triple steps (side, together, side).
- Avoid keeping your feet apart in second position throughout.

**TO INCREASE DIFFICULTY**

- Alternate first position breaks with the cha-cha half basics in an H-shaped floor path, using a minimum of two repetitions of each.
- The leader may initiate the first position break starting with either his left or his right foot and repeat at least two half basics.

*(continued)*

Drill 7 *(continued)*

### *Success Goal*

Alternate the cha-cha basics with a triple to the side with first position breaks to slow cha-cha music for 2 minutes. ___

- Clearly differentiate between second position and first position while maintaining the cha-cha rhythmic step pattern.___
- Execute two weight changes with feet together on the first position breaks. ___

# Drill 8
# Parallel (Outside Partner) Break Steps

When in a closed position, this variation permits two options: either to break forward or to break backward. The direction is determined by the leader's position. Using the basic H-shaped floor path, the leader may substitute parallel breaks during the regular breaks. In parallel, both partners' shoulders and feet should angle 45 degrees with the feet in a forward–backward stride position. From the leader's point of view, he may do his break steps either along a forward diagonal or a backward diagonal.

## *Forward Parallel Break Steps*

On both sides, the leader steps diagonally forward and outside his partner's feet during the forward parallel break steps. On the last of the *cha-cha-cha* steps to the leader's right side, he slightly angles his right foot outward and he slightly rotates his upper torso to face his right front diagonal direction. This angle facilitates a forward parallel break step with the leader's left foot to step forward in this new direction, keeping his feet parallel and outside his partner (see figure 11.6a). The leader continues with the *cha-cha-cha* steps directly to his left side and repeats the variation on the other side by angling 45 degrees to face his left front diagonal and does a parallel break step forward with his right foot and

outside his partner. To resume a closed dance position and the basic H-shaped floor path, the leader needs to keep his shoulders parallel with his partner without angling. On both sides, the follower does parallel break steps backward with her feet in fifth foot position as the leader does parallel break steps forward.

## *Backward Parallel Break Steps*

On both sides, the leader steps diagonally backward as the follower steps outside his feet during the backward parallel breaks. On the last of the right sideways *cha-cha-cha* steps, he slightly angles his right foot inward and rotates his upper torso to face his left front diagonal direction. This facilitates a backward parallel break step with his left foot (see figure 11.6b) while the follower does a forward parallel break step with her right foot outside her partner's foot. The leader repeats the *cha-cha-cha* steps to his left side and rotates his shoulders and upper body to face his right front diagonal to facilitate parallel breaks backward with his right foot (while the follower does a forward parallel break step with her left foot outside her partner's foot). The leader resumes a closed position not by rotating, but rather by remaining squared up, with parallel shoulders, to his partner.

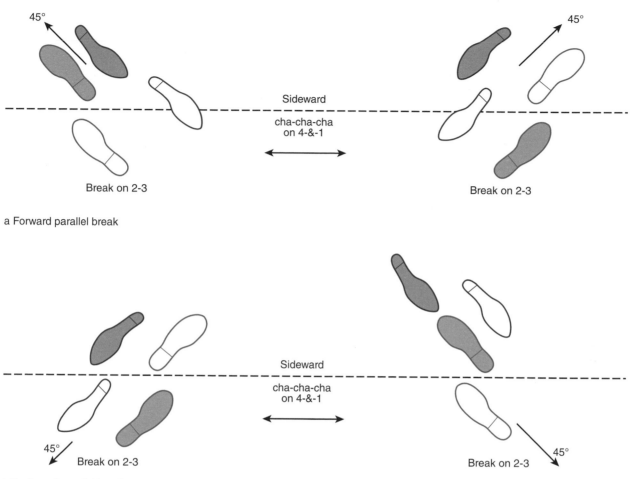

45°

Sideward
cha-cha-cha
on 4-&-1

←——————→

Break on 2-3

45°

Break on 2-3

a Forward parallel break

Sideward
cha-cha-cha
on 4-&-1

←——————→

45°

Break on 2-3

45°

Break on 2-3

b Backward parallel break

**Figure 11.6** The leader breaks (a) forward and outside his partner's foot on the forward parallel break step, and (b) backward on a backward parallel break step as the follower steps forward and outside her partner's foot.

### TO DECREASE DIFFICULTY

- Without a partner, practice your foot positions to clearly distinguish between regular and parallel break step placements for the feet and body. Ask an observer to provide feedback, or use tape on the floor or select other reference points that help show forward and backward as opposed to diagonal forward and diagonal backward directions.

- Place your arms on your partner's to feel the shoulders rotating 45 degrees CW or CCW.

### TO INCREASE DIFFICULTY

- Alternate forward parallel break steps with backward parallel break steps using any multiple of two repetitions of each.

- Combine either parallel break steps with any one other variation, such as an underarm turn at the end (when back to the basic H-shaped floor path).

*(continued)*

Drill 8   (continued)

## Success Goal

Alternate cha-cha half basics (a) with four forward parallel break steps, and (b) with four backward parallel break steps to slow cha-cha music for 2 minutes. ___

- If a proper closed dance connection is maintained, the follower will be aware of whether or not the leader's shoulders are angling 45 degrees preceding the break steps. ___

- On the last of the leader's right sideways *cha-cha-cha* steps, his shoulders angle 45 degrees CW (to parallel break step forward) or CCW (to parallel break step backward). ___

- Square up (keep shoulders parallel) with your partner's shoulders on the sideways *cha-cha-cha* steps. ___

- Execute a minimum of two parallel break steps, one on each side. ___

- Each of the parallel breaks start with the leader's left foot. ___

# Drill 9
# Fifth Position Break Steps

From a closed position, these break steps, called *fifth position breaks*, offer another variation using backward break steps by both partners at the same time. In this modification of the backward parallel break step, a fifth position foot placement angles the big toe of one foot beside the heel of the other foot.

Start with the basic step in an H-shaped floor path. At the end of the leader's right sideways *cha-cha-cha* steps, he needs to indicate to the follower to break step backward with him. His leads include releasing his left hand and gently pressing with the heel of his right hand on the follower's left shoulder blade, which causes both partners to open arms as they face the leader's left side. Keeping the outside arms symmetrical, the leader can then do the first break step backward with his left foot, and the follower can break step backward with her right foot (see figure 11.7a). The leader faces the follower on his left side *cha-cha-cha* steps as he places his left hand on the follower's right shoulder blade and releases his right hand (see figure 11.7b). Both partners open their outside arms to face the leader's right side to do the second backward break in fifth position using the leader's right foot and the follower's left foot (see figure 11.7c). Continue with another triple step to the leader's right side to do the third repetition of the fifth position break (leader's left foot and follower's right foot). After the fourth repetition of the fifth position break, resume a closed position (see figure 11.7d).

**a** Both partners do a fifth position break (on leader's right side) and open free arms

**b** Face partner as leader places his left hand on follower's right shoulder blade and releases right hand

**c** Both partners do a fifth position break (on leader's left side) and open free arms

**d** Resume closed position

**Figure 11.7** Fifth position break steps.

## TO DECREASE DIFFICULTY

- Without a partner, check that your foot placement is in the proper position.
- The leader may remain in closed position for the first fifth position break, release his right hand and bring the clasped hands through the middle on the second fifth position break, then resume a closed position.

*(continued)*

**Drill 9** *(continued)*

### TO INCREASE DIFFICULTY

- Use any multiple of two repetitions before changing to another variation such as adding an underarm turn for the follower on the leader's fourth repetition of the fifth position breaks.
- Combine the fifth position breaks with any two other variations that you know so far.

### *Success Goal*

Alternate the cha-cha basic steps with four repetitions of the fifth position break steps to slow cha-cha music for 2 minutes. ___

### *Success Check*

- Both partners break step backward at the same time. ___
- Both partners break step with a toe–heel foot placement. ___
- Keep the arms in frame and symmetrical. ___

## Drill 10
# Crossover Break Steps

The break steps may also be executed to each side, which are called *crossover breaks*. Start in a two-hands-joined position with your partner. Notice that the cha-cha also modifies the hand grasp when in a two-hands-joined position. The leader's thumb and fingers are separated (so they can open and close much like a bird's beak), with his fingers on top of the follower's hand and his thumb in her palm (review figure 11.3). The crossover breaks alternate between a two-hands-joined and a one-hand-joined position.

From a two-hands-joined position and after any backward break step (with his right foot), the leader may release his right-hand grasp and bring his left hand across his midline during the triple step to his right side. As his left hand continues to the side, both partners open to

face the leader's right side so that they can initiate a crossover break (see figure 11.8a) with their inside feet (leader's left and follower's right). During the triple step to the leader's left side, the leader can grasp both hands again (see figure 11.8b). The leader may now release his left hand grasp and bring his right hand across the midline of his body to open to his left side. Both partners execute the crossover break with their inside feet (leader's right and follower's left) while facing the leader's left side (see figure 11.8c). The leader may grasp both hands again when executing the triple step to the leader's right side (see figure 11.8d). Execute the crossover breaks a minimum of four times (twice to each side).

**a** Crossover break with inside feet on leader's right side

**b** Triple step to leader's left side

**c** Crossover break with inside feet on leader's left side

**d** Triple step to leader's right side

**Figure 11.8** Crossover breaks to each side.

## TO DECREASE DIFFICULTY

- Angle your foot on the last *cha* (count 1) toward the side in which you will be executing the crossover break.
- Focus your gaze as if you are saying hi to your partner, then to the audience on each side.

*(continued)*

Drill 10  *(continued)*

### TO INCREASE DIFFICULTY

- Combine the fifth position breaks with the crossover breaks; be sure to float away to transition from closed to two hands.
- Vary the number of repetitions with a minimum of two basic steps or two crossover breaks.
- Add an underarm turn for the follower on the fourth repetition of the crossover breaks.

## Success Goal

Alternate basic steps with four crossover breaks to slow music for 2 minutes. ___

## Success Check

- Instead of reaching, grasp a hand when coming closer to your partner. ___
- Keep your hands on the center-line that separates and defines both your own and your partner's space. ___
- Face your partner on the side triple step and open (outside arms and shoulders) to the side on the crossover break steps.

___

# Drill 11
# Walkaround Turns

A fun variation of the crossover break is a walkaround turn. This turn is similar to the half chase turns, except that both partners turn at the same time and the pivot is side to side, then another quarter turn is added at the end to face your partner again. The leader has a lot of options on this turn. The pivot turn may be executed on only one side or on both sides, using either single or multiple repetitions.

For example, during a crossover break on the leader's right side, the leader's left foot (and the follower's right foot) begins the crossover break on count 2. The leader needs to keep his left hand and forearm horizontal, releasing and gently extending the follower's

right hand (see figure 11.9a). Both partners need to keep their feet in a forward-backward stride as they pivot away from each other (CW for the leader, CCW for the follower). Think of facing each side wall. On count 3 of the pivot, notice that both partner's inside forearms may be close or slightly touching (see figure 11.9b). This helps you know where your partner is at the end of the pivot. Then continue rotating to face your partner for the side *cha-cha-cha* steps and resume a two-hands-joined position (see figure 11.9c). The leader may signal the walkaround turn on either side, or on both sides, or he may execute crossover breaks in between.

**a** Pivot with inside feet on count 2     **b** Shift weight to opposite foot on count 3

**c** Both do triple step to leader's left side

**Figure 11.9** Walkaround turn from leader's right side.

 **TO DECREASE DIFFICULTY**

- Without a partner, practice the footwork for both sides.
- Lead the walkaround turn using a set order and only one repetition, such as only on the fourth crossover break.

 **TO INCREASE DIFFICULTY**

- Randomly lead the walkaround turn to one side, to the other side, or to both sides.
- Combine the walkaround turn with any other variation that you know so far, such as after two walkaround turns, then transition to a shine position for half or full chases.

*(continued)*

Drill 11   *(continued)*

### *Success Goal*

For 2 minutes, alternate cha-cha basic steps with two crossover breaks and two walkaround turns on the third and fourth basic steps to slow music.___

### Success Check

- Keep your feet in a forward–backward stride on the pivot, using a *pivot, replace* so that you don't move your foot from its original position on count 3. ___
- Remember to meet in the middle with your hands when facing your partner. ___

# Drill 12
# Butterfly

The butterfly is a variation used during the crossover breaks. It alternately combines one crossover break with a triple step to the side, then one fifth position break with a triple step to the side. This variation is called a butterfly because both partners alternately close (face each other) and open up (face the side) like an emerging butterfly's wings. The butterfly may be led on either side. The following describes how to execute this variation off the leader's right side crossover break. Simply reverse the directions to lead off the leader's left-side crossover break.

After the leader's right-side crossover break (with his left foot), he faces his partner as usual to do the sideways *cha-cha-cha* steps with one exception: If he opens his right palm like a stop sign, this signals the follower to place her left hand in the same position. Both let their palms touch during the triple step to the follower's left side, then the leader releases his pressure and rotates 45 degrees clockwise to open his right shoulder (and the follower's left shoulder opens). Both partners do a fifth position break (leader's right foot back and follower's left foot back), then a triple step to the leader's right side. After the right-side crossover break, the leader continues to show his right palm until he wants to end this variation. To end this variation, the leader can grasp both hands on the triple step to his left side, then release his left hand to make the transition into a crossover break on the leader's left side and repeat the butterfly on that side.

### TO DECREASE DIFFICULTY
- Isolate your hand and body positioning with your partner on each part.
- Slowly add the footwork with each part.

### TO INCREASE DIFFICULTY
- Alternate the butterfly variation on both sides with walkaround turns.
- Combine the butterfly with any two other variations that you know so far.

## Success Goal

Perform cha-cha basic steps, executing the butterfly variation on both sides to slow music for 2 minutes. ___

- The leader's stop sign with open palm and fingers toward the ceiling signals that the butterfly variation is coming next. ___
- The follower needs to bring her hands back to the center for either a crossover break or to match the leader's open-palm position. ___
- Alternate a crossover break/ triple, a fifth-position break/triple, a crossover break/triple, a fifth-position break/triple, and continue with a crossover break and a side triple step in a two-hands-joined position. ___

# Drill 13
# Freeze

The freeze is a variation that adds two extra counts to each crossover break, which makes it important to repeat this variation on both sides. As the music is in 4/4 time, this adds four counts total, or one measure, to each side.

During the freeze, a crossover break is repeated twice. On the first crossover break, the leader keeps his inside hand and forearm firm and horizontal to signal both partners to rock their weight forward and backward twice. At the end of the second crossover break, the leader continues with a side triple step. He may then repeat the freeze on the opposite side.

 **TO DECREASE DIFFICULTY**

- Check that you are making four weight changes or rocking your weight from one foot to the other four times preceding a triple step.
- Check your position with a partner to start the four weight changes with your inside foot and keep your inside hands and arm approximately waist level.

**TO INCREASE DIFFICULTY**

- Alternate the freeze with walkaround turns, using any number of crossover breaks between them.
- Combine the freeze with any two other variations that you know so far.

*(continued)*

Drill 13  *(continued)*

## *Success Goal*

Alternate crossover breaks with the freeze on both sides of the body to slow cha-cha music for 2 minutes. ___

- Both partners position their feet in a forward–backward stride during the freeze. ___
- The leader's inside hand firmly remains at waist level to initiate the freeze. ___
- Remember to lead the freeze on both sides, in multiples of two repetitions. ___

# Drill 14
# Figure-Eight Turns

From a closed dance position, the figure-eight turns include three consecutive underarm turns for the follower. It alternates both CW and CCW pivot turns for the follower while the leader does the basic cha-cha step with a side triple step using the basic H-shaped floor path. After the leader's forward break with his left foot, he releases his right hand during his left-side triple step and lifts his left hand to make an arch. This signals the follower to prepare for a CW underarm turn on a crossover break step to her right side. The leader does his backward break step while the follower does a pivot turn under the arch (review figure 11.5). To continue another pivot turn on the other side, the leader must keep his left hand above the follower's head during the side triple step and gently direct the next pivot turn as he circles his left hand in a horizontal figure eight. When he wants the turns to end, the leader simply lowers his left hand. Try to do three pivot turns before resuming closed position again.

### TO DECREASE DIFFICULTY
- The follower should practice consecutive crossovers with a pivot turn on each side without a partner.
- With a partner, slowly move through the hand positions using a loose grip.

### TO INCREASE DIFFICULTY
- Lead three or more consecutive underarm turns during the figure-eight turns.
- Randomly alternate the figure-eight turns with any one other variation that you know so far, such as crossover breaks or fifth position breaks.

## Success Goal

Alternate cha-cha basic steps in an H-shaped floor path with the figure-eight turns to slow music for 2 minutes. ___

## Success Check

- The leader's left hand traces a horizontal figure-eight path in the air above the follower's head. ___

- The follower faces each side preceding the pivot, then uses her inside foot to pivot to face the opposite side, shifts weight to her other foot (she replaces it without moving it from its original location), then continues her turn to face the leader so that both can do a triple step to the side. ___

# Drill 15
# On Your Own: Linking Four Cha-Cha Variations

Your next challenge is to link at least four cha-cha variations into longer combinations. Start in a closed position and execute the basic cha-cha with a side triple using an H floor path. Try each of the following sample practice combinations:

- Fifth position breaks, crossover breaks, walkaround turns, and freeze
- Crossover breaks, butterfly, fifth position breaks, and figure-eight turns
- Crossover breaks, walkaround turn, half chase, and full chase
- Parallel forward breaks, underarm turn, crossover breaks, and butterfly

Now, it is your turn to select and link in any order at least four cha-cha variations that you can repeat at least four times. For your reference, the cha-cha variations covered in this book are categorized according to the dance position from which they are executed as follows:

| | |
|---|---|
| **Shine position variations** | • **Half basic forward and backward**<br>• **Chase (half, full or double)**<br>• **Cross and hop** |
| **One- or two-hands-joined positions** | • **Underarm turn**<br>• **First position breaks**<br>• **Crossover breaks**<br>• **Walkaround turns**<br>• **Butterfly**<br>• **Freeze**<br>• **Figure-eight turns** |
| **Closed position** | • **Basic H floor path**<br>• **Parallel breaks (forward and backward)**<br>• **Fifth position breaks** |

*(continued)*

Drill 15 *(continued)*

### TO DECREASE DIFFICULTY

- Use as many basic steps as you need between each variation to prepare for the next lead.
- Use a slow tempo.

### TO INCREASE DIFFICULTY

- Repeat the drill with different partners.
- Use a faster tempo.
- Execute all sample practice combinations.

## Success Goal

Perform at least four repetitions of any one of the sample cha-cha practice combinations listed, then select and link any four or more variations into a combination for the length of one song. ___

## Success Check

- Maintain the cha-cha rhythm with the music. ___
- Keep all transitions smooth. ___
- Practice proper partner etiquette. ___
- Write down your favorite combination. ___

# SUCCESS SUMMARY FOR CHA-CHA

The cha-cha is an interactive, flirtatious dance with styling that can be either very smooth or very staccato. The styling depends on how dramatic you want to be in your execution of the basic rhythmic step pattern, which alternates a break step with a triple step. The triple step may be executed either to the side (to follow an H-shaped floor path) or while traveling in a forward or backward direction. The break is a two-count move that propels your body in a new direction as your weight gets shifted in one direction, then in the opposite direction, such as forward to backward, or backward to forward, or side to side. In the cha-cha, the break steps occur on counts 2-3 and 6-7, when grouping two measures of music. Some dancers prefer to count each measure or break step with a triple step as *2, 3, 4-&-1*, which is repeated twice (until your starting foot is free again). Or, alternatively, the counts may be cued as *2, 3, 4-&-5, 6, 7, 8-&-1* because the last step of the *cha-cha-cha* steps becomes the starting step to the side (option one of three example starting options described). The cha-cha may be executed in a shine position (facing your partner without touching), a closed position, or in either a one- or two-hands-joined position. Connecting with the music and with your partner makes this dance exciting!

# Rumba

## *Reflecting Romance*

The rumba has been called the *dance of love* because of its sultry and romantic styling. The rumba is African in origin and was originally a courtship, marriage, and street dance with suggestive body and exaggerated hip movements. A slower and more refined version gradually evolved. Rumba music is a blend of Latin and African music with a staccato beat. Accompanying instruments typically include the maracas (originally dried gourds with seeds inside), the claves (two sticks), and the drums.

The rumba was introduced in the United States around 1913, but it did not catch on until the late 1920s. At that time, a major influence was Xavier Cugat, a famous musician who formed an orchestra specializing in Latin music. His orchestra opened at the Coconut Grove in Los Angeles, California, and his music was featured in early sound movies such as *In Gay Madrid.* The American version of the rumba uses a box rhythm with footwork similar to that used in the waltz box step, yet with the timing of the foxtrot (4/4 time).

The rumba was introduced in Europe in the 1930s by Monsieur Pierre, a leading dance teacher. He and his partner, Doris Lavelle, popularized Latin American dancing in London. Their *Cuban rumba* became the officially recognized version in 1955 and it paralleled the American version. However, soon after this, Pierre visited Havana and discovered that the rumba was danced with a rhythm and timing similar to that used in the cha-cha. He shared this discovery, which evolved into the standard *international Cuban rumba* that is used in competition today. Either version is appropriate on the dance floor. However, the American rumba is a bit easier for beginning dancers and is more often seen on the social dance floor. Both versions may use Cuban motion, which gives the illusion of taking a step without initially placing weight on that step. Cuban motion does not result from thrusting the hips sideways, but rather from alternately keeping one knee straight while the other knee is bent with each weight change. With Cuban motion, keep your feet flat on the floor and avoid lifting your heel higher off the floor than your toes. If you have trouble with the Cuban motion, keep practicing; mastery takes time.

# RHYTHMIC STEP PATTERN FOR RUMBA

The rhythmic step pattern used in the American rumba uses two repetitions of the four-count *slow, quick, quick* (SQQ), or box rhythm, until your starting foot is free again. Because the SQQ rhythm pattern involves three weight changes, make sure that the first weight change gets two counts in rumba. However, for styling, do not bring your feet together on count 2 during the *slow* as you did in the box rhythm in the foxtrot. Instead, use control to hold or extend your first weight change for two counts, then step on each of the *quick, quick* cues. This timing contrasts the quality of your slow and quick steps with sustained movement on the *slow* and sharp staccato styling on the *quick, quick,* which is characteristic of Latin dances. In general, the rumba footwork is very flatfooted with feet skimming along the floor, almost as if there is honey on the floor. Notice how the rhythmic step pattern remains the same as you make direction changes within the side basic step, the box step, and the half-box progression.

## Side Basic Step

The side basic step repeats the box rhythm twice to permit the uneven number of weight changes to be executed on both sides of the body, which takes two measures, or eight counts. The leader steps to his left side with the left foot, holds two counts for the *slow*, then brings the right foot beside the left foot in first position on the first *quick* and steps on the left foot on the second *quick*, keeping the feet together in first position. Then, the leader repeats these actions to his right side. The follower starts with her right foot to her right side for the *slow*, then brings her left foot beside her right foot in first position on the first *quick* and steps on her right foot on the second *quick*, keeping the feet together in first position. Then, she repeats these actions to her left side.

## Box Step

A box step is composed of two half boxes in two directions, alternating forward and backward (or backward and forward). The leader starts on the forward half with his left foot while the follower starts on the backward half with her right foot. It is your option whether to use Cuban motion or not. Cuban motion comes from alternating one leg bent with the other leg straight and delaying the actual weight change. If you choose to not use Cuban motion, then your weight changes (steps) are taken on each of the following cues: *forward (& hold), side, together* and *backward (& hold), side, together*. Both options are perfectly acceptable on the social dance floor.

To execute the forward half-box using Cuban motion, shift your weight onto your right foot and place your left foot forward as you press into the floor using the inside edge of your foot in a ball–heel contact with the floor on counts 1, 2. Delay the actual weight shift onto your left leg until count 2. Simultaneously, you can place your right foot with a bent knee to your right side. On count 3, shift your weight fully onto your right leg as you simultaneously bring your left foot with a bent knee beside your right foot. On count 4, shift your weight fully onto your left foot and bend your right knee, keeping the feet in first position.

To execute the backward half-box using Cuban motion, shift your weight onto your left foot as you place the heel of your right foot two to three inches (5-7 cm) backward, beyond the heel of your left foot on counts 1, 2. Delay the actual weight shift onto your right leg until count 2. Simultaneously, you can place your left foot with a bent knee to your left side. On count 3, shift your weight fully onto your left leg as you simultaneously bring your right foot with a bent knee beside your left foot. On count 4, shift your weight fully onto your right foot and bend your left knee, either keeping feet in first position to end the box step or extending the left knee slightly forward to execute the forward half box.

### Half-Box Progression

As in the waltz and the foxtrot, an alternative is to continue the box rhythm while traveling forward on the second half-box by stepping *forward, side, together, forward, side, together,* or while traveling backward using a *backward, side, together, backward, side, together*. This option becomes the forward or backward half-box progression. It is very versatile in the rumba, especially when traveling on a curved pathway. For example, on the slow underarm turn or on the open rumba walks, modify the half-box progression to let the feet pass as you repeat the box rhythm whether you are moving *forward, forward, forward* or *backward, backward, backward* on each weight change.

Figure 12.1 shows the various ways you might organize the counts and the footwork (without adding Cuban motion) for three variations of the rhythmic step pattern for rumba.

---

## Figure 12.1   **RHYTHMIC STEP PATTERNS FOR RUMBA**

### Footwork Cues

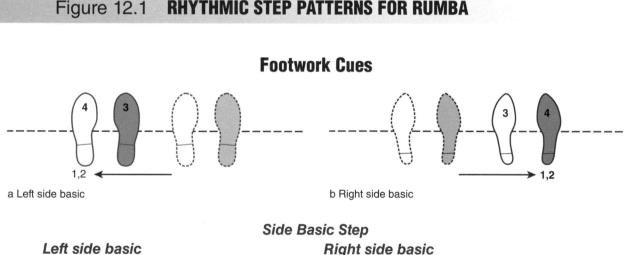

a Left side basic

b Right side basic

*Side Basic Step*

**Left side basic**
Left side (& hold), right (together), left/replace

**Right side basic**
Right side (& hold), left (together), right/replace

*(continued)*

## Figure 12.1 **RHYTHMIC STEP PATTERNS FOR RUMBA** *(CONTINUED)*

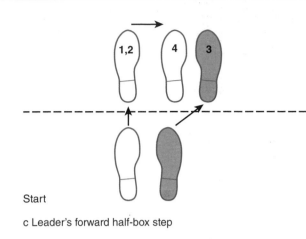

c Leader's forward half-box step

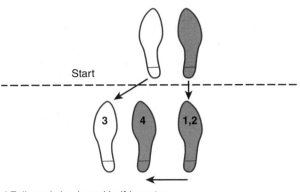

d Follower's backward half-box step

### *Box Step*

*Forward half box*
Forward left (& hold), right (side), left (together)

*Backward half box*
Backward right (& hold), left (side), right (together)

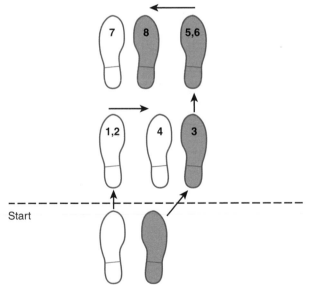

e Leader's forward half-box progression

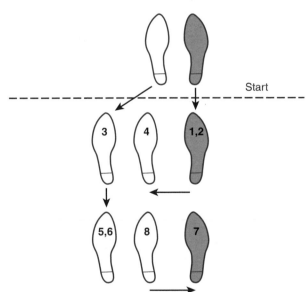

f Follower's backward half-box progression

### *Half-Box Progression*

*Forward half-box progression*
Forward left (& hold), right (side), left (together); Forward right (& hold), left (side), right (together)

*Backward half-box progression*
Backward right (& hold), left (side), right (together); Backward left (& hold), right (side), left (together)

## Timing Cues

| | |
|---|---|
| 4/4 time signature: | Four beats to a measure (group two measures) |
| Duration: | Each beat gets one count (total of eight counts) |
| Rhythm: | Slow, quick, quick; slow, quick, quick |
| Counts: | 1-2, 3, 4; 5-6, 7, 8; or 1-2, 3, 4; 2-2, 3, 4 |
| Weight changes: | Six (in two measures) |
| Direction of steps: | Side step—Left side, together, in place; right side, together, in place |
| | Box step—Forward, side, together; backward, side, together |
| | Half-box progression—Forward (or backward), side, together; forward (or backward), side, together |
| Foot positions: | Side step—Second, first, first; second, first, first |
| | Box step—Fourth, second, first; fourth, second, first |
| | Half-box progression—Fourth, second, first; fourth, second, first |

# DRILLS FOR RUMBA

The rumba is the dance of love because of its contrasting movement qualities of slow, sustained movements on the *slow* and sharp, precise foot placements on the *quick, quick*. It uses 4/4 time Latin music. For each drill, read the directions, and watch the video demonstrations on the enclosed DVD to see (a) how to execute the selected rumba variations, and (b) how to combine them into short practice combinations. Then, practice until you can meet the Success Goal for each drill. Use track 17 to practice your rumba moves.

## Drill 1
## Cuban Motion and Side Basic Steps

One of the distinguishing characteristics of the rumba is Cuban motion. A weight shift onto one straight leg automatically lets you flex, or bend, your other leg. Imagine that you are standing and waiting for someone who is very late. As you get tired of waiting, shift your weight to the other leg. Without forcing your hips to either side, notice how it feels when your weight is fully committed to the straight leg, while the other leg bends. Remain stationary and try this alternating weight shift a few times. Then, use control to slowly shift your weight in rhythm.

The next challenge is to use Cuban motion as you travel in different directions. This requires you to simultaneously combine two actions: shifting your weight onto a straight leg *and* positioning, or placing, the opposite foot with a bent knee. This is somewhat like rubbing your stomach and patting your head in that you need to slow down and control the weight shift and speed up the foot

*(continued)*

### Drill 1 *(continued)*

positioning until they coincide. Where might you place the opposite non-weighted foot? You have three options: sideways, forward, or backward. Try positioning the foot of your bent knee in the different directions as you shift your weight onto a straight leg.

Once you are comfortable doing these actions without the rumba rhythm, you are ready to use these actions to execute the side basic steps (review figure 12.1, *a* and *b*). Using the SQQ rhythm, practice your side (second position), together (first position), and in place (first position) to each side. Thus, it takes two repetitions of the rumba box rhythm before your starting foot is free again. The leader starts with the left, while the follower starts with the right. Don't worry if you can't do Cuban motion right away. It takes practice, practice, and more practice! It is most important to keep the SQQ, SQQ rhythm going for the length of a particular song.

### TO DECREASE DIFFICULTY

- Focus on alternating a straight leg and a bent knee during the *quick, quick* cues when your feet are in first position. Then, try the side basic steps. Cuban motion on the side basic step will come!
- Position the foot of the bent knee in the direction of travel and use at least two repetitions of box rhythm to move forward, then backward.

### TO INCREASE DIFFICULTY

- Repeat facing a partner without touching with the follower doing the mirror reverse.
- Repeat the side basic steps from a closed position with your partner.

## Success Goal

Practice *shift and position* steps first while stationary, and then while executing side basic steps to slow music for 2 minutes; use track 17. ___

## Success Check

- The straight leg has the weight. ___
- The foot of the bent knee indicates the direction of travel and has no weight. ___
- Simultaneously shift your weight (onto a straight leg) and position your opposite foot (with a bent knee). ___
- The side basic steps use second, first, first positions of the foot on each side. ___
- Maintain the SQQ rhythm. ___

## Drill 2
# Execution Challenge for Box Step

If you've practiced the box step in the waltz and the foxtrot, then you already know it. However, in the rumba, the timing is different and you eventually need to add Cuban motion, as well as follow a box shape on the floor (review figure 12.1, *c* and *d*). Repeat the basic rumba box step until you are comfortable without a partner, with slow music, and then with a partner in closed position.

**TO DECREASE DIFFICULTY**
- Master the basic step alone to counts until you can match the tempo of slow rumba music.
- Face a partner without touching and repeat the drill to see how your actions mirror your partner's in reverse.

**TO INCREASE DIFFICULTY**
- Use a variety of slow rumba music.
- Change partners frequently.
- Alternate four side basic steps and two box steps.

### Success Goal

Execute the rumba box step to slow music for 2 minutes; use track 17. ___

### Success Check

- Maintain the SQQ rhythmic pattern. ___
- Take small steps. ___
- Use fourth, second, and first positions of the foot on each half of the box step. ___

## Drill 3
# Execution Challenge for Half-Box Progression

The main advantage of the half-box progression is that it permits you to avoid other couples whenever there is room to travel (review figure 12.1, *e* and *f*). Try it to slow rumba music without and then with a partner in closed position. Once you get comfortable with the half-box progression execution, experiment with a practice combination such as four half-box progressions forward (16 total counts), then four half-box progressions backward (16 total counts).

*(continued)*

Drill 3   (continued)

### TO DECREASE DIFFICULTY

- Use more than two repetitions of the basic progression in any one direction to have more time to prepare for the next direction.
- Leave out the side step and let your feet pass on each SQQ step. For example, try four SQQ progressive forward steps in rhythm, then four SQQ progressive backward steps in rhythm.

### TO INCREASE DIFFICULTY

- Vary the number of repetitions in multiples of two. Thus, try six (or 4, or 2) half-box progressions forward and six (or 4, or 2) half-box progressions backward. Which combination is easiest for you and your partner?
- Add a box step to make this a longer combination.

## Success Goal

Execute the half-box progressions alternating four forward, then four backward to slow music for 2 minutes; use track 17. ___

## Success Check

- Maintain the SQQ rhythmic pattern to the tempo of the music. ___
- Make direction changes smooth transitions. ___
- Use fourth, second, and first positions of the foot on each half-box progression. ___
- Take small steps. ___

# Drill 4
# Slow Underarm Turn

An underarm turn for the follower makes this variation fun to do. Starting in closed position, the leader executes two box steps while the follower moves clockwise (CW) under the arch formed by the leader lifting his left hand. It helps to group four half-boxes when executing the follower's slow underarm turn. Both partners do the first half-box together. On the *slow* of the second half-box, the leader lifts his left arm to form an arch and keeps his right hand on the follower's left shoulder blade. On the *quick, quick* of the second half-box, the leader uses his right hand to gently guide the follower to move clockwise a half turn under the arched hands to be on the leader's left side and a half step in front of him. On the third half-box, both partners step forward on the *slow*. The leader completes his forward half-box in place while the follower continues to move forward on the *quick, quick* cues with forward progressive steps along a curved, CW path until facing her partner again. On the fourth half-box, the follower continues to move forward into a forward half-box, while the leader finishes with his backward half-box. Take your time to slowly resume a closed position when you get closer to your partner. The slow underarm turn takes four half-boxes, or a total of 16 counts.

## TO DECREASE DIFFICULTY

- The follower may trace an imaginary circular path on the floor to follow during the slow underarm turn, first without a partner, then with a partner.

- On the third (forward) half-box, the leader may rotate a quarter turn counterclockwise (CCW) to face his partner, then continue with his backward half-box.

## TO INCREASE DIFFICULTY

- Alternate two box steps with a slow underarm turn.
- Change partners frequently.

## Success Goal

Perform 10 smoothly executed slow underarm turns to music. ___

## Success Check

- Keep your free arm curved and slightly in front of your body. ___
- Keep the SQQ rhythm on each of the four half-boxes to avoid rushing it. ___
- The lead is given on the second *slow,* then the follower moves CW 180 degrees on the *quick, quick* cues.___
- Notice that both partners move in unison as the leader moves forward, backward, forward, backward; the follower moves backward, forward (and under), forward (and curve), forward.___

# Drill 5
# Left Box Turn

The left box turn is a variation of the box step, which is executed from a closed position. The box step is composed of both a forward half-box and a backward half-box. The box step takes eight beats of music before your starting foot is free again (the leader's left foot and the follower's right foot). The box turn can take two or more box steps to revolve 360 degrees. In rumba, there is no hurry to complete the left box turn in any specific number of half-boxes because the rumba is a spot dance. Start with the box step to establish a tempo. Before any forward half-box, the leader rotates his upper torso and frame CCW approximately 45 degrees. Finish the backward half-box while facing this new direction. Before each forward half-box, slowly rotate CCW approximately a quarter turn until you've turned 360 degrees. Another option is to rotate a quarter turn on each half-box.

## TO DECREASE DIFFICULTY

- Take small steps.
- Rotate in small increments only on the leader's backward half-boxes.
- Place your hands on your partner's shoulders to be aware of facing your partner and keeping the shoulders parallel in order to rotate as a unit.

## TO INCREASE DIFFICULTY

- Vary the tempo.
- Combine a slow underarm turn and a left box turn.

## Success Goal

Alternate two box steps with a left box turn to slow rumba music for 2 minutes. ___

## Success Check

- Upper torso and frame move as one unit. ___
- The left foot angles outward (to step on your front, left diagonal) preceding each forward half-box. ___
- The right foot angles inward (to step on your back, right diagonal) preceding each backward half-box. ___

# Drill 6
# Fifth Position Breaks for Rumba

You may remember the fifth position break from the cha-cha. It is also a popular variation in the rumba. The fifth position break includes a toe-to-heel (or fifth) foot position within the *quick, quick* rumba rhythm. Start in a closed position and take a forward half-box. The lead for the fifth position break is signaled by the leader stepping sideways on his right foot to his right side on the *slow*. Then, he releases his left hand grasp to facilitate a 45-degree rotation with the upper body and frame (CCW for the leader, and CW for the follower). On the *quick, quick,* both partners step back (leader's left foot and follower's right foot on count 3), then replace (leader's right foot and follower's left foot on count 4).

Repeat on the other side with a step to the leader's left side on his left foot as he releases his right hand and places his left hand on the follower's right shoulder blade. Again open the shoulders (leaser's right shoulder back, follower's left shoulder back) approximately 45 degrees. This signals both partners to break back (with the leader's right foot and the follower's left foot).

Notice that the right arm opens when the right foot breaks back and the left arm opens when the left foot breaks back. Avoid opening your arms either straight to the side or behind your body; rather, keep your free hand in front of your shoulder at approximately 45 degrees. Even though the leader is placing his hand on the follower's shoulder blades, this variation is sometimes called *waist-to-waist*.

For practice, do four repetitions of the fifth position break. The leader breaks back on each *quick, quick* starting with his left foot, and alternates with his right, left, right, while the follower breaks back with her right foot, and alternates with her left, right, left. To end this variation, both partners do a *side, together* on the *quick, quick*. Thus, the leader steps on his left foot to the left side, and brings his right foot in to first position, which frees his left foot so he can initiate another variation, such as a box step. The follower steps on her right foot to her right side, and brings her left foot in to first position on the *together*.

## TO DECREASE DIFFICULTY

- Practice without a partner to clarify your toe-to-heel foot placements.
- Practice facing a partner without touching to review the shoulder positioning (approximately 45 degrees) on the fifth position breaks. Avoid overrotating your shoulders and overextending your free arms.
- Do a half-box, step to the leader's right side, and fifth position break (face extended hands); the leader releases his right hand and brings his left hand (and follower's right hand) across his midline to open free arms (his right and her left) on the second fifth position break. Resume a closed position on the third repetition.

*(continued)*

Drill 6  (continued)

### TO INCREASE DIFFICULTY

- Start the fifth position breaks from the leader's right-side basic step.
- The leader may lead three waist-to-waists, then three hand-to-hand changes by extending his left hand to grasp the follower's right hand, then his right hand to grasp the follower's left hand, and his left hand to grasp the follower's right hand before coming out of the fifth position breaks.

## Success Goal

Alternate the box step with the fifth position breaks to slow rumba music. ___

## Success Check

- Place feet toe-to-heel (and angled 45 degrees) during the fifth position breaks. ___
- The follower keeps her arms lifted in frame so the leader can find her shoulder blades. ___
- Foot positions for the half-box fourth, second, first. ___
- Foot positions for the fifth position break (repeated 2-4 times): second, fifth, fifth. ___
- Foot positions for the ending: second, second, first. ___

# Drill 7
# Forward Parallel Break Steps for Rumba

You did the forward parallel break steps in the cha-cha. The forward direction is from the leader's point of view, while the follower does all backward break steps with her feet in fifth position. The parallel break steps use fourth position from a left parallel and a right parallel position (review figure 4.1, *h* and *i*) so that the leader can step outside his partner's feet. Start in closed position and do a half-box with your partner. On the second SQQ, the leader takes a side step to his right onto his right foot on the *slow*. Then, the leader angles his shoulders CW to be facing his front diagonal right (which brings the follower to his left side). The leader's break steps (left foot forward, right foot backward on QQ) are executed outside his partner's feet.

On the third SQQ, the leader steps on his left foot to his left side (back to closed position). Then, he continues to rotate his shoulders CCW 45 degrees to bring the follower to his right side. The leader's break steps (right foot forward, left foot backward) are executed outside his partner's feet. Repeat the parallel break steps on both sides again. To end or come out of the parallel breaks, the leader does a *slow* to his right side, then a *side, together* on QQ (his left foot steps to his left side, and brings his right foot beside his left).

The follower breaks in a backward–forward direction while the leader breaks in a forward–backward direction on each parallel break. Notice how the break steps are done in parallel with your partner's break steps along a diagonal.

## TO DECREASE DIFFICULTY

- Place your arms on your partner's shoulder to be aware of how the shoulders need to remain parallel whether in closed or in outside parallel partner positions.
- Repeat the drill from a two-hands-joined position.

## TO INCREASE DIFFICULTY

- Combine the forward parallel break steps with any two other rumba variations.
- Alternately, execute three side basics, four parallel break steps, and a side basic.

### Success Goal

Alternate a box step with four forward parallel breaks to music for 2 minutes.

___

### Success Check

- Maintain SQQ rhythmic pattern. ___
- Repeat any even-number repetitions of the parallel break steps to each side. ___
- Keep shoulders parallel to your partner's in closed position and while angled in both outside partner positions. ___

---

# Drill 8
# Crossover Breaks
# (With Follower's Underarm Turn Option)

Many transitions from the cha-cha also work with the rumba. For example, you may execute crossover breaks in the rumba too. The name of this move refers to the manner of the lead; that is, the leader brings one hand from one side to the other, crossing his midline each time. The crossover break is done on each side. Review figure 11.8 to refresh your memory. Thus, at least two repetitions (one to each side) are needed before transitioning to another variation. Typically, four repetitions of the crossover breaks are executed.

Start in a two-hands-joined position with your partner. It takes six repetitions of the rumba's basic rhythm, SQQ. Do

one half-box. On the second repetition, the leader initiates the crossover breaks by stepping to his right side onto his right foot on the *slow,* while the follower steps to her left side onto her left foot. The leader releases his right hand and brings his left hand across his midline to open both partners towards the leader's right side. Both take a break step (forward, backward) with their inside feet on the QQ while facing this side.

On the third repetition, the leader steps to his left side onto his left foot on the *slow,* while the follower steps onto her right foot toward her right side. Resume the two-hands-joined position. The leader releases his left hand and

*(continued)*

**Drill 8** *(continued)*

brings his right hand across his midline to open to his left side. Both partners do the break step (forward, backward) with their inside feet on the QQ while facing this side. For the fourth and fifth repetitions, repeat the second and third repetitions to break toward the leader's right side, then his left side. On the sixth repetition, the leader does a right-side basic step; he steps onto his right foot toward his right side, feet together, and in place.

A shorter sequence option is the pivot turn option where the leader executes one half-box and one crossover lead (only to his right side). On the third repetition of the basic rhythm, the leader lifts

his left hand and arm to form an arch (on the *slow*), which becomes a nonverbal signal for the follower to prepare her right foot for the right underarm pivot turn by rotating her right toes to face her right side. On the QQ, the follower does a CW pivot turn stepping on her left, then right foot (review figure 11.5), while the leader breaks backward starting with his right foot. On the fourth SQQ, the leader steps to his right side onto his right foot, then does a *side, together* (with his left, right foot). The follower steps onto her left to the side, then onto her right side, and together. Then both resume a box step.

### TO DECREASE DIFFICULTY

- Practice each part separately, gradually linking more parts together.
- Start with side basic steps, then lead into the crossover breaks without the underarm turn option.

### TO INCREASE DIFFICULTY

- Execute the underarm turn option and resume either a closed or a two-hands-joined position.
- Add the underarm turn option on the fifth repetition within the previous crossover break sequence.
- Both partners can do a walkaround or pivot on the fifth repetition within the previous crossover break sequence, if the leader releases his right after he brings it across his midline and lets the follower's forearm roll off his forearm. He pivots CCW (right, left foot), while she pivots CW (left, right foot) on the QQ.

## Success Goal

Perform 10 smoothly executed crossover break sequences to rumba music.

\_\_\_

## Success Check

- Maintain a SQQ rhythmic pattern. \_\_\_
- Maintain your arm positions, rather than letting your arms hang freely. \_\_\_
- On the crossover breaks, look to the side and start the break with your inside foot (closest to your partner's foot). \_\_\_
- Break steps change directions (forward, then backward) on the *quick, quick* cues. \_\_\_

# Drill 9
# One-Hand Around-the-World Variation

In this variation, the leader is the *world* and the follower moves around him. It starts with a slow underarm turn, except the leader brings his left hand over his head as if looping a lasso to guide the follower completely around his body. The follower does forward walks in rhythm while traveling in a small circle around the leader. The one-hand around-the-world variation takes eight SQQ basic steps. The leader does the box step (the equivalent of eight half-box steps or four box steps).

From a closed position, both partners do a half-box and a *slow* of the second half-box when the leader lifts his left hand and arm to form an arch. The follower moves CW under the arched hands on the *quick, quick.* At this point, the leader keeps his right hand on the follower's back as she goes under the arch and maintains contact as he continues to gently guide her in a small CW circle (see figure 12.2*a*).

To maintain the momentum, the leader keeps his left hand high and brings the follower to his right side, then guides her behind him as his left hand goes over his own head as if looping a rope (see figure 12.2*b*). On the seventh half-box, the leader does a left quarter turn to face his partner (see figure 12.2*c*) and resumes a closed position again on the eighth half-box (see figure 12.2*d*).

## TO DECREASE DIFFICULTY

- Practice just the leader's arm movements without any footwork.
- The follower can take her time moving around the leader.

## TO INCREASE DIFFICULTY

- Randomly alternate the slow underarm turn and the around-the-world variation.
- Vary the total number of basics used. For example, rotate to face the follower on the fifth half-box.
- The leader may delay moving to closed position by keeping his left hand high on the seventh (or fifth) half-box to signal another underarm turn for the follower, then resume a closed position.

## Success Goal

Perform the one-hand around-the-world variation to rumba music. ___

## Success Check

- Simultaneously, after the leader's left-hand arch, his right hand guides the follower as he brings his left hand to his right side and over his own head. ___
- The follower moves in a circular path clockwise around the leader. ___

*(continued)*

**a** The palm of the right hand remains on the follower's back.

**b** The left hand remains high to guide the follower's clockwise basic steps.

**c** The leader rotates counterclockwise to face the follower.

**d** Resume a closed position.

**Figure 12.2**   One-hand around-the-world leads after an underarm turn.

# Drill 10
# Cross-Body Lead

The cross-body lead is a useful transition to smoothly connect many variations as well as to rotate 180 degrees with your partner. Start in a closed position and do a box step. The cross-body lead takes two repetitions of the rumba's SQQ rhythm.

Both partners do the first SQQ (the leader does a forward half-box, while the follower does a backward half-box). On the second SQQ, the leader angles his right foot along his back, diagonal direction during the *slow* step. He may either keep his left hand firm or he can turn over his left hand CW and lower his left arm to indicate that a new lead is coming. On the *quick, quick*, he steps with his left foot to his left side, then he rocks back on his right foot with feet together. The leader will be facing the side wall. Thus, the leader's shoulders are perpendicular to the follower's shoulders as she

will move down the slot opened by the leader. Preceding his next forward *slow* with his left foot, he rotates a quarter turn to face the follower (and to face the back wall) and finishes his *quick, quick* steps. Then, he may either repeat the cross-body lead or lead another variation.

After the follower's backward half-box (first SQQ), she uses three forward traveling steps (left, right, left) with a swivel at the end to face the leader (second SQQ). She needs to pass her feet on each step (with the toes of alternating feet in front) and maintain the rhythm as she travels down the slot. A common error is to rotate too soon to face the leader. The follower needs to keep her left shoulder perpendicular to the leader's shoulders as she travels forward down the slot opened when the leader's left shoulder rotates a quarter turn on the second SQQ.

## TO DECREASE DIFFICULTY

- The cross-body lead takes two repetitions of the rumba's SQQ rhythm.
- The leader angles to rotate a quarter turn on the second SQQ.
- Practice your part independently from your partner using the walls as references. For example, the follower faces the back wall, then the front wall, while the leader faces the front wall, his left side wall, and the back wall.

## TO INCREASE DIFFICULTY

- Practice with a variety of partners.
- Combine a box step, a cross-body lead, two forward half-box progressions, then a side step into either forward parallel breaks or fifth position breaks.
- Add an underarm turn after the cross-body lead.

*(continued)*

Drill 10 *(continued)*

### *Success Goal*

Alternate a box step with a cross-body lead to rumba music for 2 minutes. ___

# Drill 11
# Open Rumba Walks

The open rumba walks start with the cross-body lead, then add on to keep both partners rotating around a central axis, much like a wheel. Start in closed dance position with your partner. It takes six SQQ basics to execute the open rumba walks.

## *Cross-Body Lead (Two SQQs)*

In a closed position, both partners do a half-box. On the second half-box, the leader steps on a back diagonal with his right foot on *slow,* and he takes his *side, together* steps while facing the side wall. The follower continues forward down the slot on her second SQQ basic step.

## *Third SQQ Basic*

The leader starts a forward half-box basic step with his left foot on *slow* as he releases his right hand to open the position. He finishes with a side break (on the *quick, quick* in opposition with his partner, such that he is on the right, while she is on his left side), keeping his left arm firm and horizontal. The follower steps to her right side with her right foot on the *slow*, then continues to open the position (CCW) to do a side break on the *quick, quick* (stepping left, right). The leader will be on her right side with the forearms touching.

## *Fourth SQQ Basic*

The leader backs up to walk CW in rhythm (right, left, right). The follower walks forward in a CW path (left, right, left).

## *Fifth SQQ Basic*

The leader draws his left hand toward his body on the *slow*, then out to his left side on the *quick, quick* in order to bring the follower closer to him so he can resume a closed position on the next basic. The leader needs to compress his backward walks (left, right, left) to not travel as much, which signals to the follower that he is preparing to resume a closed position. The follower steps on her right foot on *slow* as the leader helps her swivel CW to face him. She continues to walk forward on the *quick, quick* steps (left, right) while facing the leader.

### Sixth SQQ Basic

The leader does a backward half-box (right, left, right) to resume a closed position while the follower does a forward half-box (left, right, left).

Notice that the leader bends his left elbow until both partners' forearms are touching before and during the open rumba walks (see figure 12.3). The forearms are the central axis from which the leader walks backward while the follower walks forward. For styling, think of presenting the follower; thus, look at your partner as you revolve together. This is a beautiful, flowing variation.

**Figure 12.3** Open rumba walks with forearm position as a fulcrum for rotation.

### TO DECREASE DIFFICULTY

- Without any rhythm—just walking—practice the CW wheel motion when the leader's left hand and forearm is firmly in the middle, and the leader walks backward as the follower walks forward.
- Slowly add on the next SQQ basic steps until the entire sequence is completed.

### TO INCREASE DIFFICULTY

- The leader can extend the sequence to two more basics by adding two more backward SQQ walks, alternating his right foot (SQQ), left foot (SQQ), right foot (SQQ), and left foot on *slow* (to swivel the follower to face him) and resume a closed position on the *quick, quick*.
- Combine the open rumba walks with any two other rumba variations.

*(continued)*

Drill 11  *(continued)*

## *Success Goal*

Alternate box steps with the open rumba walks to music for 2 minutes. ___

- During the wheel rotation, the leader backs up while the follower moves forward. ___
- Rotate with your forearms horizontal as the central axis. ___
- Look at your partner as you both rotate. ___

# Drill 12
# On Your Own: Linking Four Rumba Variations

The next challenge is to link at least four rumba variations into a combination using smooth transitions and continuous movement. For practice, try the following sample combinations using any number of basic progressions in between each variation:

- Side basic steps, crossover break with underarm turn, fifth position breaks, left box turn
- Box step, slow underarm turn, left box turn, forward parallel breaks
- Cross-body lead, open rumba walks, fifth position breaks, one-hand around-the-world variation

Now it's your turn to link any four or more rumba variations to create your own combinations. Select from the following points when you experiment with your own combinations:

- Side basic steps
- Box step (half-box forward and half-box backward)
- Half-box progressions (forward and backward)
- Slow underarm turn
- Left box turn
- Fifth position breaks
- Forward parallel breaks
- Crossover breaks
- One-hand around-the-world
- Cross-body lead
- Open rumba walks

 **TO DECREASE DIFFICULTY**
- Start by linking two, then three variations that fit together for you and your partner.
- Write down your favorite combinations and refer to them as needed.

**TO INCREASE DIFFICULTY**
- Practice with a variety of partners.
- Vary the tempo.
- Combine more than four variations for a longer sequence.
- Start the open rumba walks with a slow underarm turn.

### Success Goal

Perform four consecutive repetitions of at least two combinations linking at least four rumba variations to music. ___

### Success Check

- Keep transitions smooth. ___
- Maintain your frame. ___
- Maintain the rhythmic pattern. ___

# SUCCESS SUMMARY FOR RUMBA

The rumba is a Latin dance done to slow 4/4 time music. It is called *the dance of love*. The rumba uses box rhythm executed in four-beat measures with its own unique styling. It is similar, but should not be confused with the box rhythm execution used in either the foxtrot or the waltz. Three rhythmic step patterns associated with the rumba are the side basic step, the box step, and the half-box progression. It takes two repetitions of the rumba's *slow, quick, quick* rhythm until your starting foot is free again, or two measures of music. Many of the rumba variations typically start and end in a closed dance position. The flavor of the rumba styling is enhanced by contrasting the *slow* and the *quick* steps. The romance of this dance comes from looking at your partner and moving in unison. Enjoy the time you share with your partner!

# Tango

## *Expressing Attitude and Flair*

From its origins in Spain or Morocco, the tango has evolved to be a popular social dance. The flirtatious music of the tango was considered immoral in the early 1800s. The ballroom version of tango was shaped by the lower class of Buenos Aires. In the crowded night clubs, the men had to lead around and between the round tables, which shows in the many curving paths used in the tango variations. The attire for the men was high boots, spurs, and chaps to protect them from riding sweaty horses. The women wore full skirts. The story goes that the gauchos didn't shower often, so the woman danced within the crook of his right arm with her head held back.

In the 1900s, the tango spread throughout Europe and to America. It became popular in New York in 1921 when Rudolf Valentino danced the tango. Over time, both the music and the dance became more subdued, which helped the tango to become more respected by society. Many movies have featured the tango including the following: *Shall We Dance* with Richard Gere and Jennifer Lopez, *Scent of a Woman* with Al Pacino, *Evita* with Madonna, and *True Lies* with Arnold Schwarzenegger and Jamie Lee Curtis.

The tango is a smooth dance that has three common styles—each executed with a dramatic flair. The American tango is slow and slinky with open positions, fans, and dips. It progresses counterclockwise (CCW) in the line of dance (LOD) and uses cat-like walks and staccato foot movements. The international tango, which originated in Buenos Aires, Argentina, has a different hold with the follower's arm lower. It is characterized by staccato head snaps, with the couple moving as a unit within a closed position and in the LOD. The Argentine tango is also danced only in closed position, yet it is more of a spot dance and uses a lot of leg and foot actions with no set basic, but rather spontaneous movement with the music. Of these three styles, the American tango is the most popular in social dance settings and is described here in more detail.

The American tango is one of the easiest dances to learn, yet it also requires a strong connection with the music as well as with your partner. It is important that you can distinguish between a heavy measure and a light measure in the 4/4 time tango music (review step 2 as needed). Once you can hear and feel the phrasing of the music, typically in 16 or 32 beats of music, you will start moving on the heavy measure of music.

# RHYTHMIC STEP PATTERN FOR TANGO

The rhythmic step pattern for the American tango uses eight counts, or two measures of 4/4 time music. During counts 7-8 of this rhythmic pattern there is a hold, or freeze, with a slow drag of the free foot. Sometimes, it is helpful to cue the four weight changes with the first four letters of the word and the close with the O as follows: T-A-N-G-O, or *walk, walk, TANG-O-Close*, or *slow, slow, quick, quick, slow.* The close on the last *slow* receives no weight change. The tango travels in the line of dance, or counterclockwise around the perimeter of the room, with stop-and-go movements executed more toward the center of the room. The tango is most often danced in either a closed position or a promenade position. Selected variations in the drill section use an open position as well.

## Closed Position

The leader starts in a closed position and with his left foot, takes two long steps forward. The long steps get two counts each and correspond to the *slow, slow* rhythmic cues. The leader then takes two short steps, one forward and one slightly to his right side (leaving the inside edge of his left big toe touching the floor). The short steps get one count each and correspond to the *quick, quick* rhythmic cues. On counts 7-8, the leader can slowly drag the inside edge of his left foot (toe) along the floor to close his feet (without making a weight change). This "close" corresponds to the "slow" rhythmic cue. At the end of the tango basic step pattern, the leader's left foot is free to repeat the eight counts of the tango rhythmic step pattern.

The follower also starts in a closed position and with her right foot, takes two long steps backward. The long steps get two counts each and correspond to the "slow, slow" rhythmic cues. The follower then takes two short steps, one backward and one slightly to her left side (leaving the inside edge of her right foot's big toe touching the floor). The short steps get one count each and correspond to the "quick, quick" rhythmic cues. On counts 7 and 8, the follower can slowly drag the inside edge of her right foot (right big toe) along the floor to close her feet without making a weight change. This *close* corresponds to the *slow* rhythmic cue. At the end of the rhythmic step pattern, the follower's right foot is free to repeat the eight counts of the rhythmic step pattern for tango.

## Promenade Position

From a promenade position, the rhythmic step pattern may also be executed to the side (leader's left and follower's right). Just before moving into a promenade position, the leader snaps his head to look toward his left side (and the follower mirrors by snapping her head toward her right side). Then both partners take two *slow* walking steps to the side. The leader steps onto his left foot, then crosses his right foot over his left foot. The follower steps onto her right foot, then crosses her left foot over her right foot. Both partners take a short step toward the side onto the ball of their outside foot (leader's left foot and follower's right), then quickly shift weight back onto the opposite foot (leader's right foot and follower's left) and face each other (in closed position). Finish by slowly dragging the outside foot (leader's left foot and follower's right foot) to close your feet. This finish, or close, is much like a period at the end of a sentence. At this point, the leader has the option of traveling either forward (in closed position) or to his left side (in promenade position).

Figure 13.1 shows the various ways you might organize the counts and the footwork for the tango rhythmic step pattern. Select those cues that most help you retain how to execute it both from a closed and from a promenade position.

## Figure 13.1   RHYTHMIC STEP PATTERN FOR TANGO

### Footwork Cues

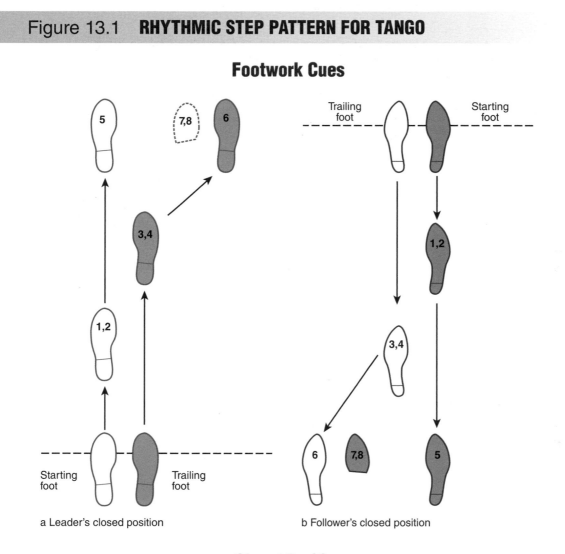

a Leader's closed position

b Follower's closed position

### *Closed Position*

**Leader**
Forward (left), forward (right), forward (left), side (right), close (drag left)

**Follower**
Backward (right), backward (left), backward (right), side (left), close (drag right)

*(continued)*

## Figure 13.1 RHYTHMIC STEP PATTERN FOR TANGO *(CONTINUED)*

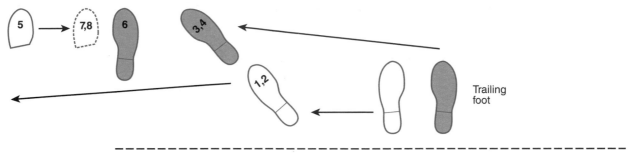

c Leader's promenade position

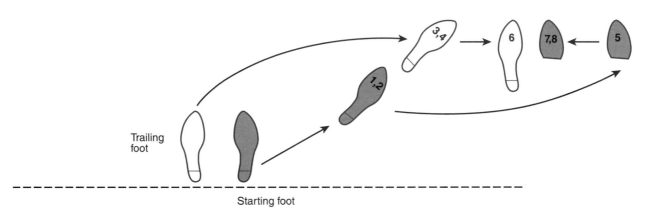

d Follower's promenade position

### Promenade Position

| Leader | Follower |
|---|---|
| Side (left), cross (right), side (left), replace (right), close (drag left) | Side (right), cross (left), side (right), replace (left), close (drag right) |

### Timing Cues

| | |
|---|---|
| 4/4 time signature: | Four beats to a measure (group two measures) |
| Duration: | Each beat gets one count (total of eight counts) |
| Rhythm strategy: | Slow (delayed single), slow (delayed single), quick, quick, slow (no weight change) |
| Counts: | 1-2, 3-4, 5, 6, 7-8 |
| Weight changes: | Four (in two measures, on counts 2, 4, 5, 6) |
| Length of steps: | Long, long, short, short, in place |
| Direction of steps: | Closed position—Forward, forward, forward, right side, in place (leader); or backward, backward, backward, left side, in place (follower) |
| | Promenade position—Left side, right across, left side, right replace, in place (leader); or right side, left across, right side, left replace, in place (follower) |
| Foot positions: | Fourth, fourth, fourth, second, first |

# DRILLS FOR TANGO

The footwork for the tango corresponds to the letters T-A-N-G-O with a weight change on the first four letters and a drag to close the feet at the end. It is an easy way to remember the rhythmic step pattern for the tango. The tango uses 4/4 time music and eight counts for the entire rhythmic step pattern. It is important to start the tango's rhythmic step pattern with count 1 of the first, or heavy, measure versus the second, or light, measure. The following drills will help you to practice the tango. For each drill, read the directions, and watch the video demonstrations on the enclosed DVD to see (a) how to execute the selected tango variations, and (b) how to combine them into short practice combinations. Then, practice until you can meet the Success Goal for each drill. For slow tango music, use track 18.

## Drill 1
## Basic Tango Step in Closed and Promenade Positions

The eight beats in the tango rhythmic step pattern are cued as *slow, slow, quick, quick, slow*. The tango basic may be executed either from a closed position (review figure 13.1, *a* and *b*) or from a promenade position (review figure 13.1, *c* and *d*).

Start in a closed position and take two forward walking steps, then a *forward, side, close*. Sometimes it is helpful to use the cue *tan-go close* to correspond to the *quick, quick, slow* finish. During the finish, when you take the side step, the heel of your opposite foot (leader's left and follower's right) comes slightly off the floor. Then, slowly drag the inside edge of the big toe of that foot along the floor to bring your feet together, or close your feet without making a weight change.

From a promenade position, take two *slow* walking steps, first stepping with your outside foot (the leader's left foot and the follower's right foot), then crossing over with your inside foot (the leader's right foot and the follower's left foot) on the next step. Continue by taking a small step with your outside foot, then shift your weight onto your inside foot. Face your partner in closed position and slowly drag the inside edge of the toe of your outside foot along the floor to close your feet. After you are comfortable with the basic step pattern to the leader's left side, the leader can snap his head before rotating into the promenade position. The follower then snaps her head just before taking the two walking steps to the side too. Thus, both partners look toward the direction they will be traveling (the leader's left side and the follower's right side).

Moving into the promenade position requires a firm frame while the lower body rotates approximately 45 degrees to face the extended hands. Try to make the timing changes distinctly different (contrast *slow* and *quick* steps) in each part of the tango rhythmic step pattern. In particular, extend your reach and try to delay contacting the floor as you take your first two steps until counts 2 and 4, which will yield more panther-like reaches.

*(continued)*

**Drill 1** *(continued)*

### TO DECREASE DIFFICULTY

- Practice alone until you can execute the basic pattern without looking at your feet.
- The leader may start in closed position facing the front diagonal wall so that multiple repetitions into promenade position will also travel in the LOD.

### TO INCREASE DIFFICULTY

- Practice with different partners.
- Vary the number of repetitions of the basic pattern in each direction (i.e., forward or sideward). Can you do one repetition in each direction?

## Success Goal

Alternate between two tango basics progressing forward in closed position and two tango basics progressing to the side in promenade position for 2 minutes; use track 18.___

## Success Check

- Keep a narrow base (feet no more than about 3 in, or 7 cm, apart) on forward and backward steps. ___
- Each *slow* gets two counts. ___
- Each *quick* gets one count. ___
- Take long strides on the *slow, slow* cues, delaying each weight change until counts 2 and 4. ___
- The tango close has two quick steps on counts 5, 6 and a slow foot drag on counts 7-8___

# Drill 2
# Left Quarter Turn

An easy variation of the tango basic progressing forward is to add a left quarter turn lead just before the tango close. This variation may be added to both the forward and side directions, which gives the leader two more options.

## From a Closed Position

Both partners do the two walking steps in closed position (forward). The leader then rotates his upper torso and frame CCW 45 degrees to make a left quarter turn. Finish with the regular tango close ending.

## From a Promenade Position

Both partners do the two walking steps in promenade position (sideways). Before the tango close, the leader rotates his upper torso and frame CCW 45 degrees. Both partners finish with their tango close ending.

### TO DECREASE DIFFICULTY

- Use any number of repetitions of the basic in each position before adding the left quarter turn.
- Use two repetitions before changing to another lead; for example, try two forward basic steps, then two forward basic steps with a left quarter turn, or two basic steps to the side in promenade, then two basic steps to the side in promenade with a left quarter turn.

### TO INCREASE DIFFICULTY

- Randomly alternate the basic step in closed position with a left quarter turn and the basic step in promenade position with a left quarter turn.
- Create a sequence that combines the basic steps in both positions with and without the left quarter turn, which means a minimum of four repetitions of the tango basic step.

## Success Goal

Perform the left quarter turn alternating from a closed position and from a promenade position to slow tango music for 2 minutes. ___

## Success Check

- The left quarter turn is led after the second walking step. ___
- The leader's rotation facilitates an angled foot position (toe out for the leader and toe in for the follower). ___
- Keep a firm frame. ___
- Maintain the rhythmic step pattern. ___

# Drill 3
# Corte and Recover

The corte is a popular tango variation when in a closed position. It is done in a small space and may be led after any tango close. To lead the corte, the leader keeps his frame and right hand firm as he steps back (see figure 13.2a) onto his left foot (*slow*). To recover, he then rocks his weight forward (see figure 13.2b) onto his right foot (*slow*). The follower does the opposite, shifting her weight forward onto her right foot, then backward onto her left foot. Then both partners do the normal tango close ending (*quick, quick, slow*, or *forward, side, close* for the leader).

(continued)

Drill 3 *(continued)*

a                    b

**Figure 13.2** *(a)* Corte and *(b)* recover positions preceding a tango close.

## TO DECREASE DIFFICULTY

- Practice without a partner to a slow tempo.
- Repeat the corte and recover at least twice preceding the tango close.
- Use as many repetitions of the forward basic step as needed between leading the corte and recover.

## TO INCREASE DIFFICULTY

- Experiment with leading the corte and recover after either of the left quarter turn options.
- Use the corte as a final pose at the end of a song.
- Experiment with adding two more *slows* preceding the corte and recover so that the leader rocks forward, backward, then backward (corte) and forward (recover), then tango close.

## Success Goal

Perform eight repetitions of the corte and recover after any tango close ending to slow tango music. ___

## Success Check

- The leader rocks back onto his left foot on the first *slow,* then forward onto his right foot on the second *slow.* ___
- Remain in closed position with the upper torso extended back. ___
- Bend one knee (more like a lunge) during the corte. ___
- Finish with a tango close. ___

# Drill 4
# Rock Steps

The tango in closed position may be modified with syncopation steps by adding two *quick, quick, slow* rhythms, or eight additional counts to the tango rhythmic step pattern. In this variation, two additional *quick, quick, slow* portions are inserted after the two forward walking steps.

After two walks forward, instead of going directly to the tango close, the leader signals forward–backward–forward rocks twice, corresponding to the *quick, quick, slow,* by keeping his frame and right hand firm and bringing his left hand beside his left hip. Also, the leader slightly angles his torso and left shoulder forward to initiate rocks with his left–right–left foot while the follower rocks with her right–left–right foot. The leader then slightly angles his torso and right shoulder forward to repeat these three rocks starting with the opposite foot (right–left–right for the leader and left–right–left for the follower) while still in a closed position. Keep your feet in a forward–backward stride (parallel fourth foot position) on the two forward steps, then use either a fourth or an extended fifth position of the foot on the two rock, or *quick, quick, slow,* steps. The leader's left foot is now free again to finish with the tango close ending with his left hand back in the closed position.

## TO DECREASE DIFFICULTY

- Practice footwork without a partner to match a weight change with each of the three cues used for the rocking actions.
- Repeat this variation at least twice.

## TO INCREASE DIFFICULTY

- Alternate the rock steps with any other variation that you know so far.
- Change partners frequently.

## *Success Goal*

Alternate two forward progressing basics in closed position and two rock steps to slow tango music for 2 minutes. ___

## *Success Check*

- Remain in closed position throughout. ___
- A total of 16 counts is needed to complete the rock step variation. ___
- After the *slow, slow* forward walking steps, insert two *quick, quick, slow* rhythms, then finish with a tango close. ___
- Quickly shift your weight three times to alternate the forward and backward directions, matching a weight change on counts 5, 6, 7 (hold 8) and 9, 10, 11 (hold 12). ___
- Use either a fourth or fifth foot position on the rock steps. ___

# Drill 5
# Closed Figure-Eight Fans

This variation starts from a closed position. The closed figure-eight fans expand on the left quarter turn to add at least two more *slow* steps preceding the tango close. The fans result from a crossover of one foot, then tracing the big toe of the other foot in an arc on the floor. The follower repeats this twice to create a figure-eight, or fanlike, motion.

The leader initiates the figure-eight fans during the left quarter turn after the *quick, quick*. Taking advantage of the CCW rotation, the leader overrotates the follower to place her on his right side in a hip-to-hip position. Then he does a rock step back onto his left foot, then forward onto his right foot, while the follower does two fans. The fans are executed on the *slow, slow,* then the partners finish with a tango close. During the figure-eight fans, the leader needs to pull with the fingers of his right hand, then press or push with the heel of his right hand, using a figure-eight motion with his right wrist to guide the follower on these two *slows.*

## TO DECREASE DIFFICULTY

- The follower can place her hands on a wall, weight on the balls of the feet, and practice the lower-body 45-degree rotation to swivel on each side that is needed on the fans.

- Practice the footwork and the hand position for leading the fans without a partner, then with a partner using a very slow tempo.

## TO INCREASE DIFFICULTY

- Execute the closed figure-eight fans after a left quarter turn from a promenade position.

- Try two consecutive figure-eight fans: After the quarter turn, the leader needs to step back on his left foot on *slow,* forward on his right foot on *slow,* do another CCW quarter turn on the *quick, quick* and bring the follower to his right side again for two more fans on *slow, slow,* then do a tango close.

## Success Goal

Alternate left quarter turns with the closed figure-eight fans to slow tango music for 2 minutes. ___

- The leader brings the follower to his right side for the fans, guiding her with a figure-eight wrist motion as he rocks backward and forward during the two additional *slow* steps. ___
- The follower does two fans using a crossover with the right foot (arcing the free, left foot along the floor to form a half circle) and point, then crossing with the left foot (arcing the free, right foot to forms a half circle) and point, and swiveling on the left foot to face the leader (and briefly closing the right foot). ___
- To end the fans, the leader keeps the follower in front of him to finish in closed position with a tango close. ___

# Drill 6
# Open Fans

The open fans variation starts from a promenade position. The open position occurs when the leader releases his right hand to permit opening to an inside-hands-joined position. Both partners then execute two fans preceding a tango close ending. It takes two repetitions of the tango rhythmic step pattern to complete this variation.

## Leader

Start in promenade and do two walks. Release the right hand and arc the right arm across your midline (like a roll-out transition in the swing) as you take two quick steps (left side, right side). With the follower on your left side in an open position (see figure 13.3a), drag your left big toe in to close the feet at the end of the first repetition of the tango rhythmic step pattern.

During the first *slow* of the next rhythmic step pattern, step toward your left front diagonal with the left foot (see figure 13.3b). Then, swivel CCW as you arc your outside foot (see figure 13.3c) and close your left foot. On the second *slow*, cross your right foot to step toward your left front diagonal onto your right foot as you arc your outside foot and rotate CW to close your left foot (see figure 13.3d). Resume a closed position with your partner during the finish with a left quarter turn on the tango close (see figure 13.3, e-g).

*(continued)*

**Drill 6** *(continued)*

### *Follower*

Do two walks in promenade. Step forward onto your right foot, then swivel CCW a half turn to step to your left side onto your left foot. With the leader on your right side in open position, drag your right big toe in to finish the close of the first rhythmic step pattern (see figure 13.3*a*).

During the first *slow* of the next rhythmic step pattern, step toward your right front diagonal with your right foot (see figure 13.3*b*), swivel 45 degrees CW, and extend your left foot for the first fan (see figure 13.3*c*). On the second *slow,* step toward your left front diagonal onto your left foot (see figure 13.3*d*), swivel 45 degrees CCW, and either extend your right foot (for the second fan) or bring it beside your left foot. Resume a closed position during the finish (see figure 13.3, *e-g*) with a left quarter turn on the tango close (*quick, quick, slow*).

**a** Open position at the end of the first basic (from promenade)

**b** Slow (diagonal step and fan)

**e** Quick (left quarter turn)

**f** Quick (side)

**Figure 13.3** Open fans in the tango use two tango rhythmic step patterns.

## TO DECREASE DIFFICULTY

- Go through just the footwork without a partner, then add a partner, and then add the arms.
- Repeat the open fans at least twice before leading another variation.

## TO INCREASE DIFFICULTY

- Add the closed figure-eight fans during the second left quarter turn.
- Alternate the open fans variation with any other variation that you know so far.

c Toe point on fan

d Slow (diagonal step and fan)

g Slow (close)

**Figure 13.3 *(continued)***

*(continued)*

Drill 6 *(continued)*

## *Success Goal*

Alternate the tango rhythmic step pattern in promenade position with the open fans variation to slow tango music for 2 minutes. ___

## *Success Check*

- Keep your extended hand in front of your shoulder and curved symmetrically with your partner's extended hand. ___
- The leader and follower alternate either the left front or right front diagonals on the cross and point or fan steps, respectively. ___

# Drill 7
# On Your Own: Linking Three Tango Variations

It is time to challenge yourself by linking at least three tango variations into longer combinations. For practice, try each of the following sample combinations:

- Basic forward, basic in promenade with a left quarter turn, open fans
- Basic forward, rock steps, corte and recover
- Basic forward with left quarter turn, rock steps, closed figure-eight fans

Now it is your turn to create your own combinations of any three tango variations using any number of repetitions and in any order. Refer to the following summary chart listing the tango variations.

| Closed position variations | • Basic forward<br>• Forward with a left quarter turn<br>• Corte and recover<br>• Rock steps<br>• Closed figure-eight fans |
|---|---|
| Promenade and Open position variations | • Basic to side<br>• Promenade with a left quarter turn<br>• Open fans |

### TO DECREASE DIFFICULTY

- Repeat each variation as many times as needed to prepare for a new lead.
- Link variations in the order that you learned them, gradually adding another variation until you can link at least three together.

### TO INCREASE DIFFICULTY

- Repeat with different partners.
- Use a variety of tempos.
- Link more than three variations together or use multiple repetitions as needed to travel in the LOD.

## Success Goal

Perform four consecutive repetitions of two different combinations linking any three variations to tango music. ___

## Success Check

- Smoothly link each variation. ___
- Practice proper partner etiquette. ___
- Maintain the rhythmic step pattern. ___

# SUCCESS SUMMARY FOR TANGO

The tango has Latin origins that are exemplified in the characteristic panther-like walks, staccato foot changes, and the dramatic tango close finish to each rhythmic step pattern. The rhythm uses a *slow, slow, quick, quick, slow* pattern. The drama is a result of contrasting the quick and slow steps, which takes a lot of control. The basic rhythmic step pattern uses eight counts of 4/4 time music with a delayed weight change on the first two walking steps in order to increase the stride length. The tango mainly uses three dance positions: closed, promenade, and open. The variations in the tango are exciting to watch and to do!

# Salsa/Mambo

## *Adding Spice and Flavor*

The word *salsa* refers to sauce, or spicy flavor, which is characteristic of this popular social dance. This Latin American dance is similar to the mambo, but not as structured. Salsa is a composite of many Latin and Afro-Caribbean dances that were influenced by a variety of Latin American music styles. Bands from countries such as the Dominican Republic, Colombia, and Puerto Rico brought their music to Mexico City and eventually to New York City. In New York, the term *salsa* became the nickname used to refer to a variety of music with Hispanic influence. Many of these types were mixed to create salsa music. Salsa music is distinguished from other Latin American styles by the New York sound developed by Puerto Rican musicians in that city. Likewise, the salsa dance has many different styles.

The salsa emerged as a contemporary, street version of the mambo. The mambo, a spot dance with compact steps, was introduced in the United States near the end of the World War II and imported from Cuba. The mambo basic pattern is structured such that the break occurs on beat 2. The mambo's more difficult timing is most often done by advanced dancers. However, the mambo helped to shape the cha-cha, which is sometimes called the *triple mambo.* In contrast, the salsa may break on either beat 1 or 2, depending on the music, which makes it easier for social dancers. Many mambo-type step variations and borrowed cha-cha step variations (including cha-cha's break step) are used in the salsa. A number of films featured the mambo and Eddie Torres, a New York professional known as the Mambo King of Latin Dance. He defines the salsa as the authentic night-club style of mambo dancing.

The basic footwork is the same for both the salsa and the mambo; the difference is in the timing. The salsa breaks on counts 1-2 and 5-6, while the mambo breaks on counts 2-3 and 6-7. Both the salsa and the mambo use a *quick, quick, slow* rhythm, which is used when describing the basic rhythmic step pattern, variations, and combinations for these dance styles. You only need to adjust the timing of the basic step when you want to execute each one.

# RHYTHMIC STEP PATTERN FOR SALSA/MAMBO

The rhythmic step pattern for salsa/mambo may be executed from a shine position, a closed position, or a two-hands-joined position. The rhythmic step pattern repeats a *quick, quick, slow* (QQS) rhythm twice before the starting foot is free again—for a total of eight counts. The salsa/mambo rhythmic step pattern has a forward break and a backward break. The leader starts with the forward break while the follower starts with the backward break. Side breaks are also popular. A break is a quick change of direction such as forward, then backward, and vice versa; or left, then right, and vice versa. The forward break is always executed moving in a forward direction with the left foot, while the backward break is always executed moving backward with the right foot.

## Leader

Step or break forward with your left foot by shifting weight forward onto your left foot. Then shift your weight back to your right foot; that is, replace your right foot in its original location. These two weight changes correspond to the *quick, quick.* Step onto your left foot for the *slow.* Your right foot is now free to execute the backward break (see the follower's directions).

## Follower

Step or break backward onto your right foot. Then shift your weight forward onto your left foot, keeping it in its original location by replacing it. These two weight changes correspond to the *quick, quick.* Step onto your right foot for the *slow.* Your left foot is now free to execute the forward break (see the leader's directions).

Figure 14.1 shows various ways you might use to organize the counts and footwork for the salsa/mambo. Select those cues that most help you retain how to execute the salsa/mambo basic step pattern.

## Figure 14.1 **RHYTHMIC STEP PATTERN FOR SALSA/MAMBO**

### Footwork Cues

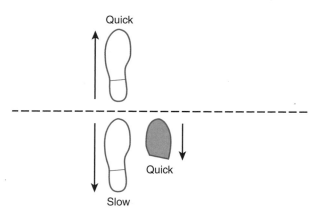

a Leader, left foot forward break and hold

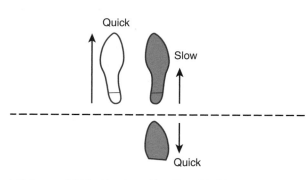

b Follower, right foot backward break and hold

*Forward break*

Left, right/replace, left & hold

*Backward break*

Right, left/replace, right & hold

### Timing Cues

| | |
|---|---|
| 4/4 time signature: | Four beats to a measure (group two measures) |
| Duration: | Each beat gets one count (total of eight counts) |
| Rhythm: | Quick, quick, slow; quick, quick, slow |
| Counts: | Salsa—1, 2, 3, hold 4; 5, 6, 7, hold 8 |
| | Mambo—2, 3, 4, hold 5; 6, 7, 8, hold 1 |
| Weight changes: | Salsa—Six, on beats 1, 2, 3, 5, 6, 7 |
| | Mambo—Six; on beats 2, 3, 4, 6, 7, 8 |
| Direction of steps: | Forward break—Forward, backward/ replace, in place |
| | Backward break—Backward, forward/ replace, in place |
| Foot positions: | Fourth, fourth, first; fourth, fourth, first |
| Floor contact: | Ball, ball, ball–flat; Ball, ball, ball-flat |

# DRILLS FOR SALSA/MAMBO

Both the salsa and the mambo use the same *quick, quick, slow* (QQS) rhythmic step pattern. Both salsa and mambo are done to 4/4 time Latin music. Review figure 14.1 for the timing differences for the salsa versus the mambo because it is your choice about which timing to use; both ways are appropriate on the social dance floor. For each drill, read the directions, and watch the video demonstrations on the enclosed DVD to see (a) how to execute the selected salsa variations, and (b) how to combine them into short practice combinations. Then, practice until you can meet the Success Goal for each drill. Use track 19 to practice both the salsa and the mambo.

## Drill 1
## Execution Challenge for Salsa/Mambo Basic Pattern

Face a partner in shine position (without touching). Verbally cue your partner when to begin. The leader starts with his left foot and the forward break (review figure 14.1a). The follower starts with her right foot and the backward break (review figure 14.1b). It helps to bend your knees slightly on the break steps and to keep your weight centered over both feet, rather than let your upper torso move either forward or backward. Time the *quick, quick* steps to be one count each, while the slow step takes two counts. Repeat on both sides of the body for a total of eight counts, or two measures of music.

Because three weight changes occur in each direction within four beats of music, there is a tendency to rush the steps together and not hold or pause on the last beat of each measure (counts 4 and 8 in the salsa, or counts 1 and 5 in the mambo). One option to help you better connect with the music is to execute a small heel dig, or low kick, at the end of each *slow,* or on counts 4 and 8 in the salsa. In the mambo, you can lower your CPB by bending your knees during the hold on counts 1 and 5. These nonweight actions give you something to do on the beat with a hold in each of the two measures. By accenting the *hold* counts, you also add a bit more styling to your dancing.

After you can move in unison with a partner to slow salsa/mambo music in shine position, practice the basic pattern with a partner in a two-hands-joined position. Then, repeat the basic steps while in a modified closed position (used for Latin dances as you did in the cha-cha and rumba). When in closed position, remember that the follower stands offset, or more on the leader's right side (not facing toe-to-toe). This will help you avoid stepping on your partner's feet. In addition, the elbows and forearms are closer together in the modified closed position.

### TO DECREASE DIFFICULTY
- Use verbal counts and gradually increase the tempo until you can move to the tempo of slow salsa/mambo music.
- Use only one partner position for the length of one song.

## TO INCREASE DIFFICULTY

- Use a variety of salsa/mambo music.
- Practice with different partners.
- Use salsa timing with a hold/pause on counts 4 and 8, then repeat the drill using mambo timing, which has a hold/pause on counts 1 and 5.

### Success Goal

Execute the salsa/mambo rhythmic step pattern with a partner first in shine position, then in a two-hands-joined position, and finally in a closed position. ___

### Success Check

- Take small steps. ___
- The leader breaks forward with the left foot to start. ___
- The follower breaks backward with the right foot to start. ___
- Salsa has either a hold or a heel dig on counts 4 and 8. ___
- Mambo has either a hold or a knee bend on counts 1 and 5.

___

## Drill 2
# Side Breaks (Second Position Breaks)

For variety, the salsa/mambo break steps may be executed to the side. These side breaks are sometimes called second position breaks because they use footwork in second position. In salsa, they have also been called *cucarachas*, which is the plural form of a Spanish word for cockroach because the quick side step mimics stepping on a cockroach (see figures 14.2 *a* and *b*). When the leader's left foot is free, he may step sideways to his left, then shift his weight back to his right foot (to replace it) during the *quick, quick* cues. On the *slow* cue, the leader brings his feet together as he steps in place with his left foot. The follower steps with her right foot to the right side and shifts her weight onto her left foot (to replace it) during the *quick,*

*quick.* On the *slow,* she brings her feet together as she steps in place with her right foot. Each partner then repeats the *side, replace, together* steps starting with the opposite foot. Remember to hold on the appropriate counts in order to match your actions with the music.

Face your partner in shine position and try the following practice combination: Do four repetitions of the salsa/mambo rhythmic step pattern (QQS) while alternately breaking forward and backward (for a total of 16 counts, or four sets of four counts), then do four salsa/mambo side basics (for a total of 16 counts, or four sets of four counts). When you are comfortable with the combined pattern, start in a closed position with a partner and repeat the combination.

*(continued)*

Drill 2  *(continued)*

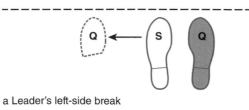

a Leader's left-side break

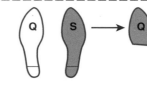

b Follower's right-side break

**Figure 14.2**  Side or second position breaks (a) to the left side and (b) to the right side.

### TO DECREASE DIFFICULTY

- Practice each part of the combination separately.
- Use slow salsa/mambo music.

### TO INCREASE DIFFICULTY

- Use a variety of salsa/mambo music.
- Practice with different partners.
- Vary the number of repetitions of the QQS rhythm, with a minimum of two measures or eight counts, before switching to the side breaks.

## Success Goal

Alternate the salsa/mambo rhythmic step pattern with side or second position breaks for 2 minutes.___

## Success Check

- Use second, second, first positions of the foot on the *side, replace, together,* respectively. ___
- The side step should be approximately the width of your shoulders. ___
- Make smooth transitions shifting weight from one foot to the other on the *quick, quick* while in second foot position. ___
- Maintain the rhythmic step pattern. ___

# Drill 3
# Cross-Body Lead

The cross-body lead is a useful transition in the salsa/mambo to smoothly connect many variations and to rotate 180 degrees with your partner. The cross-body lead takes eight counts to complete, or two *quick, quick, slow* repetitions. Try it with a partner in a closed position.

On the first QQS, the leader does a forward break starting with his left foot on the *quick, quick* as he steps forward and backward. On the *slow*, the leader rotates his left shoulder back CCW a quarter turn to face the side wall and steps onto his left foot with his feet in second foot position. This opens a slot or path for the follower to travel along. The follower does her backward break on the *quick, quick*, and a step forward on the *slow*.

On the second QQS, the leader continues to rotate his left shoulder back CCW a quarter turn to face the back wall as he steps *back, forward, forward* (stepping right, left, right). The follower takes two quick steps forward with her left foot, then right foot (moving down the slot) and rotates CCW a quarter turn to face the leader by swiveling on the ball of her left foot on the *slow*. Then, she does her backward break.

### TO DECREASE DIFFICULTY

- Practice your steps without a partner.
- Use a two-hands-joined position with a partner, small steps, and a slow count.

### TO INCREASE DIFFICULTY

- Execute two cross-body leads consecutively without any basics in between.
- Alternate a cross-body lead with two side breaks.

## Success Goal

Alternate salsa/mambo basic steps with the cross-body lead for 2 minutes. ___

## Success Check

- The leader faces the front wall, his left side wall, then transitions to face the back wall.___
- After her backward break steps, the follower moves down the slot on the second *QQS* and swivels to face the leader prior to her second *slow*.___
- Maintain the rhythmic pattern twice.___

# Drill 4
# Right Underarm Turn

The quicker tempo of the salsa/mambo music compared to the cha-cha music makes this CW underarm turn challenging and fun. Start in a closed position with your partner. It helps to break down the lead for the follower's right underarm turn according to four QQS basic steps. During the underarm turn, the leader's fingers and palm face down, while the follower's fingers and palm face up (with a slight arm bend, not a straight elbow).

## Leader

Execute two QQS basics, breaking forward and backward (for eight counts).

*(continued)*

## Drill 4  *(continued)*

On the third QQS do your forward break and place your left palm up, like a stop sign on the *slow*. This signals the follower to be ready to turn (but she doesn't turn yet). On the your fourth QQS, do a regular backward break, while the follower executes her forward break with a pivot turn and a spin. To lead the underarm turn, keep your palm approximately shoulder height and firm on the first *quick*. Extend your palm forward toward the follower's ear on the second *quick* and lift your left hand over the follower's head as she finishes the turn on the *slow*. End the turn by lowering your left hand back to the closed position.

### *Follower*

Do two QQS basics breaking backward and forward. On the third QQS, do your regular backward break and match your right hand with the leader's left hand in a palm-to-palm stop sign position on the *slow*. On the fourth QQS basic, during your forward break, place your left foot forward on the first *quick*, pivot CW 180 degrees to face the back as you shift weight onto your right foot on the second *quick* (see figure 14.3). On the *slow*, continue your CW rotation by spinning on your right foot as you move under the arched hands to face the leader and step onto your left foot. If you remember the full chase in shine position from the cha-cha, then this is similar with the exception that the leader maintains finger-to-palm contact during the pivot turn, and both partners replace the *cha-cha-cha* steps with only one weight change.

**Figure 14.3** Follower focuses on the back wall on her second *quick* of a right underarm turn.

### TO DECREASE DIFFICULTY

- Use the momentum of the shift from the left foot starting the pivot turn on the first *quick* onto an angled, or turned-out, right foot, then rotate the right shoulder back and clockwise to initiate the spin on the ball of the right foot on the second *quick*. Finish the *slow* facing your partner.
- Look in the direction of the turn: forward (toward your partner), back wall, forward (toward your partner).

## TO INCREASE DIFFICULTY

- Vary the number of basics prior to the underarm turn (the leader uses a stop sign signal at the end of any forward basic).
- Use a variety of tempos.

### Success Goal

Alternate salsa/mambo basics with the follower's right underarm turn for 2 minutes. ___

### Success Check

- Both partners keep the free arm curved and slightly in front of the body. ___
- Use a stop sign on the *slow* of the leader's forward break. ___
- The follower pivots on *quick, quick* (QQ) during her forward break, and she continues to rotate CW to finish the turn and face her partner on the *slow*. ___

# Drill 5
# Head Loops

At the end of the follower's right underarm turn, the leader changes hands to be in a right-to-right hand grasp. Then, he grasps the left hands below the right hands. Do two QQS basics in this crossed-handshake position (eight counts). On the leader's next forward basic, he lifts his right hand up and over the follower's head, releasing his right hand grasp. On the leader's back break, he brings his left hand up and over his own head with a release of his left hand at the end. Sometimes the head loop action may be called a *hair brush* or a *waterfall,* because of the image resulting from the curved shaping of the hands over the head. Resume a closed position and continue salsa/mambo basics.

## TO DECREASE DIFFICULTY

- Face your partner on the head loops and avoid any tendency to turn, by keeping the hands approximately waist level.
- Create the illusion of a curved arc such as brushing or smoothing the hair without actually touching the hair when you release the hand grasps above the head of your partner on each of the head loops.

## TO INCREASE DIFFICULTY

- Leave out the two basics before the head loops.
- Randomly lead a right underarm turn, or lead the head loops.

*(continued)*

Drill 5  *(continued)*

## Success Goal

Alternate salsa/mambo basics with head loops for 2 minutes. ___

## Success Check

- In the crossed-handshake position, grasp right-to-right hands on top and left-to-left hands underneath. ___
- Loop ladies first, then over the gentleman's head. ___
- Take four counts for each head loop. ___

# Drill 6
# <u>Right Turn (Behind-the-Back Pass) for the Leader</u>

The leader can turn, too—and have as much fun as the follower! It is easy to extend the head loop combination above by adding a behind-the-back pass for the leader and a second right underarm turn for the follower (for a total of eight QQS basics). Start in a closed position for the following She–He–She turn combination. The following directions are for the leader.

## First Basic

The leader breaks forward with a stop sign palm lead on the *slow*.

## Second Basic

The leader breaks backward as the follower does a right underarm turn.

## Third Basic

Leader breaks forward and does a behind-the-back pass. On the QQ, he pivots CW from his left foot to his right foot to face the back wall as he places the follower's right hand from his left hand into his right hand. Avoid sharply bending the elbows; instead, lower the arms to pass low behind your back. Spin on your right foot to face the follower and step on your left foot (on the *slow*).

## Fourth Basic

The leader breaks backward and uses his right-hand grasp to lead the follower into another right underarm turn.

## Fifth Basic

The leader breaks forward, keeping right-to-right hands on top and joining left-to-left hands below.

## Sixth Basic

The leader breaks backward, maintaining crossed-handshake grasps.

## Seventh Basic

The leader breaks forward with the right-hand head loop over the follower's head.

## Eighth Basic

The leader breaks backward with left-hand head loop over his head.

## TO DECREASE DIFFICULTY

- Without a partner, practice only the footwork for the CW pivot on a forward break, then do a backward break.
- In shine position, both partners can alternately practice the right turn when your left foot breaks forward, similar to the full chase in the cha-cha.
- Practice the leader's behind-the-back pass on any forward break basic, do the follower's underarm turn on the leader's backward break basic, then switch hands to resume a closed position.

## TO INCREASE DIFFICULTY

- Leave out the fifth and sixth basics to go immediately into the head loops.
- Alternate the She–He–She turn combination with any other salsa/mambo variation.

### Success Goal

Alternate salsa/mambo basics with the She–He–She turn combination for 2 minutes. ___

### Success Check

- Each basic QQS gets four counts. ___
- Eight total basics in the She–He–She turn combination___
- Maintain the rhythmic step pattern___

# Drill 7
# Fifth Position Breaks

The fifth position breaks from the rumba and the cha-cha are also used in the salsa/mambo. Both partners start the fifth position break by stepping back to position the leader's left and follower's right foot in a toe-to-heel foot position, and replace the other foot on the second *quick*. Face your partner on the *slow* step. Repeat the fifth position breaks alternating from side to side. Do a minimum of two basics, one to each side. The following combination uses four basics and gives the leader the option of leading the fifth position breaks using a waist-to-waist position, a hand-to-hand position, or both.

### Waist-to-Waist Position

Execute the basic in closed position. At the end of any backward basic step, the leader may step to his right side with his right foot and release his left-hand grasp. Figure 14.4 shows both partners' open arms in a semicircle facing the leader's left side as they do a fifth position break (with the leader's left foot and the follower's right foot stepping back). Face your

*(continued)*

### Drill 7 *(continued)*

partner on the *slow* step as the leader places his left hand on the follower's right shoulder blade. While facing the leader's right side, both partners do a fifth position break using their outside feet (with the leader's right and the follower's left foot stepping back). For practice do two repetitions to each side (four total QQS basics). Whenever the leader's left foot is free, he may resume a closed position and execute the basic forward and backward breaks.

## Hand-to-Hand Position

Another option for the leader is to open up the space between him and his partner by moving apart to a two-hands-joined position (see figure 14.5a) on each *slow*. Then, he can grasp her inside hand on each fifth position break (see figure 14.5b). Repeat at least four times before resuming a closed position again.

**Figure 14.4**   Waist-to-waist option during fifth position breaks.

a

b

**Figure 14.5**   Hand-to-hand option moving (*a*) from a two-hands-joined position into (*b*) fifth position breaks.

## TO DECREASE DIFFICULTY

- Practice your footwork without a partner.
- Start in a two-hands-joined position.

## TO INCREASE DIFFICULTY

- Do three fifth position breaks in a waist-to-waist position, then do three fifth position breaks in a hand-to-hand position.
- Alternate the fifth position breaks with any other salsa/mambo variation.

## Success Goal

Alternate salsa/mambo basics with four fifth position breaks first in a waist-to-waist position, and then in a hand-to-hand position for 2 minutes. ___

## Success Check

- Use toe-to-heel foot position (fifth position) on the break (QQ) steps. ___
- Face your partner on *slow* step. ___
- Open your shoulders approximately 45 degrees on each fifth position break. ___
- Keep your arms curved and in frame; don't let gravity take over. ___

# Drill 8
# Crossover Breaks (With Walkaround Turn Option)

From a two-hands-joined position, the leader has the option of breaking forward, but also of breaking while facing each side, called crossover breaks. Just like crossover breaks in the cha-cha and the rumba, the leader brings one hand from one side to the other, crossing the midline of his body each time. For practice, repeat the basic QQS rhythm a total of six times: one forward break, one backward break, and four crossover breaks.

Execute one basic with the leader breaking forward. On the second basic, the leader breaks backward with a direction change taking his *slow* step to his right side with his right foot and still facing his partner. The leader then swivels on the ball of his right foot as he releases his right-hand grasp and brings his left hand across his midline to face his right side.

On the third basic, the leader does a crossover break starting with his left foot (and the follower's right foot). He shifts weight from his left to his right foot as he breaks on the QQ, then swivels back to face his partner and grasp both hands on the *slow*. Preceding the fourth basic, the leader brings his right hand across his midline, releasing his left-hand grasp, and swivels on his left foot to face his left side. On the fourth basic, during the leader's crossover break, he

*(continued)*

**Drill 8** *(continued)*

shifts weight from his right to his left foot on the QQ, then swivels on his left foot to face his partner and resume a two-hands-joined position again on the *slow*. Repeat the crossover breaks at least two more times (fifth and sixth basics).

For the walkaround turn option, both partners may do a pivot turn during either or both crossover breaks. However, it is common to lead a walkaround turn on the fourth crossover break. Execute a pivot turn (rotating away from your partner) during the QQ, then face your partner on the *slow* step. Keep your outside foot stationary on the pivot, then finish the turn to face your partner.

### TO DECREASE DIFFICULTY

- Without a partner, practice the pivot turn facing each side wall on the QQ steps, keeping your outside foot stationary to spin on that foot to complete another half turn preceding to the *slow*.
- Use a slow count and check your position with your partner on each basic.

### TO INCREASE DIFFICULTY

- Randomly add a walkaround turn, such as on the fourth crossover break, or on both the third and fourth crossover breaks.
- Use a variety of tempos.

## Success Goal

Alternate two salsa/mambo basics with four crossover breaks for 2 minutes. ___

## Success Check

- Maintain the QQS rhythm. ___
- Break forward toward the side wall with your inside foot (closest to your partner) on the first *quick* of the crossover breaks. ___
- Replace your weight onto your outside foot on the second *quick* of the crossover breaks. ___
- Keep your weight over the balls of your feet and face your partner on the *slow*. ___

# Drill 9
# Side Cross Basic (Cumbia)

The side cross basic, or *cumbia,* is a versatile variation that may be used from a variety of partner positions: closed, two-hands-joined, or shine position. Notice that the cumbia must be repeated twice until your starting foot is free again. The leader starts with his left foot while the follower starts with her right foot. The footwork is the same for both the leader and the follower, yet it is the mirror reverse when facing each other.

### Left-Side Cross Basic

To travel to your left side, your left foot must be free. Slide your left foot diagonally backward and step onto your left foot (*quick*). Bring your right foot toward your left side to cross it over your left foot, then step onto your right foot (*quick*). Step again to your left side on the *slow* and leave your right foot on the floor. During the second-count hold of the *slow,* you may either point the toes of your right foot (without a weight change) or dig the heel of your right foot (without a weight change) toward your right side.

## Right-Side Cross Basic

To travel to your right side, your right foot must be free. Slide your right foot

diagonally backward and step onto your right foot (*quick*). Bring your left foot toward your right side to cross it over your right foot, then step onto your left foot (*quick*). Step again to your right side with your right foot and hold the fourth count (with either a left toe point or a left heel dig toward your left side). Figure 14.6, *a-c* shows the leader's right side cross (or cumbia) basic footwork from a two-hands-joined position. Repeat these actions on both sides in order to free your starting foot again; that is, complete at least two basics before leading another variation.

**a** Diagonal side (quick)

**b** Cross (quick)

**c** Side and point (slow)

**Figure 14.6** Side cross basic (cumbia) executed to the leader's right and the follower's left side.

*(continued)*

**Drill 9** *(continued)*

Mirror your partner's actions when in a shine position. When in a two-hands-joined position, the leader gently guides both hands to the appropriate side. When in a closed position, both partners need to take small steps and open their shoulders slightly toward the direction of travel. For example, open your left shoulder when traveling to your left. Try the cumbia variation from each of these three partner positions and select your favorite one.

### TO DECREASE DIFFICULTY

- Practice in shine position to review the footwork.
- Start in a two-hands-joined position.

### TO INCREASE DIFFICULTY

- Alternate four repetitions of the cumbia with four crossover breaks.
- Repeat the cumbia and transition to each of the three partner positions using at least four repetitions in each position to create a continuous sequence.

## Success Goal

Perform eight repetitions of the cumbia in each of three partner positions: shine, two hands joined, and closed. ___

## Success Check

- The first side step is diagonally back to make room to cross your opposite foot. ___
- On the *slow*, leave your non-weighted foot in the center. For example, keep either the toes or the heel of your free foot on the floor during the hold on the *slow*. ___
- Use four counts for each cumbia. ___

# Drill 10
# Open Break and Inside Left Turn

An open break and inside left turn is a variation that combines both a backward break with the leader's left foot and a cumbia to the leader's right side. With multiple repetitions of this variation, the leader ends up making a quarter turn CW to face a new wall each time. The open break and inside left turn is led from a one-hand-joined position. An option to this variation is a shoulder-check turn that ends with an open break and inside left turn. Another option is to add a second inside left turn on the leader's right side cross (cumbia).

## Leader

Instead of breaking forward with your left foot, break backward with your left foot (see figure 14.7). This action creates a rubber-band effect on the *quick, quick* such that both partners move apart, then toward each other. You need to take advantage of directing the follower's forward motion toward your right side to lead the inside left turn during the *slow* step. To start the turn, bring your left hand toward your right shoulder with either one or two fingers pointing down, lift your left hand up higher to make an arch, then loop it CCW over the follower's head. As you step forward with your left foot, rotate CW a quarter turn to face your partner (and your right-side wall). To end the turn, bring your hand down. Finish with a cumbia (step right, cross left, step right) to the leader's right side (review figure 14.6, *a-c*).

## Follower

Break backward as usual with your right foot on the first *quick,* then step diagonally left during your forward step on the second *quick.* Step forward again onto your right foot on the slow. With your weight on your right foot, rotate CCW approximately three quarters of a turn to face your partner. Square up your shoulders with your partner with your left foot free at the end of the turn. Then, execute a left-side cumbia by stepping diagonally back onto your left foot, right foot crosses, and left foot to the left side leaving your right free foot touching the floor (review figure 14.6, *a-c*).

**Figure 14.7**   On an open break both partners break backward to create a rubber band effect prior to the inside left turn for the follower.

For the shoulder-check turn option, the leader may stop the inside left turn and reverse it by placing his right hand on the follower's left shoulder blade or upper back on the *slow* step. Thus, a minimum of two basics are needed to execute the shoulder-check turn option. On the first basic, the follower does a backward break step, a replace onto her left foot, and a half turn CCW on her right foot (four counts). On the second basic, the follower does a backward break step with her left foot, replaces her right foot, and rotates a half turn CW on her left foot (four counts). To get out of this option, the leader lets the follower complete her inside left turn on the third basic, and both do a cumbia on the fourth basic.

*(continued)*

**Drill 10** *(continued)*

### TO DECREASE DIFFICULTY

- On the inside left turn, isolate the *slow* rhythm cue into two parts: turn CCW on the ball of the right foot, then square up to face your partner, giving each action one count.
- The leader can practice his part without a partner, using left foot breaks back, right foot replace, and quarter turn right as he steps onto the left foot on the *slow*.

### TO INCREASE DIFFICULTY

- Lead consecutive open breaks and inside left turns (e.g., on two, three, then four walls to form a square to get back to where you started).
- Lead a right underarm turn after any number of open break and inside left turns. The leader does his open break and steps to his left side on the slow and lifts his left hand to form an arch. The follower does her right pivot turn as the leader does his backward break.
- Add in two repetitions of the shoulder-check turn preceding the inside left turn and cumbia (with double left turn option).

## *Success Goal*

Alternate salsa/mambo basics with the open break and inside left turn for 2 minutes. ___

## Success Check

- Use two measures of 4/4 time music, or a total of eight counts for each open break and inside left (CCW) turn. ___
- At the end of his open break, the leader rotates a quarter turn CW to face a new wall each time. ___
- Both partners square up (with shoulders parallel) before executing the cumbia to the side in unison. ___

# Drill 11   On Your Own: Linking Four Salsa/Mambo Variations

It is time to challenge yourself by linking at least four salsa/mambo variations into longer combinations. For practice, try each of the following sample combinations using any number of repetitions of each and any number of basics in between each variation:

- Basic forward and backward in closed position, side breaks, right underarm turn, and head loops
- Basic forward and backward in shine position, side cross basic (cumbia), join to two

hands for crossover breaks, and walkaround turn(s)

- Basic forward and backward in closed position, She–He–She turn combination, open break and inside left turn, fifth position breaks (waist-to-waist, or hand-to-hand leads)

Now it is your turn either to modify these sample combinations or to create your own combinations of at least four salsa/mambo variations. Use the following points to refer to as you select the salsa/mambo variations.

- Basic steps (forward and backward)

- Side breaks (second position breaks)
- Cross-body lead
- Right underarm turn
- Head loops
- Right turn (behind-the-back pass) for the leader
- She–He–She turn combination
- Fifth position breaks (waist-to-waist and hand-to-hand position)
- Crossover breaks (with walkaround turn option)
- Side cross basic (cumbia)
- Open break and inside left turn (with shoulder check and double turn options)

## TO DECREASE DIFFICULTY

- Use a minimum of four repetitions of each variation.
- Use as many basics in between each variation as needed.
- Combine two variations, then gradually add another variation until you can link at least three together.

## TO INCREASE DIFFICULTY

- Repeat the drill with different partners.
- Use a minimum of two basics before leading another variation.
- Link more than four salsa/mambo variations.
- Experiment with other cha-cha variations that also work in salsa/mambo. For example, add a full chase turn (or half-chase) when in shine position. Just remember to modify it by using the QQS salsa/mambo rhythm.

## Success Goal

Perform four consecutive repetitions of each of two different combinations linking any four salsa/mambo variations to music. ___

## Success Check

- Maintain a salsa/mambo rhythmic step pattern.___
- Smoothly link each variation. ___
- Practice proper partner etiquette. ___

# SUCCESS SUMMARY FOR SALSA/MAMBO

The salsa is a Latin dance that is similar to the mambo. Both are done to a fast tempo and a *quick, quick, slow* rhythm. The salsa has emerged as a contemporary, street version of the mambo. The mambo helped shape the cha-cha. The main difference is that the salsa may break on either the downbeat or the upbeat—count 1 or 2—whereas the mambo breaks on count 2. The break and replace steps are executed on the *quick, quick* steps; each gets one count per change of direction, such as forward to backward/replace, or backward to forward/replace. The leader starts the forward break with his left foot, while the follower starts the backward break with her right foot. Each *slow* portion of the salsa/mambo's rhythmic step pattern uses two counts of music, including one weight change and a hold, or pause. The precise salsa/mambo timing is dependent on the music and on one's preference. Both are welcome on the social dance floor. Many of the same transitions and variations from the other Latin dances, especially the cha-cha, can be done in the salsa and the mambo. The characteristic Latin styling of the salsa/mambo variations make them fun, exciting, and a bit spicy!

# PART III

## Etiquette on the Dance Floor: Adding the Finishing Touches

**N**ow that you know how to do many, if not all, of the 10 social dances described in part II, the next steps are to transition your skills from a practice setting to the social dance floor, to refine your technique, and to add appropriate styling. Using a building analogy, you've laid a solid foundation in part I and set up strong support walls in part II. In part III, you add the roof and other finishing touches. The following learning steps will help you stand out from the crowd.

- *Step 15:* Dance Floor Etiquette—Knowing a lot of variations in practice may not help you on the social dance floor when spontaneous decisions have to be made in response to the changing locations of the other couples. Because the other couples are each doing their own thing, the flow of traffic becomes unpredictable and random. Thus, there are rules of the road that all dancers need to follow in order to make the social experience enjoyable for all. Knowing these rules can help reduce the amount of decision making needed on the dance floor. The drills identify specific practice situations that you will encounter on the dance floor and provide strategies so that you can adjust more quickly.

- *Step 16:* Turn Technique, Styling, and Timing Options—Because you can look better doing a few things well, this learning step helps you hone your turn technique to maintain balance and control. Selected tips and applications are given to help you refine your technique and to provide timing options for adapting to different music styles and new dance settings. Lastly, it is important to revisit the styling characteristics of each dance so that they are qualitatively different. Each dance that you do should not look the same. The drills help you practice specific situations where you can apply turn technique and styling. Once you understand how styling can improve your dancing image, you're on your way to becoming an accomplished dancer!

# Dance Floor Etiquette

## *Moving From Practice to Social Dance Settings*

In a practice setting, many couples are executing the same set combination at the same time. However, once you are ready for an evening of dancing, you'll soon find that a set combination does not necessarily work when the other couples on the dance floor are doing different combinations at different times because the flow of traffic is random and unpredictable. For example, if one of your favorite combinations includes variations that facilitate travel in the line of dance (LOD) and another couple moves immediately in front of you, blocking your forward motion, what should you do? Or, when given a choice, where should you stand on the social dance floor to start your combination? In the social dance setting, the type of dance dictates both where couples may locate on the dance floor and what types of movements to select. There are two basic categories of dances: progressive and spot dances. You are now ready to make the transition from a practice to a social setting, including how to modify your dancing to prevent collisions, use the floor space effectively, and practice good floor etiquette.

# IMPORTANCE OF DANCE FLOOR ETIQUETTE

Dance floor etiquette entails certain rules of the road that make social dancing more enjoyable for all couples. Once you know these rules, you can become a better social dancer by either following the rules or modifying them to fit the situation. But the rules don't work if you are the only one who knows them. Thus, at times it is beneficial to bend the rules a bit to prevent any accidents on the dance floor. In these cases, you must become a defensive driver and watch out for the unexpected. However, when the rules are known and followed, social dancing becomes a more enjoyable experience for all involved.

The ability to avoid collisions (bumping into other couples) on the dance floor is known as demonstrating good floor craft. To avoid collisions, the leader needs to focus externally to be aware of others, use peripheral vision to survey the field (observe other couples' locations on the dance floor), and make spontaneous decisions about which moves to execute for the particular situation (or configuration of couples) encountered. The follower needs to recognize the various leads, to trust the leader to make the correct decisions, and to respond to the leads (without anticipating or initiating them). Both partners need to dance with control, including being aware of when the floor is too crowded to travel very fast or to extend their arms too far out into another couple's space.

Demonstrating good floor craft is part of the etiquette expected on the social dance floor. Typically, the outside lane is for progressive dances that travel in the LOD, such as the foxtrot, waltz, polka, and tango. The inside lane is for slower dances that travel in the LOD and include some stationary as well as LOD traveling movements. If you are in the fast lane, avoid moving in a reverse LOD; rather, move to the slower, inside lane. The center of the floor is for spot dances such as various forms of swing and line dances. You may dance anywhere on the floor within your own small area for dances such as the merengue, swing, cha-cha, rumba, and salsa/mambo. These dances are sometimes called spot dances because a spot is staked out on the dance floor. In some instances, particularly with fast foxtrot tempos, it is your option whether to do a swing or a foxtrot—and a choice about where to start and execute these dance styles on the dance floor. As spot dances, the swing dance forms need to be executed in the center of the floor, particularly when other couples are executing the foxtrot in the progressive lanes. Figure 15.1 shows a diagram of the locations for executing various dance styles on the social dance floor. Following these rules of the road will make it more enjoyable for all dancers.

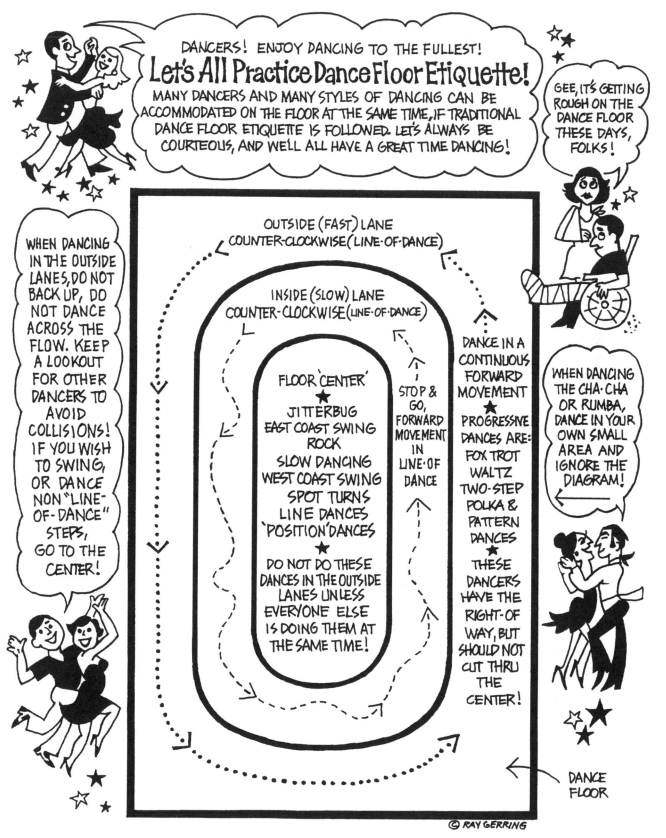

**Figure 15.1** Good floor etiquette is a must.

# STRATEGIES FOR ADJUSTING TO THE FLOW OF TRAFFIC

The social dance floor represents a dynamically changing setting. In an instant the leader needs to decide which variation to select and to signal the follower to execute it—all while avoiding bumping into other couples, keeping in time with the music, and moving in unison with the follower. At first, these decisions may seem like reactionary responses that can be disruptive to the flow of movement on the dance floor. However, with a proactive approach, the leader can plan ahead to have a strategy for adjusting to the common situations encountered on the dance floor. The following sections describe two strategies that can help the leader improve his decision making to make more spontaneous adjustments to the traffic encountered. For each dance style, you start by categorizing the dance variations into one of two options: progressive, or traveling, variations and spot, or stationary, variations. The advantage of using these two categories is that it narrows down the options for the leader, making it easier for him not only to recognize the situation, but also to select an appropriate variation.

## Progressive Dance Strategies

The ultimate goal for progressive dances that travel in the LOD is to travel—whenever there is space to do so. However, when another couple suddenly blocks your progression, you need to slow down and mark time or remain relatively stationary until the path is open again. You may pass other couples, but avoid cutting across the center of the room. Thus, one strategy for selecting the appropriate variation for the situation encountered is to separate the variations that you know so far according to whether they progress you forward in the LOD or keep you relatively stationary. As a review, the following strategies may be used when progressing in the LOD:

- The leader needs to use his peripheral vision to survey the floor to be aware of where other couples are on the dance floor. At all times, keep your head and eyes focused toward the direction of travel.

- When another couple abruptly moves into your path, select any of the stationary variations to execute. Continue with stationary variations until your path opens up again.

- When no other couple is immediately in your path, select any of the traveling variations to execute. Continue with traveling variations until your path is blocked or the traffic has slowed down.

- Avoid getting too close to other couples. Regulate the pace of your moves to adjust to the speed of the other couples. If they are moving slowly, select more stationary variations and avoid showy moves with extended arms and hands. If they are moving quickly, select more traveling variations to execute. If you happen to bump into another couple, excuse yourself and apologize at a convenient time.

## Spot Dance Strategies

One of the characteristics of spot dances is that they are executed within a small space, or spot, on the dance floor. In comparison with progressive dance styles, spot dances have fewer decisions involving other couples. Assuming each couple remains in their own area, the leader's decisions revolve more around which dance variation to select, including those that rotate or can be used to redirect the follower's motion in a new direction to avoid crashing into another dancer. For spot dances, when selecting a variation to execute with a partner, the leader may use the following strategies:

- The leader needs to be aware of the location of other couples before starting to dance in a particular spot.

- Select variations that help you remain within or return to your small circular area.

- Be ready to adjust the direction that you send the follower, such as in an underarm turn, so that she doesn't bump into another dancer or get bumped. For example, use the CW and CCW rotations in the swing to change your location within your spot.

- Adjust the size of your small area depending on the number of other couples on the floor at the same time.

- Avoid getting too close to others. If an unavoidable bump occurs, excuse yourself and apologize at a convenient time.

# DRILLS FOR DANCE FLOOR ETIQUETTE

Whether you are the leader or the follower, you both will be more comfortable on the social dance floor when you are aware of typical situations that may arise when dancing with others. The following drills will help you to be prepared with a plan of attack for addressing some common situations. You may make your music selections either from tracks 7 to 19 on the enclosed DVD, or select your own music when completing the drills.

## Drill 1
## Find a Starting Spot

Be aware of how you enter and exit the dance floor in order to avoid bumping into other dancers. Find an open space, or spot, on the floor that you can temporarily stake a claim to prior to dancing. Review figure 15.1 to identify the floor etiquette for where to stand to start according to the dance you will be doing. The progressive dances, such as waltz, foxtrot, tango, and polka travel in the LOD. Remember that for some foxtrot music selections, either a swing or a foxtrot may be executed. In this case, the swing dancers need to move to the center of the floor so that the foxtrot couples may progress in the LOD. With spot dances,

*(continued)*

**Drill 1** *(continued)*

such as the merengue, swing, cha-cha, rumba, and salsa/mambo, social dancers typically execute the same basic step pattern within a small area. Ask a friend to select music from two progressive dances and two spot dances without telling you either the name of the music or the dance style to use with it. Listen to each music selection, identify the appropriate dance, then dance and enjoy the music being played without bumping into other couples.

**TO DECREASE DIFFICULTY**

- Ask that the dance name be announced before hearing the music.
- Select any one progressive dance and any one spot dance.
- Gradually increase your repertoire.

**TO INCREASE DIFFICULTY**

- Practice with a variety of partners.
- Use a variety of tempos and variations.
- Execute a variety of dances.

## *Success Goal*

Play four different songs; select and dance two progressive dances (use tracks 9, 13, 14, 15, or 18) and then two spot dances (use tracks 7, 8, 10, 11, 12, 16, 17, or 19).___

## *Success Check*

- Listen, and select the appropriate dance style that best fits the music played. ___
- Select an appropriate open space on the dance floor to start. ___
- Dance to each music selection using the appropriate rhythmic step pattern. ___
- Practice avoiding collisions each time you're on the dance floor.

___

# Drill 2
# Progressive Dance Options

Rarely will you be able to do either all stationary or all traveling variations on the dance floor with progressive dances. It is more likely that a spontaneous decision will need to be made in response to the traffic encountered. As the leader, you have two options when dancing progressive dances: travel or remain stationary. This drill will help the leader to be prepared to make spontaneous decisions that are typically encountered when on the dance floor during progressive dances such as the waltz, foxtrot, polka, and tango. Three typical situations are described next.

## No Room to Travel

If the dance floor is very crowded and you cannot travel forward in a counterclockwise direction around the perimeter of the room, or in the LOD, the leader needs to select from the stationary variations that are known so far. For this practice situation, imagine that you are surrounded by other couples or find yourself trapped in a cluster of other couples. Thus, the leader can stand two or three feet (0.6-1 m) from and facing an outside wall with his partner in closed position. Now it is your turn to experiment with different stationary variations that will help you keep the rhythm, maintain your stationary position, and eventually get back facing the LOD. Selected stationary variations from four progressive dances are listed here:

- *Waltz*: Box step, balance step (forward, backward, sideward), left box turn, right box turn, cross step, weave step
- *Foxtrot*: Box step, left box turn, right box turn, rock step, left rock quarter turn, sway step, cross step, weave step
- *Polka*: Basic in place, around-the-world, reverse around-the-world
- *Tango*: Corte and recover, closed figure-eight fans, basic steps in promenade, promenade with a left quarter turn

## Room to Travel

If no other couples are blocking your forward motion, the leader's goal is to select traveling variations that progress in the LOD. In this practice situation, the leader starts in closed position with a partner facing the LOD. Assume that nothing is preventing forward travel in the LOD. Thus, the goal is to link traveling variations in any order to make at least two counterclockwise passes around the entire dance floor. Selected traveling variations from four progressive dances are listed here:

- *Waltz*: Half-box progressions (forward and backward), rollovers, scissors
- *Foxtrot*: Half-box progressions (forward and backward), two left quarter turns followed by two right quarter turns, promenade or conversation step, basic forward, rollovers, parallel forward and backward basics, zigzag
- *Polka*: Basic with underarm turn, front-to-front and back-to-back half turns, gallops, swivels, couples' turn
- *Tango*: Basic forward, forward with a left quarter turn, rock steps, open fans

## Spontaneous Decisions

Be alert as the traffic is unpredictable and unexpectedly another couple may move in front of you. Each time that you dance with other couples the situation will be different. Notice what works best for particular situations. Are there certain combinations that you tend to repeat over and over—your favorites? The leader can be proactive to identifying how to respond to these common situations, including how to intermix both stationary and traveling options when needed. In this practice situation, randomly place chairs or other physical objects around the room, including some in the LOD. Start in a closed position with a partner facing the LOD. The goal is to complete two CCW passes around the room by selecting appropriate variations that help you avoid contacting any of the stationary objects as you maintain the appropriate rhythm.

*(continued)*

Drill 3 *(continued)*

## TO DECREASE DIFFICULTY

- One strategy is to select the variations according to the order as listed.
- Use as many basic steps between each variation as needed to prepare for the next lead.

## TO INCREASE DIFFICULTY

- Experiment with a variety of combinations to find those that link most naturally.
- Use any order and any number of repetitions of each variation that is best suited for the situation.

## Success Goal

For at least two of the four progressive dances listed, demonstrate a solution to each of the practice situations: (a) Combine stationary variations (assume no room to travel), (b) combine traveling variations (assume room to travel), and (c) intermix variations to best fit the situation (either dance with other couples, or dance around objects such as chairs, poles, or other obstacles placed randomly on the dance floor that need to be avoided).

## Success Check

- Avoid impeding the flow of traffic within LOD or progressive dances. ___
- Select fluid, spontaneous combinations as appropriate to the flow of traffic encountered. ___
- Maintain the appropriate rhythmic step pattern. ___

# Drill 3
# Practice Good Floor Etiquette

Good floor etiquette involves sharing the dance floor with other dancers without interfering with their dancing. Once you have found your spot on the dance floor, the leader's task is to use peripheral vision to notice how the surrounding space changes as other dancers do their own moves. The leader may need to adjust the direction within the spontaneous combinations to accommodate the shifting floor locations of other dancers.

The previous drill focused on floor etiquette with progressive dances. However, the leader also may need to select appropriate variations and adjust his

leads for spot dances as well. For example, in the swing, if the leader is preparing to lead a single under, but another couple suddenly moves into the space where he and his partner intended to move, what might the leader do? One option is to repeat the rhythmic step pattern and rotate in either direction until enough space is open for a single under to be executed. Another option might be to do the single under without getting very far apart in order to reduce the amount of space used.

In addition, remember to practice good communication and etiquette with your dancing partner. For example, politely ask a partner to dance, introduce yourself (if you have a new partner), be responsible for your role in the partnership, and thank your partner after the dance. Other common courtesies are to avoid eating, drinking, or standing and talking with other dancers on the dance floor when other couples are trying to dance. If you want to talk with other dancers, just move off the dance floor. In this practice situation, politely ask six different partners to do six different spot dances, select appropriate variations, maintain the rhythmic pattern, and thank each partner after the shared dance.

## TO DECREASE DIFFICULTY

- Do short combinations of two or three variations.
- Use a slow tempo.

## TO INCREASE DIFFICULTY

- Execute both progressive and spot dances.
- Link four or more variations.
- Use a variety of tempos.

## Success Goal

Create spontaneous combinations using appropriate variations for the situations encountered during one song for each of the following spot dances: merengue, four-count swing, six-count swing, cha-cha, rumba, and salsa/mambo. ___

## Success Check

- Practice good floor etiquette each time you are on the dance floor. ___
- Excuse yourself if you happen to collide with another dancer. ___
- The leader needs to select variations that fit the dynamic situations encountered. ___

# SUCCESS SUMMARY FOR DANCE FLOOR ETIQUETTE

Whenever you move from a structured practice setting to a social setting, it is important to be aware of certain dance floor etiquette *rules of the road* to make everyone's experience more enjoyable. The ability to avoid collisions, or bumping into other couples on the dance floor, requires the leader to demonstrate good floor craft. This means knowing the basic steps and variations so well that the leader can focus more on the traffic encountered, which is constantly changing.

As a general rule, progressive dances that travel in the LOD should use the outside lane. Stop-and-start dances that travel in the LOD should use the inside lane. The center of the floor is for spot dances that remain more stationary or within a restricted area, especially if other dancers are traveling in the LOD. For some spot dances, especially when other dancers are not traveling in the LOD, the dancers may use the entire floor as long as they don't bump into other couples.

Lastly, be ready to modify the rules in order to blend with other dancers' interpretations or unawareness of the rules. Use the appropriate social etiquette needed to prevent collisions and confrontations on the dance floor. Be ready to be a defensive driver and enjoy the ride.

# Turn Technique, Styling, and Timing Options

## *Looking Good*

At some point in the search for new variations and combinations to do on the dance floor, you'll soon realize that it is more important to do a few moves well instead of many moves poorly. In particular, how you execute turns and how precisely you project the characteristic styling of each dance will make you stand out on the dance floor. An obvious indicator of poor execution with turns is when something goes wrong, such as loss of balance on turns (dizziness) or lack of control with timing (being late or out of sync with your partner or the music, or both). An indicator of poor styling is when it is difficult to identify the dance style being performed. For example, even though the same rhythmic pattern is used in different dances, such as the box rhythm within the box steps for the waltz, foxtrot, and rumba, each dance style should look qualitatively different. You can more accurately demonstrate the styling traditionally associated with different dance styles by becoming more aware of the unique characteristics of each style.

The goal in social dancing is to dance with a variety of partners and treat each other with respect as you are having fun on the dance floor. This means you need to find out where you can go dancing in your community. Look in the newspaper and ask around about clubs or studios or sponsored dances that you might be able to attend. Sometimes this means being creative at using the resources available to practice your dancing and get to know other people.

You'll soon find that some timing modifications and spatial adaptations are necessary to go with the flow of other dancers when you are in certain situations. Besides having to know the rules of the road and the proper etiquette, you might encounter additional situations such as dancing to unfamiliar music; adjusting the timing to better fit the tempo of the music being played; moving within a restricted space; and modifying rhythmic step patterns, variations, and combinations to fit the specific situations encountered. These challenges require problem solving, which takes time and practice. Each time you dance, try to focus on the three-way partnership that you are blending together— yourself, your partner, and the music. Make it an enjoyable experience that is appropriate to the social situation.

# IMPORTANCE OF TURN TECHNIQUE, STYLING, AND TIMING OPTIONS

A popular variation in most dances is some sort of turn (rotating 360 degrees). Once you understand a few turn technique tips, you can not only improve your confidence and timing, but also avoid getting dizzy on turns. It helps to know where to place your feet, how to align your body, where to focus your eyes (or spot), how fast to turn, when to turn, and how to grasp hands with your partner. Once you know how to execute a single turn, the next challenge is to execute a double turn. With practice, you'll be able to do multiple consecutive turns without difficulty.

During the early stages of learning to dance, you need to break down moves into parts and to memorize what to do on each move. During the middle to later stages of learning, the basic rhythmic patterns become more automatic. Once you have fewer things to think about, make sure that you demonstrate the flavor and essence of each dance rather than perform each dance qualitatively the same. This contrast reflects the transition between practice (more mechanical) and performance (more expressive) situations. Once you get on the social dance floor, you are performing. Wouldn't you like to hear compliments about your dancing?

If you can increase your opportunities to dance, you can increase your rehearsal time and have a better chance of polishing your skills. So as you survey your community to locate places where you can practice or perform, you may need to be flexible so as to adapt to a variety of dance settings. Many basic rhythmic step patterns may be executed either exactly the same or slightly modified to match the music. The most important goal is to work in unison with your partner to create fluid movements that fit the music.

# TECHNIQUE STRATEGIES AND TIPS

Good dancers make it look easy when there is always a trick or strategy into how, when, where, and to what extent that a particular move is executed. If you want to bump up your dancing skills a notch, then you need to be aware of how you execute your moves, or the technique that you use. In particular, the technique that you use on turns, styling, and timing with the music will set you apart from the rest. In the following sections you will find specific strategies and technique tips on how to execute a variety of turns, add characteristic styling to each dance, and offer timing options for a variety of situations you may encounter.

# Turn Technique

Using a foot-to-head order, there are at least five areas that contribute to your ability to execute a turn with finesse: foot placement, alignment, body torque, spotting, and timing. Don't expect to be able to tackle these areas all at once. Start with your footwork and gradually focus on another aspect. If your footwork is not balanced, everything else will be off too. After focusing on your personal techniques, it is important to work with your partner. Hand grips can often be too tight, especially with underarm turns. Thus, your hand positions with your partner affect your ease of execution.

## Foot Preparation and Placement

When the leader signals a turn, it is a cue for the follower to position her feet in preparation for the turn. Angling the foot approximately 45 degrees sets up the turn so as to overcome inertia and gain momentum. An angled foot is also a more stable foot because it widens your base of support. Typically, turns are set up from either an extended third or an extended fifth position of the foot to improve balance and control. Prep your foot in the direction of the turn; the left foot angles (an eighth of the turn) to the left on left turns, and the right foot angles (an eighth of the turn) to the right on right turns.

Generally, three types of turns are popular in social dance: pivot turns, three-step turns, and spins. A pivot turn is a half turn, as you've seen in a number of variations so far (e.g., in the half chase or the walkaround turns used in the cha-cha, rumba, and salsa/mambo). For practice, start in fourth position with your left foot forward. Transfer your weight from the ball of your left foot to your right foot during the CW pivot turn. You can also pivot CCW by shifting weight from the ball of your right foot to your left foot.

The three-step turn is sometimes called a *chaîné turn*. Keep your weight on the balls of your feet throughout. The amount of turn on each step is quarter, quarter, half. Aim for a first position in the middle, especially if speed is important. Use the cues *step, together, step*. You might lead this turn during a side balance in the waltz.

The most difficult turn is a spin, or a 360-degree turn on the ball of one foot. For example, you did a complete turn within the tuck and spin variation used in the six-count swing. It is important to keep your body's weight over your base of support during a spin turn. Avoid stepping beyond the width of your own shoulders to prep the turn.

## Alignment and Center Point of Balance (CPB)

Review Step 1, as needed, to reinforce how to achieve the following concepts during turns:

- Vertical alignment

- Centering, or keeping your CPB over your base of support (your feet)

- Maintaining your individual frame (arm and shoulder placement)

Your posture during turns is foundational for balance and control. Other aspects that affect your balance on turns are body torque, spotting, and timing.

## Body Torque and Contra-Body Positioning (CBP)

Your shoulders provide body torque to facilitate your turn execution, especially on spins. As you step with your foot angled outward to set up the turn, notice that your opposite shoulder also rotates in the direction of the angled foot. This opposition is called contra-body positioning, or CBP (see figure 16.1). You use CBP each time that you walk, as opposite arms and legs move together. Other sports use body torque as well, such as ice skaters when spinning, baseball players swinging a bat, or golfers swinging a club. In each case, the shoulders provide torque for the turns through the twist, or rotation of the upper torso one way, then unwind in the opposite direction. Think of either your right shoulder rotating backward on right, or CW, turns or your left shoulder rotating backward on left, or CCW, turns.

Another tip is to commit your weight onto your angled foot as you prep the turn such that your center of gravity is above the ball of that foot. If you don't shift your weight onto your angled foot, you will not be able to complete the turn. The combination of CBP and weight over the angled foot along with shoulder torque will create momentum for any turn.

**Figure 16.1**　To set up for a left turn, the right shoulder is rotated toward the angled left foot, which is an example of using CBP.

## Spotting

Typically, you need to look in the direction that you are going to turn. Once you know the direction of the turn, it helps if you focus your eyes on one spot throughout the turn rather than let your eyes wander so that you become dizzy from seeing everything in the room. This focusing technique is called *spotting*. Spotting technique is the same whether you want to execute a single turn or multiple turns. It involves the ability to isolate your head from the rest of your body—which sounds more difficult than it is. Without worrying about any footwork, select a spot in front of you at approximately eye level (see figure 16.2*a*). Keep watching that spot as you rotate your right shoulder back and look back over your left shoulder for a right or CW turn (see figure 16.2*b*). Continue watching the spot in front until you get to the halfway point where you might not be able to watch your spot if you rotate any farther. Then quickly snap your head around (faster than your body) to visually locate your spot again as you look over your right shoulder (see figure 16.2c). Let your shoulders rotate to finish the turn as you continue to watch your spot (see figure 16.2d). Spotting permits you to watch one spot throughout the turn, or one point that you are traveling toward, which helps you avoid getting dizzy. Try this without a partner. Practice spotting while turning both CW and CCW. It also helps to open and close your arms before and during the turn, respectively. With very fast turns, use a narrow base with your feet closer together.

**a** Look at a spot that is eye level

**b** Look back over your left shoulder

**c** Look back over your right shoulder

**d** Look at your spot

**Figure 16.2** Head and shoulder positions while spotting during a right or clockwise turn.

On the dance floor and with a partner, you have several choices on where to spot. In progressive dances, either the LOD or the RLOD are useful spots. In spot dances, either your partner or the general direction of the turn may be used. When spotting on turns, your head (and focused eyes) lags behind your shoulders, then is first to arrive (before your shoulders).

## Timing on Turns

The speed of your turn will also affect your balance and overall execution. On spin turns, practice moving quickly through the spin as you spot. Since a spin is executed on the ball of one foot, the less time you balance on one foot, the less likely it is that you will lose your balance. It is helpful to use the cue *spot through* as a reminder to move quickly through each turn. To stop your momentum at the end of the turn, slightly lower your center of gravity by softening and bending your knee. You might also widen your base of support by stepping onto your other foot at the end of the turn.

As you know, a pivot turn is a half turn within two beats of music. You can coordinate the timing of the turn with where you focus your eyes. For example, on the half chase in the cha-cha, look, or focus, forward (on count 2), backward (on count 3), then forward again (or partner, back wall, partner) as you complete the turn. Or, on walkaround turns in the cha-cha (and other Latin dances), look, or focus, on the side wall (on count 2), side wall (count 3), then partner (to finish the turn).

On three-step turns, be aware of the rhythmic step pattern and where the turn comes within that basic pattern. For example, you could make three weight changes, one on each beat of music within the side balance in the waltz (using 3/4 time music). Or, the timing could be syncopated (faster) such that your three weight changes are done within two beats of music (using 4/4 time music). For example, if you add a three-step turn during the *cha-cha-cha* portion of the rhythmic step pattern, the turn occurs on counts *4-&-1*.

## Hand Positions on Underarm Turns

If you grip your partner's hand too tightly, it will be difficult to do any underarm turn. For right underarm turns, a palm-to-palm connection is useful. Start with an arch (leader raises his left arm). Let the follower do a CW or right underarm turn. Figure 16.3 shows the leader's palm facing downward while the follower's palm faces upward. You must have enough downward and upward pressure so that your hands stay connected. Notice how the fingertips are able to rotate freely on the underarm turn. You need to stay connected with your partner throughout the turn. Avoid straightening your elbow on the turn; both partners need to keep their elbows slightly rounded. Try this palm-to-palm connection with all your right turns and see how it works with your partner.

With an inside, or left, turn like you did in the swing dances and in the salsa/mambo, it is useful to use a cup-and-pin technique. The leader extends one or two fingers while the follower makes a cup, or C shape, with her hand. The leader can rotate with his fingers to control how many turns and lowers his hand when he wants to end the turn. Again, it is important to stay connected with your partner and to avoid straightening elbows. Put this lead-and-follow technique in action to make your left turns smoother and easier to execute.

**Figure 16.3** Palm-to-palm hand position on the right underarm turn in the cha-cha.

## Styling

Once you know the basic step patterns and can execute a few variations, you need to remember that each dance has its own unique styling. The challenge now is learning how to demonstrate the characteristic styling for each dance so that your dances don't all look alike. Any knowledgeable observer should be able to recognize which dance you and your partner are executing. If you execute every dance with the same quality, such as everything is smooth, you will be less expressive on the dance floor than dancers who play with the timing to contrast fast and slow movements and demonstrate the characteristic styling.

Following is a summary of selected descriptions to support the desired images that are characteristic of the dance styles covered in this book.

- Merengue—constant motion, fast tempo, turns without letting go of hands, and rotation as a couple

- Four-count swing—fast, rhythmic, and steady

- Waltz—stately posture, wavelike rise-and-fall motions, and an accent on the downbeat

- Six-count swing—torso leans, jazzy, and syncopated

- Foxtrot—smooth, gliding, and regal

- Polka—lively, fun, and springing

- Cha-cha—staccato, Latin, and flirtatious

- Rumba—sultry, romantic, and the dance of love

- Tango—dramatic moves, slow catlike walks, and staccato foot movements

- Salsa/mambo—*hot*, Latin, expressive, and compact moves

## Timing Options

As you found out in step 3, the music's tempo dictates how fast you need to move, while the timing of your steps (weight changes) in relationship with the beats of the music creates the basic rhythms used in all social dances. Each social dance has a unique rhythmic step pattern, or basic step. If the dance style has more than one rhythmic step pattern to choose from, give each a try as one of them will usually fit the tempo of the music better than the other. For example, two dances, the foxtrot and the six-count swing, have more than one basic step pattern to select. In the foxtrot, you may choose between or intermix two rhythmic step patterns: six-count, or basic, rhythm, and four-count, or box, rhythm. In the six-count swing, you have three rhythmic step patterns that are appropriate for slow, moderate, or fast tempos. Because each of these three swing basics are executed in six counts, it is each partner's decision about which basic step pattern to execute—even if you do a different basic step pattern than your partner to the same tempo.

Whenever you find that the music is either too slow or too fast to execute your regular rhythmic step patterns, you need to make some timing adjustments. For example, in the foxtrot, if the tempo seems very slow, the leader has the option to make all of the steps *quick* steps (one count per weight change). Or, if the tempo seems very fast, the leader has the option to make all of the steps *slow* steps (two counts per weight change). Remember that *quicks* and *slows* are relative to each other and are not absolutes.

You may have noticed that advanced dancers often vary, or *play with*, the timing. For you, this means that the more automatic your rhythmic step patterns become, the more aware you need to be of the rolling count (review step 2 as needed). The rolling count is especially useful whenever you execute a triple rhythm or a triple step (i.e., three weight changes in two beats of music). For example, in 4/4 time music, there are four beats to a measure. You can break any one beat into halves, or syncopate (speed up) the timing. You can also break any one beat into thirds, by counting *&-a* preceding each beat. When you use this rolling count, you delay your weight change until the *a* before the beat. Thus, in cha-cha, you would break forward on counts 2-3, then *cha-cha-cha* (counted as 4-&-a-1) yet you would move only on counts 4, a-1. Pausing during the *&* count and then moving during the *a* count gives surprise and excitement to your dancing. Try this with the triple swing. Have fun, and enjoy playing with the timing!

The following general guidelines will help you make appropriate selections or adjustments to the timing of your rhythmic step pattern(s) to best fit the tempo played:

- The faster the tempo, the shorter the step.

- The slower the tempo, the longer the step.

- Very fast tempos in the foxtrot may be altered to all slow steps.

- Very slow tempos in the foxtrot may be altered to all quick steps.

- Any six-count swing basic step pattern may be used with the three tempos of swing music. Use the rolling count on the triple swing.

- Delay your weight changes during the tango's *slow, slow* walking steps to extend your stride length and land on the second and fourth counts.

- As necessary, create your own rhythmic step pattern that fits the music and the situation.

# DRILLS FOR TURN TECHNIQUE, STYLING, AND TIMING OPTIONS

The following drills will help you practice your technique for executing two different turns, including examples of how they are used within selected dances. You also will get a chance to listen to different music selections (without knowing the type of music or dance style) and to select a specific rhythmic step pattern that you can execute for the length of that music selection. Lastly, you will be asked to demonstrate appropriate technique, timing, and styling to qualitatively distinguish four different dance styles.

## Drill 1
## Three-Step Turn Execution

The three-step turn is completed with three weight changes while moving to either side. To execute a three-step turn CW, angle your right foot toward the right side (making a quarter turn) and step onto that foot. Continue rotating a quarter turn CW and step onto your left foot with feet in first position for the second weight change. Finish with a half turn CW on the third weight change and face the front. However, the timing of these weight changes will vary according to the selected dance variation executed. For practice, try adding a three-step turn in the following selected dance styles. Followers will need to spot to avoid getting dizzy.

### Foxtrot

Execute the promenade, or conversation step using the six-count, or basic, rhythm. On the next basic step the leader lifts his left hand to form an arc on the first *slow*, while the follower angles her right foot toward the LOD. The follower continues rotating CW on the second *slow* to face the outside wall. She completes the CW turn on her third weight change on the *quick* step. While facing the leader, the follower moves in unison with the leader to bring the feet together on the second

*quick* count. During the three-step turn, her foot positions are second, first, and second. Remember that the leader uses his right hand to gently guide the follower in the direction of the turn (CW), and he lowers his left hand to end the turn.

### Waltz

Execute two side balance steps (three counts to each side) in 3/4 time. On the next side balance, the leader lifts his left hand to signal a right underarm turn. The follower executes her three weight changes by rotating CW and stepping on each count. The leader may bring his left hand CCW to lead a CCW three-step turn for the follower. The foot positions are second, first, and first.

### Cha-Cha

Using crossover breaks, add a three-step turn for the follower on the *4-&-1* counts. At the end of any right-side crossover break, the leader brings his left hand across his midline and releases the follower's right hand (much like throwing a Frisbee). The follower can use this momentum to rotate CW on the *cha-cha-cha* steps as the leader does his regular *4-&-1* counts to his left side.

*(continued)*

**Drill 1** *(continued)*

At the end of the leader's left-side crossover break, he brings his right hand across his midline and releases the follower's left hand (again like throwing a Frisbee). The follower uses this momentum to do a CCW three-step turn on the *cha-cha-cha* steps as the leader does his regular *4-&-1* counts to his right side. To stop the turns, the leader resumes a two-hands-joined position after each crossover break. Use small steps on the turn. As an option, the leader may also turn at the same time as the follower. Remember to spot!

## TO DECREASE DIFFICULTY

- Maintain the rhythmic timing and tempo regardless of foot positions during the turns.
- Execute only the foxtrot turn because the timing is on the *slow, slow* then side–together is on the *quick, quick.*

## TO INCREASE DIFFICULTY

- Lead two consecutive underarm turns during any one conversation step.
- Identify and experiment with other variations where the three-step turn might be useful. For example, add a three-step turn during the *quick, quick, slow* of a cumbia (side-cross basic) in the salsa/mambo.

## Success Goal

Perform two consecutive repetitions of the three-step turn as an option when executing first the conversation step in the foxtrot, then the side balances in the waltz, and finally the crossover breaks in the cha-cha. ___

## Success Check

- Feet are in either extended third or fifth position to set up the turn.
  ___
- Spot in the direction of the turn.
  ___
- Maintain the appropriate rhythmic step pattern.___

# Drill 2
# Double-Turn Execution

A fun variation in many dances is a double turn. It is the leader's job to initiate and end turns. Thus, for a double turn, the leader needs to keep his left hand high longer. Generally, as long as the leader keeps his hand above the follower's head, the turn is to be continued. This can be a problem for the follower, however, especially if she doesn't spot. Once the leader lowers his hand below his partner's head, the turn is over. The challenge in this drill is to lead two consecutive turns, or a double turn. Examples from four different dance styles follow.

## Six-Count Swing

With slow music and the triple swing rhythmic step pattern, the leader may lead a CCW double turn for the follower from a one-hand-joined position. After any ball–change, the leader brings his left hand across his midline toward his right shoulder. The leader starts the follower's CCW turns with a small circle above the partner's head for the follower's first turn during the first triple step, and without lowering his hand, he can continue making another small circle above the partner's head for the follower's second turn during the second triple step. The leader lowers his left hand to end the turn so both partners can do their ball–change step. The leader needs to continue rotating CW to face the follower during his execution of the two triple steps. Also, try a CW double turn for the follower.

## Four-Count Swing

The leader can repeat the previous leads for a CCW double turn, except that the timing is different. The follower does four walks as she steps on each beat, taking two walks on each left turn. Remember to spot on the leader. Also try a CW double turn.

## Cha-Cha

From a shine position, a CW double turn may be used as a variation of the chase.

Start with a regular half chase (or half turn), then add another 1 1/2 turns on the *cha-cha-cha* steps in order to face your partner again. As in the regular chase variations, the leader executes a double-turn chase, then the follower executes a double-turn chase. After his double turn, the leader remains facing his partner to execute his forward break. Spotting can break this double turn into parts for easier execution. On the first half turn focus forward, then to the back wall. Do a full turn while spotting on the back wall. Then, finish the last half turn and spot forward again (on your partner).

## Polka

From a closed position, execute the polka basic step pattern on both sides of your body (i.e., four counts). To signal a double turn, the leader lifts his left hand to form an arch and gently presses with the heel of his right hand on the follower's left shoulder blade to indicate the direction of the turn (CW under the arch and toward the LOD). As long as the leader keeps his left hand high, the follower knows to continue turning a half turn on each basic step. After two turns using four basic steps, or eight counts until the leader's left foot is free again, the leader may lower his left hand and resume a closed position with his partner. If you are ambitious, the double turn may be executed in a total of four counts, one turn on each polka basic step. Spot on the leader on each turn. The leader needs to do his basic steps in place to give the follower space to execute the turns.

### TO DECREASE DIFFICULTY

- Without a partner, practice spotting on the double turns, using both CW and CCW directions.
- Use torque to get through the turn faster such that your right shoulder rotates back on a right turn, while the left shoulder rotates back on a left turn.

*(continued)*

Drill 2 *(continued)*

### TO INCREASE DIFFICULTY

- Create a combination of any four to six variations that includes at least one double-turn variation (as appropriate to the selected dance style).
- In the polka, experiment with two polka basic rhythms, or four counts, for a couple's turn, then two polka basic rhythms for the follower's double turn.

## *Success Goal*

Perform eight repetitions alternating basics with a double turn variation in each of the following dances: four-count swing, six-count swing, cha-cha, and polka. ___

## *Success Check*

- Maintain the tempo throughout your turn. ___
- Keep your free arm extended from your center. ___
- Select a specific spot or focus during the turns (e.g., on the LOD, the RLOD, or your partner). ___
- Prep or angle your foot in the direction of the turn (i.e., left foot angles on left turns, right foot angles on right turns).

___

# Drill 3
# Assessing Which Step Pattern Fits the Music

During an evening of social dance, rarely will anyone announce the type of dance appropriate to the song being played. You'll need to be able to quickly assess which rhythmic step pattern best fits the music. Obviously, some types of dances, such as the waltz or the polka, are easier to identify than others. However, when in doubt, especially with unfamiliar music, you may need to experiment with different rhythmic step patterns that you think might work. Try out each rhythmic step pattern that might be a solution until you find one that fits. For example, the six-count basic step patterns used in the foxtrot and in the six-count swing or the four-count swing are very versatile basic step patterns that may work with a variety of music styles.

Sometimes at weddings or other events that include dancing, you may be limited to spot dances. Usually this occurs when the majority of the guests are unaware of the rules to follow on the dance floor for how to progress in the LOD. You can still choose to do stationary variations, such as the box step or the rock step variations in foxtrot. Or, for contemporary music, the four-count swing/hustle is a good choice to try. You might try just the box rhythm and move any way you want on the two walks, then a step and a touch, which is also called the nightclub foxtrot.

It is typical to have slow dances at social events. What can you do to these types of songs? You might try a sway step (from the foxtrot) or just the first portion—the step and touch to each side. It is easy to rotate as a couple to do these steps and remain within a small spot on the floor. Give it a try.

Listen to 10 different songs (randomly selecting social dance music as well as popular music) and experiment with various rhythmic step patterns until you find one that fits, or can be modified to fit, the music being played. Use tracks 7-19 and any other music sources for your selections.

### TO DECREASE DIFFICULTY

- Listen to contemporary music on the radio or ask a partner to play random selections of songs for you to identify which basic step pattern would best fit the music.

- Count the underlying beats to determine the time signature and listen for accents in the music that might give a clue.

### TO INCREASE DIFFICULTY

- Listen to unfamiliar music and test yourself on which rhythmic step pattern would best fit that music.

- Once you've found an acceptable match with the music, include the appropriate variations associated with the selected basic step.

- Experiment with the foxtrot's rock steps, the left rock turn, or the right rock turn during slow dances.

- Create a rhythm by modifying the sway variation; for example, two slow sways (using a side step and touch), then four quick sways to each side rocking weight from one foot to the other (for a total of eight counts).

## Success Goal

Execute an appropriate rhythmic step pattern, variations, and combinations that best fit each of 10 different music selections for 2 minutes.___

## Success Check

- Move in unison with your partner and the music. ___
- Change to another basic step pattern if one doesn't work. ___
- Practice good floor craft and demonstrate good partner etiquette. ___

# Drill 4
# Demonstrate Characteristic Dance Styling

How you move on the dance floor can make your dancing more dramatic and engaging for you, your partner, and spectators. The flair with which you execute both the basics and the variations in each dance style will bring your dancing to life and make it more exciting to do and to watch. Now is the time to shift your concentration toward expressing the characteristic styling for each dance you execute.

For example, listen to music appropriate for a waltz, foxtrot, and rumba (use tracks 9, 13, and 17). Each of these dances has a box step variation, yet the styling should be very different. Use imagery as necessary to achieve a different look for each of these dance styles. Then, execute the box step to each music selection and add the appropriate styling for each dance.

In another example, with German, Polish, or country-western polkas, the same basic polka step is used, but the styling needs to be different. The German polka uses stomps for heavy accents. The Polish polka uses dainty, light steps, while the country-western polka eliminates the hop entirely and only uses the triple steps, which are called *shuffle steps.* The latter dance styling offers a low-impact option for polka dancers. Try these polka variations for yourself (use tracks 14 and 15).

## TO DECREASE DIFFICULTY

- Select only one dance style to work on at a time.
- Without music, execute the box step three different ways.
  Ask a partner if he or she can identify which dance style you demonstrated.

## TO INCREASE DIFFICULTY

- Use the rolling count and experiment with the timing.
- Dance with different partners.
- Add appropriate turns within your selected dances.

## Success Goal

For 2 minutes each, demonstrate characteristic styling and timing for differentiating the box step within the waltz, foxtrot, and rumba and for three different polka styles.___

## Success Check

- Match styling with your partner.
  ___
- Position your free arms. ___
- You, your partner, and the music should all connect. ___

# SUCCESS SUMMARY FOR TURN TECHNIQUE, STYLING, AND TIMING OPTIONS

The fun begins when you are able to execute both single and double turns as variations within a variety of dance styles. It is also the time to hone your turn technique to maintain balance and control. Specific turn technique tips address five typical concerns: where to place your feet to initiate turns, how to maintain balance, how to create body torque to get more speed on turns, where to focus your attention during the turn to avoid getting dizzy, and how fast or slow to execute the turn.

Now that you are more comfortable with the basics and selected variations within a variety of dance styles, it is important to review and concentrate on how well you are projecting the characteristic styling associated with each dance style. The selected descriptions provided will give you a sense of the flavor or image to achieve with each of the ten dance styles covered in this book.

Whenever you get the opportunity to go to a dance, take advantage of it. Go to as many dances as you can and practice your social dancing skills. Accept the fact that it is normal for mistakes to occur on the dance floor. Even advanced dancers make mistakes, but they cover them so well that most people do not notice anything went wrong. So, try to learn from your mistakes, including how not to *telegraph*, or make them stand out. Try to do at least one thing better each time you dance. Remember to demonstrate good partner and floor etiquette, including thanking your hosts for the evening. Social dancing is more than just executing dance steps. Have fun and enjoy your journey; it can last a lifetime!

# Rating Your Progress

Congratulations on your journey through the 16 steps to success. You have covered a lot of material in this book. In particular, you have explored rhythm and timing elements, and you have learned the rhythmic step patterns for 10 different social dances, how to communicate with your partner verbally and nonverbally, and how to use your new dance skills in various situations. Take time to evaluate your progress by completing the following charts.

## TECHNIQUE AND EXECUTION

| | Very good | Good | Fair | Poor |
|---|---|---|---|---|
| 1. Move with good posture. | ☐ | ☐ | ☐ | ☐ |
| 2. Center weight over base of support. | ☐ | ☐ | ☐ | ☐ |
| 3. Position arms to create frame. | ☐ | ☐ | ☐ | ☐ |
| 4. Hear and walk to an underlying beat. | ☐ | ☐ | ☐ | ☐ |
| 5. Practice and demonstrate proper etiquette. | ☐ | ☐ | ☐ | ☐ |
| 6. Execute the rhythmic step patterns for 10 social dances while moving in unison with a partner to music. | ☐ | ☐ | ☐ | ☐ |
| 7. Smoothly transitions between the appropriate partner dance positions according to the dance style. | ☐ | ☐ | ☐ | ☐ |
| 8. Execute the appropriate variations according to the dance style. | ☐ | ☐ | ☐ | ☐ |
| 9. Demonstrate short combinations for each social dance style. | ☐ | ☐ | ☐ | ☐ |
| 10. Follow the etiquette "rules of the road" when on the dance floor. | ☐ | ☐ | ☐ | ☐ |
| 11. Add appropriate style according to the dance style. | ☐ | ☐ | ☐ | ☐ |
| 12. Dance with fluidity and confidence. | ☐ | ☐ | ☐ | ☐ |

# OVERALL SUCCESS

In general, how do you feel about your overall progress at this point?

_____Very successful

_____Somewhat successful

_____Fairly successful

_____Unsuccessful

Look over all of your previous ratings and identify not only your strong points, but also those points that may need a little more practice. Place a star beside your three strongest points, and circle your three weakest points. Decide how you can improve any weak areas, including whether you need to add or refine your techniques for selected dance styles. Start by reviewing the appropriate sections in this book. Then, keep practicing to reach your new goals. As you continue your journey, remember to have fun along the way—social dancing is a great way to express yourself and meet others who share your passion—enjoy every shared moment!

# Glossary

**accents**—Selected beats within a measure of music that are emphasized, or made to stand out, e.g., are stronger.

**alignment**—Correct body posture while standing stationary. From a side view, visualize an imaginary plumb line aligning with the ear, shoulder, hips, knees, and ankles.

**ball–change**—Two weight changes in a backward, then forward direction. Step onto only the ball of one foot (leader's left foot and follower's right foot), then replace by stepping onto the other foot while keeping it in the same location (leader's right foot and follower's left foot).

**ballroom dance**—A partner dance typically done in a ballroom.

**broken rhythm**—A recurring pattern that takes more than one measure, such as the six-count swing rhythmic step patterns (which take one and a half measures of 4/4 time music).

**basic step**—Another name for the rhythmic step pattern that is associated with a particular dance style.

**carriage**—Correct alignment of body parts while moving.

**center point of balance (CPB or center)**—Refers to a three-dimensional point that ties together the upper and lower body, which is located below your sternum, above your solar plexis, and aligned over your base of support.

**centering**—Moving your entire body as a unit over your base of support.

**clockwise (CW)**—Rotating or turning to the right.

**close**—To bring the free foot beside the supporting foot without a weight transfer onto that foot.

**closed position**—A partner dance position with right sides facing and with the following points of contact: leader's left (and follower's right) hand; leader's right hand on follower's left shoulder blade; leader's right (and follower's left) elbow; and the follower's left hand on the leader's right upper arm.

**contra body positioning (CBP)**—Using the position of your shoulders to create torque to facilitate turns and spins, such that the opposite shoulder rotates in the direction of the turn. For example, the right shoulder rotates counterclockwise on left turns, while the left shoulder rotates clockwise on right turns.

**counterclockwise (CCW)**—Rotating or turning to the left.

**downbeat**—The odd-numbered beats, i.e., one and three, in 4/4 time music, or the first beat of any measure.

**even rhythm**—A steady pattern in which each count gets an equal time value, such as stepping on each beat.

**frame**—The placement of your arms in relationship to your torso, shoulders, and head.

**free foot**—The foot without any weight on it.

**heavy measure**—The first measure of a two-measure miniphrase in 4/4 time, which is stronger than the second measure.

**inside foot**—The foot closest to your partner.

**inside hands joined**—A partner dance position with the leader on the left side and the follower on the right side and his right hand holding her left hand or vice versa.

**leading foot**—The foot in front, or ahead of, the other foot.

**light measure**—The second measure of a two-measure miniphrase in 4/4 time, which sounds weaker than the first measure.

**line of dance (LOD)**—An imaginary line that refers to the flow of traffic, which is counterclockwise around the perimeter of the room.

**measure**—A certain number of beats grouped together according to the time signature, typically identified as two, three, or four beats per measure within social dance music.

**nonweight change**—An alternative action such as a tap, kick, or point, etc., without shifting weight onto that foot.

**outside foot**—The foot farthest away from your partner.

**phrase**—Two or more measures grouped together.

**progressive dance**—A dance that travels in the LOD, such as the waltz, foxtrot, polka, or tango.

**promenade (also conversation, or semiopen position)**—A variation of the closed partner dance position with a 45-degree hip rotation toward the extended hands and arms.

**quick (Q)**—Within 4/4 time signature music, this cue is usually equal to one beat, but it is a relative term.

**receiving foot**—The foot that receives your weight as you take a step.

**rear line of dance (RLOD)**—Facing or moving clockwise around the perimeter of the room.

**rhythm pattern**—A recurring series of slow and/or quick cues, such as box rhythm (SQQ).

**rhythmic step pattern**—A recurring series of weight changes or actions coinciding with selected beats of music that are universally recognized, for example, a box step with footwork that outlines a box shape on the floor.

**replace**—After lifting one foot, put it down in the same location and transfer weight onto that foot.

**rolling count**—The triple division of a beat, i.e., *&-a-1* used to modify the timing between each beat.

**sending foot**—The foot that supports your body weight prior to taking a step, or weight change from one foot to the other.

**shine position**—A partner dance position that is facing, yet partners are standing apart without touching and shoulders parallel.

**slow (S)**—Within 4/4 time signature music, this cue is usually equal to two beats, but it is a relative term.

**social dance**—A partner dance done for recreational purposes.

**spot dance**—A dance done within a small area on the floor (as opposed to traveling in the LOD).

**spotting**—A focusing technique used to facilitate turn execution by keeping your eyes focused on one point, or *spot,* throughout the turn and by isolating your head and shoulders.

**step**—A transfer of weight from one foot to the other.

**starting foot**—Typically, the leader takes his first step with his left foot, while the follower takes her first step with her right foot.

**supporting foot**—The foot with weight on it.

**sweetheart position**—A side-by-side partner dance position with the leader on the left side and the follower on the right side. The follower's hands are placed with palms out in front of her shoulders. The leader's fingers lightly connect with the follower's fingers.

**tempo**—The speed of the music typically expressed as beats per minute.

**time signature**—The number and duration of beats in a measure.

**together**—To bring the free foot beside the supporting foot and transfer weight onto it.